Reading in a Foreign Language

Edited by

J. Charles Alderson and A. H. Urquhart

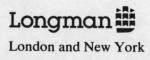

London and New York

Longman Group Limited
Longman House, Burnt Mill, Harlow,
Essex CM20 2JE, England
and Associated Companies throughout the world

Published in the United States of America by
Longman Inc., New York

First published 1984
ISBN 0 582 55372 5

BRITISH LIBRARY CATALOGUING IN PUBLICATION DATA
Reading in a foreign language. —
(Applied linguistics and language study)
1. Reading
I. Alderson, J. Charles II. Urquhart, A.H. III. Series
428'.4   LB1050

LIBRARY OF CONGRESS CATALOGING IN PUBLICATION DATA
Main entry under title:

Reading in a foreign language.
(Applied linguistics and language study)
Bibliography: p.
Includes index.
1. Language and languages — study and teaching —
Addresses, essays, lectures.
2. Reading — Addresses, essays, lectures.
I. Alderson, J. Charles. II. Urquhart, A.H. III. Series
P53.75.R42 1984 418'.007 83-18712

Set in Linotron 202 Times Roman 10/12pt.

Printed in Singapore by
Selector Printing Co (Pte) Ltd

Applied Linguistics and Language S

General Editor: C. N. Candlin

The Contributors

J. Charles Alderson
University of Lancaster

John A. Bates
University of Massachusetts

Ruth A. Berman
Tel Aviv University

John D. Bransford
Vanderbilt University

Malcolm Cooper
The British Council

Don Dallas
Longman Group Ltd.

Alan Davies
University of Edinburgh

Warwick B. Elley
University of Canterbury

Anders Fransson
University of Goteborg

Sheila Harri-Augstein
Brunel University

Carol Hosenfeld
*State University of New York at Buffalo and
University of California at Los Angeles*

Chitra Joag-Dev
University of Illinois at Urbana-Champaign

Clifford E. Konold
University of Massachusetts

James M. Royer
University of Massachusetts

Tommie Shelton
Vanderbilt University

Margaret S. Steffensen
University of Illinois at Urbana-Champaign

Barry S. Stein
Tennessee Technological University

Laurie F. Thomas
Brunel University

A. H. Urquhart
University of Aston

H. G. Widdowson
University of London

Ray Williams
University of Aston

Contents

Preface

Although this most recent contribution to the *Applied Linguistics and Language Study* Series focuses unequivocally on reading, and in particular in a foreign language context, I would like to begin in this Preface by arguing for its more important general relevance to applied linguistics research. In their own most valuable Introduction the Editors isolate the three centres around which they have clustered, with great care, the papers in this collection: a centre on the reader, a centre on the text and a centre on the interaction of the reader and the text and, by extension, beyond to the writer of the text. Reading, whether in the mother tongue or in the foreign language, sets these centres in motion and if we are to explore what reading is we need to continue to see them, as the Editors do, not as isolated but as interactive and interdependent. Each of these centres, however, is a crucial point of focus for applied linguistics research, as, indeed, is their interdependence. In fact this is why reading research is so important a testing ground.

On text, the papers in the collection take for the most part what is by now a commonplace view that although we can identify a residual quantum of meaning within the text itself, the words on the page, what expands and develops this minimum is the meaning-making capacities of the language user, in this case the reader of the text. Text thus has, in Halliday's terms, potential for meaning. How then does a focus on reading permit us to make more concrete this speculation? I think in two ways; firstly that research evidence points to textual description being a necessary but not sufficient guide to readers' problems with understanding text. Here the evidence is oblique: readers, insofar as their linguistic knowledge allows them access to the text, cannot prevent their extra-textual experience, their reading purposes and their affective involvement from complexifying the reading process beyond their capacity to tolerate. Meaning-making, paradoxically, inhibits understanding. Secondly, empirical observation emphasizes the variation in the meaning made from texts. Texts do not have unitary meanings potentially accessible to all, they rather allow for variety in interpretation by different readers, governed by factors such as purpose, background knowledge, and the relationship established in the act of reading between the reader and the writer.

On the reader, the papers emphasize heterogeneity, divergence rather than convergence. This orientation, as we shall emphasize, stands most at odds with the view taken by the majority of foreign (and mother tongue) reading manuals and exercises. Whatever variable one takes, texts themselves, background knowledge, cultural and social inheritance, age, preferred reading strategy, linguistic competence, purposes, affective involvement, other- or self-set tasks, one distinguishes readers. For applied linguistics research this variability has important messages. It suggests that we should temper large-scale quantitative research which seeks for generalization across at most one or two variables with more qualitative and exploratory case-studies of particular subjects across a range of variables; more particularly, that we cannot expect to understand the use and the comprehension of language in isolation from these non-linguistic variables. Applied linguistics research cannot and ought not to take place in some social vacuum.

Turning now to the interaction of the reader and the text, the conclusion of the papers is that we need to see reading as cooperation and negotiation, as a layered series of processes whereby from the discourse of the writer a text is created from which text the reader by his or her discourse creates a (potential) 'text' — a cycle of production and interpretation, evidenced by text and 'text'. Now such a cooperative and negotiative process has its (social) psychological and its sociological dimension. Readers engage their purposes, knowledge and affects and employ their varying strategies on the reading task, entering into a dialogue not only with the writer but with their own knowledge and their own experience. Many of the papers document this negotiative process, emphasizing in turn the quality of the cognitive processing, the influence of the conditions of the reading moment and the naturalized pressures of social conditioning towards particular interpretations. Such a rich environment has, again, important general applied linguistic consequences. It accustoms us not only to variability and dynamism in our research objects as a fact of life, but it signals that for our explanation of such phenomena we shall need a multi-disciplinary perspective.

In reading in a foreign language, therefore, a focus on text, on reader and on interaction has an important contribution to make to applied linguistics research.

What now of the teacher of reading? Perhaps the most significant and far-reaching implications which Dr Alderson and Dr Urquhart draw from the research papers in this collection relate to the reading classroom in the foreign language context. Consistently, their well-argued Postscripts emphasize the pedagogic courses of action which can be inferred from the research evidence. As they say unequivocally at the outset they are concerned to examine competing hypotheses on the nature of reading and to draw practical conclusions where they can. The papers are designed to offer at least a partial answer to the reader who announced: 'I got 100% on the questions but I didn't understand the passage'. What, then, is to be done? Of greatest significance is the re-evaluation of the teacher's role. If we are to focus on the learner–reader's attempts at meaning-making then teachers will necessarily become engaged in evaluating variable interpretations of the meanings to be made from texts. Furthermore, the link established by research between products of reading and readers' purposes suggests a teaching role of advising, guiding and ultimately evaluating readers' goals and routes, and, most difficult of all for a pedagogy accustomed to assessment against common yardsticks, the acceptance of a variety of provisional interpretations. Indeed, given the significant variation of purpose and background knowledge among readers in terms of the readings they derive we will have to question whether we can seriously expect to determine when a reader has 'understood' a text, and, in consequence, experience difficulty in determining what problems readers will have in texts and where they may occur. This uncertainty can, however, be turned to advantage, as several of the papers and the Editors' Postscripts indicate. We can, as teachers, concentrate our attention, and that of our readers, on the monitoring and exploring of the personal process of reading by our foreign language learners. These conclusions from the particular reading perspective can be used to inform a more generally valid pedagogy of foreign language teaching, one in which the teachers and the learners cooperate in what can only be an experimental activity. 'Teaching' reading becomes itself an investigation, drawing perhaps on some of the research techniques made so explicit in the papers in this collection. These conclusions put at question, moreover, how we make use of tests to assess reading skill; the viability of much product-oriented testing must be in doubt, especially if the results of such tests are deemed to be revelatory of reader strategy. By the same token, we will need to re-examine the materials with which teachers and foreign language readers are engaged in classrooms. Presumably, on the evidence, we will wish to favour materials which lay a premium on varied reading tasks, activating and enhancing a variety of reading strategies, applicable to texts at least in part learner-selected and learner-purposed.

It is for the readers of *this* volume to ask themselves the question to what extent in their own reading teaching, and, indeed, in their own reading experience, such conclusions are warranted and such changes in common and traditional pedagogy motivated.

A characteristic of this collection of specially prepared papers is the valuable way in which the Editors have identified and cross-referenced in their Postscripts the conclusions for our understanding of the reading process and its accompanying pedagogy that I have adumbrated above. Indeed, the Postscripts serve an additional purpose as a consequence. They offer to the organizer of in-service and pre-service language teacher training a collection of questions to be applied to practice. They are in themselves an exploratory and experimental programme. It is in the spirit of this exploration and experiment that I would like, in this Preface, to identify some additional questions to which the 'teachers as experimenters' I characterize above could now address themselves. The first is from a sociological perspective, the second psychological and the third methodological.

1.   In our examination of the relationships between writer and reader do we not need, in our interpretations, to take account of not only readers' and writers' purposes and background knowledge but also the social conditions of production and interpretation of the texts? To *explain*, as it were, *why* the text is as it is and the particular reader interpretation is as it is? Such an approach would stress the social and subject-matter constraints on the writer to create the particular text he or she has, and would emphasize the importance of what could be called an 'ethnography of reading', in our attempt to probe further into particular readings. What Hall refers to as 'incorporated' and 'oppositional' readers do not, as it were, appear by chance; indeed this contrast is itself variable according to varying social conditions.

2.   We should take further the point made from time to time in the papers here, that *recall* does not equal *comprehension* or *understanding*. Not only does recall need to be itself differ-

entiated at least to identify recall of actual words/strings, of 'idea units' and of rhetorical structures, but the act of recall is itself a creative task, dependent on memory, and as such a poor or deceptive indicator of the cumulative process of understanding. Much more, as well as much less, is recalled than has been understood from the particular text.

3. Research into the nature of the reading process is research into the unobservable; reading after all is a private matter. We need to be cautious in our reliance on readers' accounts, as a consequence, in evaluating understanding. There are too many distorting variables, linguistic, psychological and social psychological, for us to rely with equanimity on what our readers tell us that they are doing when they read. We have difficulty, after all, even in determining the appropriate 'units' in which to analyse the protocols we do obtain. We should look at the triangulation procedures in sociological method to see how we can make our reader accounts as rich and as warranted as possible. Taking our accounts back to our informants is not only a reflexive desirability, it is indispensable.

Christopher N Candlin　　　　　　　　　*Lancaster*
General Editor　　　　　　　　　　　　*February 1983*

But this is bound to lead to delayed-retrospectively-created reasons for things. What value can this have in uncovering the reading process as it actually occurs. Also slightly at odds with comment on p. x calling for more qualitative research.

Introduction: what is reading?

This book on reading, with particular reference to reading in a foreign language, consists of a set of specially commissioned papers reflecting up-to-date thinking and research in this area. It is hoped that a great deal of what is reported in this volume will be of relevance to the reading of a second or foreign language. Much of the research reported, however, is from studies of first-language readers, which we consider to be of particular relevance to the foreign language reader. We do not, and indeed find it difficult to, draw a clear distinction between first and foreign language reading — in fact, it is not clear to what extent reading in a foreign language is different from reading in a first language. Alderson's paper in this volume addresses this issue, discussing to what extent problems in foreign language reading are due to problems with the foreign language and to what extent they are due to reading problems in general. The focus of Alderson's paper is typical of the book as a whole — it examines empirical evidence for competing hypotheses about the nature of reading, to see how far these are justified by the evidence.

An overview of that area of academic investigation that has come to be called reading research is fast becoming impossible, because of the vastness of the area. The volume of research is simply awe-inspiring, for its quantity and variety, and it is beyond the capacity of the editors of this book to summarize or synthesize, or indeed simply read, the studies that are being conducted at present and that have been carried out particularly in the past ten years, and especially in the study of reading in one's first language. Having said that an overview is impossible, it might then seem foolish to attempt to answer the question 'What is reading?'. The aim of this introduction is not to provide a dangerously simplified answer to this question, but rather to raise further questions in our readers' minds which might help them towards their own answers in the light of the papers in this volume.

Reading undeniably and incontrovertibly involves two necessary elements: a reader and a text. A third element is often important and influential, namely the writer: although our book does not focus upon this third element, the reader will find that Widdowson in particular deals with writers from the perspective of the writer's purpose: how and why messages in writers' heads are turned into texts. These texts are processed by readers in an *interaction* of, incontestably, the reader and the text and, equally plausibly, the reader and the writer. This book, although not explicitly, is organized around the first two elements of reader and text, and the interaction of the two. The reader and related factors are covered by the first five papers, from Alderson to Fransson; the text is looked at more specifically in papers 6 to 10 (Cooper to Williams and Dallas); the interaction of reader and text is, broadly speaking, the topic of the final four papers in the book. Inevitably this is an arbitrary division, since texts must have readers, readers must have something to read, and 'reading' is necessarily interactive. Nevertheless, we have found such an arbitrary, tripartite division useful in guiding our own thinking, and so it is offered for the reader's consideration.

The reader

Traditionally, reading researchers focusing on the reader have attempted to analyse the reading skill into a series of subskills. Teachers are familiar enough with approaches that distinguish between the ability to understand or recall details from a passage, or facts from a text, and the ability to understand the main idea of a passage, i.e. to get the gist of a text. Research has attempted to discover whether reading is composed of different subskills that might relate to one another within a taxonomy or hierarchy of skills. The usual approach is to give learners a series of passages to understand, and ask them a variety of questions afterwards. These questions are then subjected to factor analysis, to see whether identifiable factors emerge. Many different taxonomies or lists have been drawn up over the years, varying in content from three or four, up to the outstanding 36 drawn up by the New York City Board of Education, quoted in Lunzer and Gardner (1979, p. 42). Typical of such taxonomies is that of Barrett (1968). Barrett reportedly distinguishes five skills: literal comprehension, reorganization of the ideas in the text, inferential ability, evaluation, and appreciation. Davies and Widdowson (1974) come up with a similar list of types of reading comprehension questions, relevant to the testing of reading ability: direct reference questions, inference, supposition and evaluation questions. A longer list of feasible levels of questions is exemplified by Adams-Smith (1981), using the Bloomian taxonomy. Royer, Konold and Bates (this volume) also refer to the notion of higher-order questions. Typically, textbooks purporting to teach reading in a foreign language will consist of a variety of texts, with a set of questions (often in multiple choice format) which aim to test the learner's ability to understand the text at various levels, and the levels often relate to the sorts of taxonomies that research has established. The point seems to be that it is desirable for readers to read at different levels, not just at the level of understanding explicitly stated facts within one sentence.

There are, however, problems with trying to define reading as consisting of a series of subskills in this fashion.

Firstly, recent research has failed to find evidence for the separate existence of these skills. Lunzer and Gardner (1979) report an attempt to identify a hierarchy of skills by creating questions on passages aimed at different levels of meaning. The researchers failed to prove that the different questions called upon different subskills: they did not find people who could answer 'word-meaning' questions, but not questions higher up the hierarchy; or readers who could make inferences, and do lower level tasks, but could not make judgements about what they were reading.

Secondly, there is a problem mentioned by Lunzer and Gardner as a possible explanation for their failure to find distinct subskills in reading: the skills approach typically proceeds by giving subjects tests on their understanding of passages, yet doing a comprehension test and actually reading are probably not the same thing. Research that bases itself upon the former can only with difficulty be related to the latter.

Thirdly, although establishing the level of understanding that a learner has achieved may be a relevant and worthwhile occupation for a *tester*, it is not obvious that such an activity is relevant to teaching, since knowing what a student has understood does not, of itself, help one decide how he has or has not understood this, and cannot provide information on how the learner might be helped to understand at a higher level if he has failed to achieve that level.

Fourthly, these levels of understanding do not relate to the *process* of understanding but to the *product*, what the reader has 'got out' of the text. A description of what a student has understood of a text is not the same as a description of how he arrives at such an understanding. The product of reading may vary in terms of levels of meaning and comprehension, but it does not follow that the levels of comprehension reflect different skills. It is at least possible that readers use similar *processes* for getting at different *products*. The so-called skills approach to reading offers us no insights into how the reader arrived at his level of comprehension; we are not in a position to describe what the reader was doing as he was reading, in order to arrive at his particular product. Recent research, consequently, has attempted to investigate the *process* of reading, rather than focusing upon the *product* or outcome. The papers in this volume by Hosenfeld, Harri-Augstein and Thomas and Fransson are concerned with gathering evidence about the nature of the process.

Fifthly, the product of reading will vary according to the reader. Different readers will arrive at different products because they start off from different positions (Strang 1972). Bransford *et al.* and Steffensen and Joag-Dev all refer to the effect of what might generally be termed background knowledge on the product of reading. Steffensen and Joag-Dev, in particular, clearly demonstrate the effect of cultural knowledge on the product of comprehension, appealing to the processes of distortion and elaboration to account for the differences between a recall of text and the original text. Bransford *et al.* show that not only is relevant knowledge important to processing, but also that such knowledge needs to be activated before it can contribute to understanding.

Sixthly, the product of reading will vary according to the reader's purpose and motivation, as both Royer *et al.* and Fransson show in their contributions to this volume. Royer *et al.* report attempts to manipulate the reader's intent in order to influence what the learner learns, and show that the purpose a reader has in reading a text will affect the outcome of his understanding: the product. Fransson shows that the reader's motivation (rather than the experimenter's attempts to manipulate purpose) has an effect, not only on the product of comprehension, but also upon the process of understanding. Variables such as different background knowledge, adherence to different tasks, different motivation, all cast doubt on an attempt to describe reading comprehension simply in terms of a set of hierarchically ordered skills.

One final point to be made about the tradition of research into 'skills' is that it is based upon the assumption that texts have predictable meanings, which can be extracted if only the reader is sufficiently skilful. Widdowson (1979) suggests that text does not have *meaning*, but *potential for meaning*, which will vary from reader to reader, depending upon a multitude of factors, but crucially related to purpose and knowledge. In this view, meaning is actually created by the reader in his interaction with the text.

In sum, then, it is possible to view reading both as product and as process. Research has tended to focus upon the product rather than the process but we argue that this is inadequate because of the unpredictable and normal variation in product, and because knowing the product does not tell us what actually happens when a reader interacts with a text. It is this latter knowledge, we claim, which is essential in the teaching — as opposed to the testing — of reading. This is not to say that a product approach to reading does not have its uses: apart from the value in the testing of comprehension, it is clear that an awareness of the existence of other levels of meaning, or of different interpretations of a text, can help readers by directing their attention to other aspects of comprehension, and it can serve as a stimulus for interpretation of text. The process, we argue, underlies the product (which will vary from reader to reader, purpose to purpose, time to time and so on). The value of concentrating on process in research and teaching is that if processes can be characterized, they may contain elements that are general across different texts, that learners can learn in order to improve their reading. The basic rationale behind attempts to describe process is that an understanding should lead to the possibility of distinguishing the processing of successful and unsuccessful readers. This in turn should lead to the possibility of teaching the strategies, or process components, of successful readers to unsuccessful ones, or at least making the latter aware of the existence of other strategies, which they might then wish to try for themselves. This is the rationale behind the papers of Hosenfeld, Harri-Augstein and Thomas, Fransson, and possibly Bransford *et al.*

The problem with research into process is that the process of reading is elusive: reading is essentially, at least in the twentieth century, in most cultures, a silent, private activity. Attempts have been made, in the history of research in reading, to investigate the process of reading. A strong tradition continued for some considerable time of eye movement photography, where the eye's movements were recorded, analysed, and, less usually, related to the text being processed. It has been established that good readers make fewer fixations, with less duration, than do weak readers. A reduction in eye fixations — when the brain is processing text, presumably — is matched by a rise in comprehension. Both good and poor readers show fewer regressions. The interesting questions, however (What causes regression? What information are the eyes processing when fixating? What is going on in the head when the eyes are not fixating?), have barely begun to be asked. Relatively little is known, even about the point in text where eyes fixate: do they fixate at linguistically random points? on certain sorts of words? at certain points within linguistic structures? and so on. Recent research by Just and Carpenter (1980) suggests that almost all content words in text are fixated, and that longer fixations occur on infrequent words, and at sentence ends when inferences are being made. These authors have developed a model of reading related to studies of eye movements. However, even their model is merely confirmed — or rather, not disconfirmed — by the eye movement studies. (They posit a process model of several stages: moving the eye to the site of next input; encoding the visual features of the word; accessing the lexicon, in what is called the working memory, for conceptual information; assigning case roles of the word in question — i.e. determining the relation among words in a structure; integrating clauses to each other; sentence wrap-up.) Such attempts to examine process through eye-fixations should not, of course, be confused with early attempts to improve comprehension by 'widening eye-span' and discouraging regressions. It is now almost universally accepted that frequent fixations and regressions are symptoms of poor comprehension, rather than causes of it (see M. and E. De Leeuw 1965).

Another technique that has been used to gain insight into the reading process is miscue analysis, developed by the Goodmans (see Goodman 1974). Oral reading errors are analysed for their similarity to or difference from the words in the text, and inferences are made about the process that must have been occurring. Such work has shown that readers use graphic, syntactic, semantic and discourse information in text during their processing. Readers can be seen to be creating language (miscues are often dialect or idiolect-related) on the basis of their predictions about what language will actually occur; to be constantly trying to make sense of what they read (even good readers make miscues, but such miscues are of high quality: they are usually syntactically and semantically acceptable in the context); and to be monitoring their creation of language in order to see whether it makes sense. The basic reading strategies that miscue analysis appears to reveal are: prediction — what the next chunk of language will be; sampling — selecting the minimum information from text consistent with the prediction; confirming — testing the prediction against the sample; and correction — if the prediction is not confirmed, another prediction is generated. It should be emphasized, however, that these strategies are *inferred* by researchers, rather than displayed by readers. Goodman (in Smith 1978) asserts that 'only in special circumstances is oral reading free of miscues, and silent reading is *never* miscue-free'. However, the connection between reading aloud and silent reading is somewhat difficult to prove, since there is a lack of information about the nature of the silent reading process, the process after all in which most reading researchers are interested. New methodologies have been developed in recent years for the study of the reading process — see Harri-Augstein and Thomas, Hosenfeld, and Fransson in this volume for details and comments — and it is in this area that we feel much interesting and useful work will concentrate in the near future.

The text

Whatever the reading process, the reader must engage with text, the second element in the interaction, and a considerable body of research exists which has examined the text in detail and related its nature to the reading process. Particular attention has focused upon those features of text that cause difficulty to readers. The study of text readability has a considerable history, and the articles by Urquhart, Berman, and Williams and Dallas derive from this tradition. An area related to readability is that of simplification: if a text is found not to be readable, attempts may be made to alter it in order to make it more readable, or simpler. The topic of simplification is the central issue in Davies, Williams and Dallas, and is also touched upon by Urquhart. Davies suggests, however, that simplification may be a more complex process than has been traditionally assumed.

The variables studied in most readability research have been linguistic, and rather unsophisticated linguistic variables at that. The typical readability study (see Klare 1974, 1975 and Gilliland 1972, for reviews) takes a range of passages, determines their 'difficulty' for a range of readers by means either of multiple

choice questions or, more recently, cloze tests, and then attempts
to find the best predictor or group of predictors of text difficulty,
by statistical means. The passages are usually analysed in terms
of their linguistic units: structures, words, clause and sentence
relationships, or whatever. The variables that have emerged as the
best predictors of difficulty, often combined in regression equa-
tions for readability formulae, have proved to be related to word
difficulty, and to complexity of sentence structure. Word difficulty
may relate to infrequency of occurrence, and has been indexed
either by reference to frequency lists, or by reference to word
length, usually measured in number of syllables, since, on the
whole, longer words tend to be less frequent and therefore might
be expected to cause processing problems. Sentence complexity
can be measured by a variety of devices, ranging from the number
of transformations required to produce the surface string from a
posited deep structure (see Chomsky 1965) to a simple count of
the number of words in a sentence, since, again, on the whole, the
longer the sentence, the more complex it is likely to be, with
embedded and subordinate clauses, and the like. One typical readability formula is the Fog Index (referred to in Urquhart's paper)
whose formula is

$$\frac{\text{No. words}}{\text{No. sentences}} + \frac{\text{no. 3-syllable words}}{\text{no. words}} \times \frac{100}{1} \times \cdot 4$$

and the result is interpreted as $12- = $ easy, $13-16 = $ undergrad-
uate, $16+ = $ postgraduate.

Although considerably more complicated formulae have been
established, their rationale, construction and validity are not very
different. The rationale, of course, corresponds to the layman's
view of difficulty of text, that simple English is written in short
easy sentences with not too many long words.

It should be emphasized that readability studies result in *indices*
of difficulty and do not claim to be indicative of causes of difficulty: that is, if one applies a readability formula to a text, finds
it too difficult for a given audience, and then manipulates the text
to shorten sentence length and remove long words, it will not
necessarily follow that the cause of difficulty has been removed:
the text might actually have been made more difficult, although
the readability index would be lower. A clear example of this is
the index discovered by Bormuth (1966) to be his single best
predictor of difficulty. This turned out to be the number of letters
in a passage. One would not wish to suggest that it was the number

of letters that made the text difficult, but presumably, that the number of letters indicated a variety of different causes of difficulty.

More illuminating research into causes of difficulty with text has been carried out recently without the goal of producing indices of difficulty or readability formulae. Urquhart's paper in this volume shows how certain principles of text organization — in this case, based upon the advice given by rhetoricians for the improvement of writing — can affect the recall of information in text. Other studies (Kintsch and van Dijk 1978; Meyer 1975; Rumelhart 1977; Thorndyke 1977) have shown how the global organization of a narrative text can influence how a reader recalls the text.

Berman, in this volume, examines syntactic causes of difficulty for non-native speakers of English. She suggests the importance of transparency — the opposite of her term opacity — of the kernel sentence: the basic subject–verb–object ordering of sentences. If decomposing a sentence into its basic svo consti-tuents is delayed by, for example, deletion of relative pronouns, *wh* + *be* deletion in post-noun modifiers, or '*one*' or '*do*' sub-stitution for repeated lexical material, and the like, then the sen-tence will be more difficult to process.

Cooper, in this volume, compares what he calls practised and unpractised readers and examines the linguistic features of texts that might be thought to give problems: interestingly he found little difference between the two sorts of reader in terms of the processing of syntactic features like tense, aspect, modality, complementation, but he did find differences in the problems caused by some cohesive devices and particularly in the relation-ships between sentences.

Alderson, in this volume, reviews research with foreign language readers which suggests that the lexical and conceptual difficulties of texts are greater than the syntactic difficulties, and to some extent Cooper's conclusions agree with this. Alderson and Richards (1977) have shown vocabulary problems to be the most important contributors to text difficulty, but they also found that there were many foreign language readers who did not have 'language problems', including difficulty with vocabulary, but who still found text difficult to process. They suggest, in fact, that a linguistic description of a text is a necessary but not sufficient guide to the problems that readers might have with that text. It would seem not unreasonable to suggest that in the interaction of a particular reader and a given text, predicted syntactic complexity, lexical density or infrequency and rhetorical anomaly or opacity might not prove to cause difficulty or incomprehension. This may be because of other text factors. If the syntax is complex, the lexis may be simple; the lexis may be infrequent in terms of word lists, but its meaning predictable in the given text perhaps because it belongs to the same semantic field. The writer may have predicted reader difficulties and therefore provided textual — verbal or non-verbal — assistance with the predicted difficulty. Alternatively, it may come about because of reader factors like a high interest level in the text's content, which might then overcome predicted 'linguistic' difficulty, or the reader's familiarity with the topic, the genre, the author and so on (see Bransford *et al.* in this volume for an account of some of these reader factors).

In the general area of psycholinguistics, attention has recently turned to discovering the heuristics that readers might use in order to process certain linguistic structures, and a body of knowledge is slowly growing that looks specifically at the *process* of reading *language*. Interest has centred on sentences rather than longer texts, and particularly upon the case relationships of nouns and verb phrases. Schank (1972) suggests that readers use the verb as a pivotal source of information to establish the case roles of associated noun phrases. Bever (1970) does not assign particular significance to verbs, but suggests that the frequent sequence animate noun–verb–noun is heuristically assigned the case roles of agent–action–object, and this frequently results in misinterpretations of text. The suggestion is that readers develop strategies for handling particular types of linguistic organization, which may cause problems when the expectancy is not confirmed by the ongoing text.

Carpenter and Just (1977) and Kintsch and van Dijk (1978) have attempted to go beyond the sentence to look at the way readers might relate old information to new information. Just and Carpenter (1980) suggest, for example, that readers are constantly attempting to integrate new information with the ongoing text, and that such integration is facilitated at points where a linking relation can be made. Thus one would predict that explicit connections across text — in the form, for example, of marking of rhetorical relationships and other forms of text coherence — might aid the reader in his processing. On the other hand, Meyer (1975) found that the presence of rhetorical 'signalling' in texts had no apparent effect on recall.

Consideration of how the reader might be helped in his processing of the language of text brings us to the area of simplification, covered in this volume by Davies, and Williams and Dallas. Urquhart also in this volume addresses the issue of how readers might be assisted in their learning of relevant items by optimal textual organization. Many of the factors identified by research as leading to difficulties, as discussed above, would conceivably become candidates for revision and alteration in a project aimed at reducing linguistic difficulty. As both Davies, in this volume, and Mountford (1975) point out, however, such simplification is not without its hazards. Making a text syntactically less complex may actually have the effect of distorting the 'message' or, indeed, increasing difficulties in other aspects of the text. If it is important that a simplified text be 'true to the original' in the sense of 'meaning', then perhaps more attention needs to be paid to characterizing the meaning of the text and ensuring that such meaning be not distorted and, better, that it become easier to arrive at. Klare (1963) points to the need for a satisfactory 'unit of content' in readability studies. If, however, as we have suggested above and elsewhere in this volume, and as other authors have also suggested, for example Widdowson (1979), meaning does not reside in text, but rather text has potential for meaning, then it is difficult to see how such an endeavour might begin to analyse 'meaning'. Such is, however, the implication if one agrees with Mountford that the locutionary force, at least in speech act terms, of text should be preserved if simplifications are not to result in distortions.

Whatever the solution may be to the problems of simplification (and beyond it, of authenticity of text and task, especially in a foreign language context), the fact remains, as both Cooper and especially Elley, in this volume, point out, many readers have considerable difficulty with texts, and this is particularly important in those situations where, as Elley, and Williams and Dallas describe, the learner–readers are obliged to become educated through the medium of a foreign language.

The interaction

We are still left with the question: what is reading? Widdowson's definition — 'the process of getting linguistic information via print' (Widdowson 1979) — is an attractive one, and a useful corrective to more restricted approaches. But as it stands, it is probably too general and all-embracing to be of much practical value. There are so many different kinds of information, so many purposes for reading, that a general definition is in danger of being trivial or banal. In most contexts, then, it would seem necessary to specify what sort of reading is being considered, and for what purpose. In this volume, the emphasis is on reading for formal learning.

Underlying Widdowson's definition is the traditional linguistic view whereby linguistic information can be transmitted either via print (reading) or via sound (listening). This view implies a close relationship between reading and listening. This is the view taken by Fries (1963) who sees learning to read as simply a transfer of linguistic knowledge from the aural medium in which it was first acquired to the written medium. More recently the case has been argued by Sticht (1972), who produces empirical evidence for a strong correlation between reading and listening abilities. However, while the relationship unquestionably exists, there may well exist important differences between reading and listening, as is argued by Widdowson himself in this volume, and it may be dangerous to assume that at all levels apart from the phonemic/graphemic level, they represent the same set of activities and skills.

Fries rigorously excluded mention of syntax and lexis from his initial reading syllabus, on the grounds that the learner already knew them and did not need them repeated. Goodman (1976) has argued that learners be encouraged to use their knowledge of syntax, etc., in the decoding process. The apparent argument is not, however, about the nature of reading; Fries would certainly have agreed that syntactic knowledge is involved in reading. The disagreement is a pedagogical one about the best way to effect a transfer of learning.

Similarly, Fries wished to exclude 'thinking' and 'evaluating' from the initial reading programme, while Goodman and others have stressed the mental activities involved in reading, such as hypothesis formation, testing and confirmation. Fries believed that activities such as evaluating had a place in the general language programme, which would presumably include written material, but were not exclusive to reading, and so should be kept out of the initial transfer stage.

The view of reading as complex cognitive activity is comparatively old. Thorndike (1917), for example, argued that reading was similar to mathematical problem solving. Yet again there is a danger that an equation drawn between reading and very general cognitive activities, common to a myriad other human activities, will result in the end in vagueness and non-falsifiable hypotheses. Again we need to specify what particular mental operations we are talking about, and how they are carried out in particular reading situations (cf. Urquhart 1981).

A major problem arises, however, if one does not limit one's definition of reading to the ability to relate phonemes to graphemes, for then not only does any satisfactory definition of reading become all-embracing, it also implies that readers can go on becoming better readers. They do not simply have to learn, as it were, translation rules, but far more: how to relate what is being processed to one's existing knowledge, emotions, etc. and to do so with an appropriate degree of flexibility.

It follows from our positing that reading is a complex activity, that the study of reading must be inter-disciplinary. If the ability involves so many aspects of language, cognition, life and learning, then no one academic discipline can claim to have the correct view of what is crucial in reading: linguistics certainly not, probably not even applied linguistics. Cognitive and educational psychology are clearly centrally involved; sociology and sociolinguistics, information theory, the study of communication systems and doubtless other disciplines all bear upon an adequate study of reading. We have attempted to reflect this reality in the range of interests and backgrounds of our authors, from engineering to psychology, linguistics to psychometrics.

The main focus of this book is on evidence: evidence for theories, ideas and assertions. The literature on reading abounds with speculations, opinions and claims, particularly in foreign language reading, but relatively little evidence is brought to bear on specific issues. We hope that this volume will contribute to debate and theory both by providing relevant research evidence in certain areas and also by encouraging an empirical frame of mind. Authors in this volume have been encouraged to be as explicit as possible when supporting their opinions, both to allow replication of their research by interested readers and to allow the reader to make up his own mind about conclusions that may be offered, either in the papers themselves or in the postscripts.

The postscripts

Each paper is followed by a postscript written by the editors. They point out what we consider to be the salient points of the paper, and relate these salient points to the teaching and learning of reading. They are not intended as judgement on the papers — that would be pretentious and inappropriate — but as the interposition of personal views on the relevance and interest of issues raised (and supported by evidence) in the papers.

The other purpose of the postscripts is to relate any one paper to other papers in the volume as a means of emphasizing the interconnected nature of the subject (which we have argued is a complex subject necessarily involving a variety of disciplines and approaches). To this end we indicate what we think are connections between topics and papers in this volume, for the reader to use as a guide to his reading if he so wishes.

J. Charles Alderson
A. H. Urquhart

1 Reading in a foreign language: a reading problem or a language problem?

J. Charles Alderson

The problem

In many parts of the world a reading knowledge of a foreign language is often important to academic studies, professional success, and personal development. This is particularly true of English as so much professional, technical and scientific literature is published in English today. In fact, it is frequently the case that the ability to read in English is *required* of students by their subject departments, often assessed by a test of reading comprehension. A reading ability is often all that is *needed* by learners of English as a Foreign Language (EFL), as well as of other foreign languages. (This is not to say that students/learners do not *want* to speak or write English as well.) Yet despite this specific need for the foreign language, it is the common experience, at least of EFL teachers, that most students fail to learn to read adequately in the foreign language. Very frequently, students reading in a foreign language seem to read with less understanding than one might expect them to have, and to read considerably slower than they reportedly read in their first language.

Results of research also support the view that reading in a language which is not the learner's first language is a source of considerable difficulty. MacNamara (1970) found that the Irish–English bilingual students he studied were reading in their weaker language (in this case, Irish) at a slower rate and with lower comprehension than students reading in their first language. Besides taking considerably longer to read their second language, students who understood the words and structures of the texts under study (their understanding of the words and structures was tested separately) were still unable to understand what they read in the second language as well as in their first language. In a further study reported in the same paper, this time with French–English bilinguals, MacNamara found certain differences between reading in the native language and reading in a second language — 'in the rate at which individual words are interpreted, in the rate at which syntactic structures are interpreted, and in ability to anticipate the sequence of words' (p. 114) (an ability which MacNamara takes to be related to syntactic knowledge). There would appear to be some conflict between the results of the two studies. On the one hand, subjects have difficulty understanding text despite knowing the words and structures, and on the other hand the interpretation of words and syntactic structures — that is, grammar and vocabulary — seems to be the main factor in poorer reading performance in the second language than in the first language. The problem seems to be whether reading in a foreign language is 'simply' a problem of knowing the words and the grammar of the language, or whether there are other causes of the difficulties learners experience.

It is commonly asserted by many teachers (at least in Latin-American countries — I am thinking particularly of my experience in Mexico) that the reason their students cannot read adequately in English is that they cannot read adequately in the native language, in the first place. If only, so the argument goes, they learned to read 'properly' in their first language, the problems of reading in English would be vastly reduced.

Speculations

Jolly (1978) claims that success in reading a foreign language depends crucially upon one's first-language reading ability rather than upon the student's level of English 'if this is identifiable'. He asserts that reading in a foreign language requires 'the transference of old skills, not the learning of new ones'.Therefore, it would follow, students who fail to read adequately in the foreign language fail because they either do not possess the 'old skills', or because they have failed to transfer them.

This view is shared by Coady (1979), who asserts that foreign language reading is a reading problem and not a language problem.

> We have only recently come to realize that many students have very poor reading habits to transfer from their first language, and thus, in many cases, we must teach reading skills which should have been learned in first language instruction. (p. 12).

Coady is indirectly supported by the 'reading universals hypothesis' put forward by Goodman (1973), who claimed that 'the reading process will be much the same for all languages'. This position has been strengthened by the work in EFL of people like Pat Rigg (1977), who, using miscue analysis, found considerable similarities in reading miscues for EFL learners from a variety of different language backgrounds. If the reading process is the same or very similar in all languages, then one would expect reading ability to transfer across languages. That is, as Clarke (1979) states, 'If the reading process is basically the same in all languages we would logically expect good native language readers to be good second language readers. Furthermore we would expect good readers to maintain their advantage over poor readers in the second language'.

Yorio (1971) takes a contrary view. He claims that the reading problems of foreign language learners are due largely to imperfect knowledge of the language, and to native language interference in the reading process. He subscribes to Goodman's view of the reading process as involving the reader, 'guided by his knowledge of the native language', picking up graphic cues and relating them to syntactic, semantic and phonological cues. In Yorio's view, reading involves four factors: knowledge of the language, ability to predict or guess in order to make the correct choices, ability to remember the previous cues and ability to make the necessary associations between the different cues that have been selected. According to Yorio, the process is made considerably more complex for the foreign learner because of new elements:

> the reader's knowledge of the foreign language is not like that of the native speaker; the guessing or predicting ability necessary to pick up the correct cues is hindered by the imperfect knowledge of the language; the wrong choice of cues or the uncertainty of the choice makes associations more difficult; due to unfamiliarity with the material and the lack of training, the memory span in a foreign language in the early stages of its acquisition is usually shorter than in our native language: recollection of previous cues then is more difficult in a foreign language than in the mother tongue; and at all levels, and at all times, there is interference of the native language. (p. 108).

These new elements can be summarized as interference from the native language and inadequate knowledge of the target language.

Unfortunately, the views of Yorio, Coady and Jolly remain assertions: they are eminently researchable assertions, but do not base themselves upon empirical evidence.

What is needed is the development of a series of researchable hypotheses, from which not only empirical evidence should flow but hopefully also a series of pedagogic implications might be derived for the teaching or learning of reading in a foreign language.

Hypotheses

Two such hypotheses have already been suggested:
1. Poor reading in a foreign language is due to poor reading ability in the first language. Poor first-language readers will read poorly in the foreign language and good first-language readers will read well in the foreign language.
2. Poor reading in a foreign language is due to inadequate knowledge of the target language.

At least two modifications of these hypotheses are possible:

1a. Poor foreign language reading is due to incorrect strategies for reading that foreign language, strategies which differ from the strategies for reading the native language.
2a. Poor foreign language reading is due to reading strategies in the first language not being employed in the foreign language, due to inadequate knowledge of the foreign language. Good first-language readers will read well in the foreign language once they have passed a threshold of foreign language ability.

Implications

These competing hypotheses have importantly different implications for the teaching of reading.

If the cause of foreign language reading problems is poor target-language knowledge, it would make sense in the teaching of the foreign language to concentrate upon improving language knowledge. Thus a reading course would be more properly concerned with teaching language competence, rather than reading strategies as such. Similarly, if the hypothesis is correct that there is a threshold beyond which learners have to go before they can apply their (appropriate) first-language reading strategies, then the language competence of poor readers needs to be raised. It also follows that if language is the cause of difficulty in reading the foreign language, then perhaps reading texts need to be simplified linguistically, to encourage the use of appropriate reading strategies.

If, however, the cause of poor reading in the foreign language is poor reading in the first language, then presumably the teaching of foreign language reading should include instruction in appropriate reading strategies. Thus learners would be encouraged to adopt successful reading strategies (as done by Hosenfeld, 1979 and this volume), and to become flexible in their approach to text (as is done in the SQ3R technique of teaching learners to survey, question, read, revise, review). Moreover, if there is a strong transfer of reading strategies from one language to the next, then one might most efficiently teach reading strategies in the first language, and expect them to transfer automatically to the foreign language. Alternatively, especially if reading strategies are the same in all languages, then one could apply first-language reading teaching methods in the foreign language, or improve first-language strategies by teaching efficient strategies in the foreign language. Further, it follows from the positing of the transfer of reading from first to foreign language that if learners are known to be good readers in their first language one need not worry about teaching reading as such, but can concentrate on the teaching of the language that is considered necessary to the processing task. If, conversely, learners are known to be poor or indifferent readers in their first language, one needs to teach both the language and reading strategies. If, however, hypothesis 1a, above, is correct, then the strategies needed for reading the foreign language are different from the strategies needed in the first language, and presumably need to be taught separately. In this case, the learner's ability to read in the first language is irrelevant to foreign language reading teaching to the extent, at least, that the foreign language reading strategies are different from the first-language strategies.

In summary, when dealing with foreign language reading problems:
— If poor first-language reading is the cause, we must improve first-language reading.
— If poor foreign language knowledge is the cause, we need to improve FL competence.
— If first-language reading ability is short-circuited by low FL competence, we need to improve FL competence first, then improve the reading strategies of poor first-language readers.
— If processing is different for different languages, then we need to teach reading of the foreign language, regardless of the first-language ability.

— If transfer of reading ability takes place across the native/non-native language divide, then we can teach reading in either first or foreign language to those readers who are poor in their first-language reading. Readers who are poor in foreign language reading but not in their first language are either logical impossibilities or merely in need of familiarization with the foreign language code.

If a pedagogical treatment is derived from theory, then its justification must depend upon the validity of the theory, which means: to what extent does the research evidence support one theory over another? The rest of this paper will examine the extent to which empirical evidence is available to support the various possible hypotheses.

Evidence for hypothesis 1

Some research evidence is available from studies of bilingualism which suggests the transferability of reading ability across languages (although the studies were not specifically designed to prove this). Such transferability would, as we have suggested, lend support to a hypothesis that poor foreign language reading is essentially a reading problem.

Both the Tarascan study (Barrera-Vasquez 1953), where Mexican Indians were taught to read first in their native language before being introduced to Spanish, and the similar study by Modiano (1966) seemed to show that teaching children to read in their first language will result in eventual improved reading ability in the second language when compared with children who first learned to read in their second language. These findings would imply that there is indeed a transfer effect of reading ability from first to second language. However, some Canadian studies have shown that children taught to read initially in a second language (in this case, French) eventually do as well in reading in their first language (English) as do monolingual speakers of that language. In these studies (see Barik and Swain 1975) children of English-speaking parents were taught in French immersion programmes, where *all* school subjects were taught in the second language (French). After an initial fallback in achievement, the students in French immersion programmes eventually were able to display equivalent subject achievement to monolingual controls, despite having been taught in a second language. Not only, as expected, were their reading and spoken communicative abilities in the second language far superior to the control group (in fact, approaching native speaker competence) but also, perhaps more unexpectedly, the immersion group did not show any disadvantage *vis à vis* the control group in reading ability in their first language, an ability which had not been directly taught in school.

It is important to bear in mind, when examining and comparing results of research into 'bilingualism', the caveats of Cummins (1976) regarding the interpretation of apparently conflicting results. Cummins points out that there is no one single phenomenon or state called 'bilingualism', and that each bilingual learning situation is, in fact, unique. He points out, further, that many studies into 'bilingualism' did not control, or in some cases, even measure, the subjects' proficiency in the first and second languages. Some studies used what he calls 'balanced bilinguals' — those equally proficient in the first and second language (for example, conceivably, the Canadian studies) — whereas other studies do not (for example, MacNamara 1970). Whether the subjects studied were balanced bilinguals will clearly affect the nature of the generalizations one can legitimately draw from the data, and will limit the comparisons one can make. Moreover, the notion of additive or subtractive bilingualism is important in this regard (Lambert 1975): where positive effects of bilingualism have been noted (like the transfer of reading ability from the second language to the first, *inter alia*), the second language has been a socially relevant language which was unlikely to lead to replacement of the first language, itself a prestigious or dominant language. Such a situation is known as additive bilingualism, since the individual adds a language to his repertoire without diminution of the first language. Subtractive bilingualism, on the other hand, results from a situation where the first language is in some socially significant sense inferior, and is gradually replaced within the individual by the second language. In the latter circumstance (conceivably the case with the Mexican Indian studies) learning to read in a second language might not be expected to transfer to the first language, whereas initial reading instruction in the first language might serve to upgrade, or add prestige to, that first language, and thus have positive effects upon learning skills, including reading, whose transfer might then be facilitated.

Bearing in mind these remarks on the problems of interpretation of research results, the results of the Mexican studies on the one hand and the Canadian studies on the other are not necessarily contradictory, as Hatch (1973) seems to suggest, if one posits the possibility of transfer of reading ability *in either direction*. That is to say, the Mexican Indian was able to transfer his first-language reading ability to the second-language reading task, just as the French Canadian immersion children were able to transfer the strategies learned in the second language back into their first language. That transfer occurs seems to be undeniable from these results; the direction of transfer will depend upon the sorts of factors mentioned above, upon the social distance between the languages (Schumann 1976) and so on. To the extent that language-related skills do transfer across languages, then, one would expect that students who were good readers in their first language would have a better chance of becoming good readers in their second or foreign language than students who were poor readers in their first language, *other things being equal*.

In another paper Cummins (1979) claims that what he calls cognitive/academic language proficiencies (CALP) underlie language proficiency in *both* first and second languages. He further claims that the first and second CALPs are manifestations of the same underlying dimension. Thus development in second-language proficiency is 'partially a function of the level of first language proficiency at the time when intensive exposure to the second language is begun'. An extension of this hypothesis, involving the assumption that reading ability is related to or indeed part of the cognitive/academic language proficiency dimension, is that students who are proficient readers in their first language are more likely to become good readers in the second language than are poor first-language readers. Cummins supports his hypothesis with reference to correlations between various measures of CALP and measures of first and second-language proficiency. In particular, the Canadian Test of Basic Skills (CTBS) Reading Test is reported to have shown correlations of ·66 and ·61 with first and second-language proficiency respectively in an English–French bilingual study (Carey and Cummins 1979), and correlations of ·61 and ·69 with the first and second language in another study (Lapkin and Swain 1977). In addition moderate correlations are reported of performance on cloze tests in first and second language (Carey and Cummins, ·57; Lapkin and Swain, ·61; Swain, Lapkin and Barik (1976), ·67). In other words, there is a fair degree of relationship between one's reading ability in the first language and in the second language.

Lapkin and Swain (1977) found no differences between bilinguals' reading ability (as measured by cloze tests) and control native speakers, for both the first language and the second. Similar cloze errors in similar frequencies were made by bilinguals and native speakers. Correlations of the English (first language) cloze test with the CTBS Reading Test were ·68 for bilinguals and ·64 for monolingual natives, and correlations with the same cloze test and CTBS Vocabulary Test were ·56 for bilinguals and ·64 for native speakers. The French cloze test correlated with achievement in French at ·57 and with a French reading measure at ·59. The suggestion is that, since no *glaring* differences were discovered between native and non-native reading performances, it can be assumed that the same ability underlies both languages. The authors would presumably claim that a reading ability learned in the second language transfers to the first language, and that there is no evidence that bilingual reading behaviour is different in kind from native-speaker reading behaviour. They are, however, unable to conclude on their evidence that first-language reading behaviours are the same as or similar to second-language reading behaviours since individuals were not compared on these dimensions. Nevertheless these studies would seem to provide evidence for some relationship between first and second-language reading abilities if one takes the cloze test to give a measure of reading ability. If, however, the cloze test, as has been claimed (Alderson 1978, 1979a, 1979b, 1980), is more a measure of lower-order language ability than of higher-order reading ability, then the force of the argument is somewhat reduced.

Evidence for hypothesis 1a

In a study which produced counter-evidence to the Canadian studies, Cowan and Sarmad (1976) found that bilingual English–Farsi children did not read as well in either first or foreign language as their monolingual controls. This would argue against complete transfer of reading ability across languages. However, the authors did not specifically compare the bilingual child's ability in one language with his/her ability in the other. Nor did they have any usable evidence on the linguistic proficiency (English or Farsi) of their subjects. It was thus impossible to relate a lack of reading ability to a lack of control of the language. However, Cowan has posited elsewhere (Cowan 1976) a *parallel processing theory of reading*, which accommodates the apparent contradiction between the Canadian studies and his own. He claims that the strategies (sometimes referred to as perceptual strategies by

Cowan) which readers employ to process text must be to some extent language-specific. That is, the expectancies set up in the reader when sampling syntactic clues in text must be related to one's knowledge of the structure of that particular language. Thus he claims that confusion in reading in a foreign language often results from the predictions that are made by the reader being based on the strategies associated with the native language of the reader (what Yorio (1971) might call native-language interference). For example, English readers will expect subject–verb–object ordering, even when reading German, and so will be confused by a sentence with object–verb–subject ordering. In a sentence like 'Das Mädchen liebt der Junge nicht', an English reader will expect, and initially interpret, that the first noun phrase in the sentence is the subject (and his expectancy will not be altered by the initial article, since 'das' can indicate either sentence subject or sentence object for neuter nouns), and he will ignore the fact that the second NP is marked by its article as being the sentence subject. He will thus interpret the sentence to mean something like 'The girl does not love the boy', instead of 'The boy does not love the girl'. This theory of Cowan's corresponds to the hypothesis that poor foreign language reading is due to incorrect strategies for reading that foreign language.

Thus, if the strategies are language-specific, it follows that to the extent that the languages concerned are markedly different in their structures, so too will be the strategies required to read texts written in the respective languages.

The proposal is therefore that bilingual children have two sets of processing strategies, one for each language. To the extent that the languages are similar, transfer of reading strategies will be facilitated. This would account for the Canadian results (since English and French are relatively similar). To the extent that the languages are different, transfer is likely to have a negative effect — this would account for the Farsi–English results. This theory would not, however, explain the Mexican Indian results. (It is important, however, to remember at this point the caveat mentioned earlier regarding the interpretation of results from studies with different populations. In particular, it is likely that Cowan and Sarmad's subjects were different bilinguals from the Canadian subjects, although we do not have the evidence necessary to confirm this suspicion.)

The corollary of the parallel processing theory is that the know-ledge of the foreign language will affect the development of the foreign language strategies: the less of the foreign language you know, the more likely you are to read as in your first language.

If Cowan is right, we must consider the structural characteristics of the first language and the foreign language if we wish to understand the nature of perceptual strategies and the manner in which they operate in foreign language reading.

His theory would lead one to predict that the variation among first-language readers would be greatest at low levels of foreign language competence, for similar languages, since first-language strategies could be used in the foreign language, but this would not be true for very different languages since differences between languages lead to different processing strategies: the greater the differences between two languages, the less likely one is to read the first language in the same way as the foreign language, and therefore the less likely it is that there will be a positive effect of transfer of reading strategies from first language to foreign language. Increasing the knowledge of the foreign language would lead to an increased ability to read in that language. However, a good knowledge of the linguistic structure of the foreign language would then be expected to lead to good reading in the foreign language, regardless of the first-language ability. This prediction does not correspond to reported experiences of students who know the language but cannot read it with adequate speed and comprehension. One further problem with this theory is that it is not clear what it would lead us to predict about the difference between *good* first-language readers whose FL competence is low, and *poor* first-language readers whose FL competence is high: presumably, for markedly different languages, the difference in L1 reading ability would be irrelevant, but for similar languages, like Spanish and English, would one expect the *good* L1 reader to be better than the *poor* L1 reader when reading the foreign language, regardless of foreign language proficiency? The problem is that the theory does not specify the amount contributed to foreign language reading by transfer from first language and that contributed by increased knowledge of the foreign language's structures.

Evidence for hypothesis 2

Ulijn (1978) presents evidence which contradicts Cowan's theory. His study suggests that contrasting structures (between first language and foreign language) are much less problematic for the foreign language reader than the parallel processing theory predicts. He did not find that points of linguistic contrast caused comprehension difficulties or slower reading rates. In one experiment his subjects, Dutch students reading French, and French native-speakers, showed the same pattern of difficulties in reading the French text, although the text contained structures predicted to cause processing difficulty because of the lack of equivalent structures in Dutch. In a further experiment, he manipulated the presence of what he called 'conceptual information' — a city map to accompany instructions for finding one's way in an imaginary French town. The instructions were constructed in two versions, one containing structures that were parallel in French and Dutch, and the other containing structures that do not exist in Dutch, and which would be predicted, by Cowan's parallel processing theory or a contrastive analysis hypothesis, to cause reading problems. It was hypothesized that in the contextualized condition — with a city map — contrasting structures would cause difficulty only if the contrastive analysis or parallel processing hypotheses were correct. He also hypothesized that the text with less conceptual information — without the city map — would force the reader to use more syntactic analysis when reading, and therefore the text containing syntactic contrasts rather than parallel structures would be expected to cause foreign language readers greater difficulty. He failed to find significant differences between the contrasting and parallel structures, for either native speakers or foreign language readers, thus failing to confirm Cowan's theory. Whilst the addition of the conceptual information — the city map — did significantly influence reading speed for both groups of readers, he did not find the lack of conceptual information forced foreign language readers into syntactic analysis of the text, or, at least, if it did, the contrasting syntactic structures contained in one text did not affect reading speed (or, presumably, comprehension). Ulijn and Kempen (1976) conclude that:

> Under normal conditions reading comprehension is little dependent on a syntactic analysis of the text's sentences. It follows that second language reading comprehension is possible without mastery of the contrasting parts of the second language's syntax. Usually, the reader's conceptual knowledge will compensate for the lack of knowledge about linguistic contrasts between L1 and L2. (p. 499).

This conceptual knowledge, they claim, underlies the two major processes of comprehension that they posit (following Schank 1975): sentence parsing and inference, or reconstruction of the complete message from the partial message contained in the text. This conceptual knowledge appears to be both the reader's 'knowledge of the text's subject area' (p. 495) and knowledge of word meanings, particularly content words rather than function words. Thus, according to Ulijn (1978) and Ulijn and Kempen (1976), poor foreign language reading comprehension is not due to insufficient knowledge of grammar, but to lack of conceptual knowledge: the meanings of words and subject knowledge. It follows that, since native speaker readers may also lack knowledge of the subject matter, the only difference between first and foreign language readers is in their knowledge of vocabulary. Thus foreign language reading programmes need to concentrate on improving students' vocabulary, and their procedures for recognizing unknown content words. The authors have nothing to say about the role of first-language reading ability, although their conclusions suggest that they would consider such ability to be irrelevant. They did not compare first and foreign language reading ability within the same individuals, but their evidence from native and non-native speakers of French suggests that there is no difference between the groups in terms of reading ability.

Alderson, Bastien and Madrazo (1977) provide evidence which suggests that a student's knowledge of the foreign language is more important to the comprehension of foreign language texts than is reading ability in the first language. Mexican university students were tested for their English proficiency on the TEAL test (Clapham 1975) and their reading performance in both English and Spanish (the first language) was measured by multiple choice questions on texts. To control for knowledge of subject matter, and to reduce the effect of the text variable, students were given texts in their area of study (Business Administration), in English, and translated into Spanish. The questions on the text were checked by the subject department who confirmed that knowledge extraneous to the passages did not appear to be involved. The correlation between reading in English and reading in Spanish was significant, but only moderate: ·44 and ·56. (Interestingly, the higher correlation was obtained with a Spanish text that appeared to be conceptually more demanding.) A higher correlation was found between English language proficiency and reading comprehension in English (rho = ·67). The study concluded that the best predictor of reading ability in a foreign language was not reading ability in the mother tongue, but rather proficiency in the foreign language. However, a text effect was observed, such that comprehension of an easy foreign language text related much less closely to foreign language proficiency (rho = ·42), suggesting that knowledge of English is less important to the understanding of easy texts. In the reading of easy texts, one might expect first-language reading ability to be more important. As the linguistic or conceptual difficulty of the text increases, the importance of foreign language proficiency increases and that of first-language reading ability reduces. We will return to this point later.

A study by Aron (1978) offers some tentative corroboration of part of Alderson et al.'s results, namely that there is little relation between reading ability in the first language and that in the foreign language. Aron compared Spanish-speaking EFL students' reading abilities on two reading tests, the reading subtest of the Comparative Guidance and Placement Program (designed to measure reading skills of native-speaker community college entrants) and the Spanish version of the high school equivalency practice test *Programa de Equivalencia para la Escuela Secundaria*. Proficiency in English as a foreign language was not measured. Both reading tests contained questions aimed at testing three 'skill areas': recalling details, understanding a main idea not explicitly stated in the text, and making inferences.

Low correlations were found between skills in the two languages: for detail, ·50; for understanding the main idea, ·37; and for inference, ·28. This lack of relationship between abilities in the first language and abilities in the foreign language is attributed by the author to possible differences between 'the differing models of the world which are held by differing language/culture groups' (p. 3). Unfortunately no evidence is presented to support this interesting conjecture, and one could equally well speculate that the lack of relationship between the reading abilities in the two languages was due to inadequate language knowledge.

Consistent with the hypothesis that foreign language reading ability will be affected by competence in the foreign language, is the prediction that foreign language readers, who lack competence in the language, will have difficulty in making full use of contextual constraints. The use of contextual constraints is held to be crucial to the reading process (Cziko 1978) and to the extent that foreign language readers are not able to utilize such constraints, they will be ineffective/inadequate readers.

Chihara, Oller, Weaver and Chavez-Oller (1977) compared native speakers of English and Japanese learners of EFL on their ability to handle what they called sequential prose (i.e. a normal text) and scrambled prose (the original sentences in a scrambled sequence) where the texts had been subjected to cloze deletion procedures. They found that the difference between scores for scrambled and sequential prose increased as subjects became more proficient in English, from beginner EFL learner to native English speaker. This is interpreted by the authors to mean that as learners become more proficient in the foreign language, they are more able to utilize context constraints. However, they were unable to show that increased proficiency led to increased ability to handle discourse constraints, for the foreign language learners. For the native speakers, the scrambled cloze was always harder to handle than the sequential cloze, but for the foreign language learners, regardless of ability (i.e. including advanced learners), one text in scrambled order was easier to cloze than another text in sequential order. This suggests that for non-natives, the text variable is more important than the utilization of discourse constraints. Although native speakers were consistently better at handling scrambled sentences than the foreign language readers, they were also better at handling the sequential texts. It is not clear from this study whether the difference between native speakers and foreign language learners is due to the ability to handle discourse constraints, or to something else, like reading ability in the first language, which was not measured, or to the type of foreign language instruction the learners had undergone (or to a host of other uncontrolled variables).

Cziko (1978) identifies three types of contextual constraint: syntactic, that is, the constraints provided by the rules of the language and the preceding words (such that the word *the* will most likely be followed by a noun); semantic, that is, constraints provided by the meaning and selection restrictions of preceding words (for example, the words *The boy* at the beginning of a sentence will most likely constrain the following verb to an action that a boy is likely to carry out); and discourse, that is, 'constraints provided by the topic of the text' (p. 473). Cziko compared the abilities to use such constraints of native speakers of French and of learners of French at various levels of proficiency. He found that although even beginners and intermediate learners were able to make use of syntactic constraints when reading French, only the advanced foreign language readers and the native speakers were able to make use of semantic constraints. In addition, intermediate students were not aided in their performance on a cloze task by the 'additional discourse constraints present in normal prose' (p. 483).

Cziko suggests that 'a relatively high level of competence in a language is a prerequisite to the ability to use discourse constraints as a source of information in reading' (p. 484). Interestingly, Cziko was not able to find differences between advanced foreign language readers and native readers in ability to use discourse, or other constraints, unlike Chihara *et al*. If we assume that Cziko's subjects were good readers in their first language — and unfortunately we have no evidence of this — it would appear that students of a foreign language at a low level of competence are not able to use their good first-language reading strategies, one of which would presumably involve the ability to utilize contextual constraints, *because of* their low level of competence. This finding, if it had been made, would have enabled us to argue that it is important to improve the foreign language competence of foreign language readers before they can be expected to display effective reading. However, Cziko's results do not allow us to draw this conclusion, since we know nothing about the first-language reading ability of the subjects, and we are not able to compare the same individual's reading ability in two different languages, for varying levels of foreign language competence.

Evidence for hypothesis 2a

Clarke (1979) provides some evidence which enables us to explore the question of the relationship between first and foreign language reading ability in the same individual. Since his subjects were all at the same approximate level of proficiency in English as a foreign language, however, it is not possible to examine directly the connection between reading ability in first and foreign language and levels of proficiency in the foreign language.

Clarke's subjects were compared for their reading ability in their first and foreign languages (Spanish and English) using a modified cloze procedure, and a miscue analysis, to attempt to discern differences in strategies among readers that might transfer across languages. It was assumed that, 'given equivalent proficiency in the second language, the superior reading skills of the good readers would provide them with an equal advantage over the poor readers in both languages'. This position is based on the reading universals hypothesis that reading is the same in all languages.

Clarke found that the good first-language readers (as measured by their performance on the Spanish cloze test) got a significantly higher mean score on the foreign language cloze test than did the poor first-language readers (at least on the acceptable word score — no tests were reported on the exact score means, which appear not to have produced a significant difference). In other words, the good first-language readers as a group are better foreign language readers than the poor first-language readers.

When the unacceptable cloze responses were analysed, it was found that good L1 readers produced more semantically accept-able responses in their first language than did the poor readers. However, there was no difference between good and poor readers in the production of unacceptable responses in the foreign language. Good readers did not demonstrate the expected advan-tage over poor readers in their foreign language.

> When reading in English, the good readers were superior to the poor readers in that they were able to produce more acceptable cloze responses. Yet when confronted with difficult blanks the good readers appear to be little better than the poor readers in producing high quality guesses. (p. 130).

Secondly Clarke carried out miscue analysis on two readers of equal EFL proficiency, one a good L1 reader, one a poor L1 reader. The analysis was carried out on readings in both the first and the foreign language. The good L1 reader produced fewer miscues in both languages than did the poor L1 reader, and he produced more syntactically and semantically acceptable miscues than the poor reader. However, the difference between the two was greatly reduced in the foreign language. Clarke suggests on the basis of the cloze and oral reading results that there may exist a 'language competence ceiling' which 'hampers the good L1 reader in his attempts to use effective reading behaviours' in the foreign language. 'Limited control over the language "short circuits" the good reader's system causing him to revert to poor reader strategies when confronted with a difficult or confusing task in the second language.' Thus a poor foreign language reader could be one of at least two types — a poor L1 reader, or a good L1 reader who has not been able to transfer his L1 reading ability to the foreign language because of his problem with the foreign language.

The implications of Clarke's work are that there is no direct transfer of ability or strategies across languages, and that foreign language competence is required before transfer can occur. Further research is needed to see if the difference between good and poor L1 readers does indeed exist in the foreign language, whether it exists at low levels of foreign language competence, and whether it increases as learners progress in foreign language proficiency.

The limitations of Clarke's research are (i) that good and poor readers are defined purely in terms of their cloze performance, (ii) that the subjects have approximately the same levels of EFL proficiency, (iii) that the miscue analysis produced results which were very similar to those produced in native speaker studies and ESL studies with children (Rigg 1977), which leads one either to believe that reading processes are universal, or that the findings are instrument-induced, and other, more interesting differences between readers actually exist which are not being shown by the miscue analyses. The only information Clarke produces on reading behaviours — that is, the *process* of reading rather than the *product* or result of reading — are the miscues. Additional techniques are required for getting at reader behaviour.

Nevertheless, the short-circuit hypothesis advanced by Clarke appears to be supported by the results obtained by Cziko, where it appeared that only with increasing proficiency were subjects able to use discourse constraints, an ability held to be important in the reading process in general. Clarke's hypothesis also receives theoretical and empirical support from Cummins (1979) who puts forward the notion of a 'threshold level of linguistic competence' which bilinguals need to achieve before the supposed benefits of bilingualism can appear. This notion is based upon a survey of apparently contradictory empirical studies of the effects of bilingualism. By re-interpreting and comparing the data, Cummins finds that those studies which have shown positive effects of bilingualism have been associated with balanced bilinguals in additive bilingual settings where the bilinguals are likely to have had high levels of second-language competence; by comparison, earlier studies which suggested that bilingualism might adversely affect cognitive and scholastic progress tended to involve subtractive bilingual settings, and often the bilinguals had not attained high levels of second-language competence or indeed of first-language competence.

> One implication of the threshold hypothesis . . . is that pupils who have attained the threshold may perform very differently on cognitive and academic tasks from pupils who have failed to attain the threshold. (p. 26).

Thus, synthesizing Cummins and Clarke, we could arrive at a statement of the relationship between reading ability and language ability in foreign language reading that predicted that foreign language readers will not be able to read as well in the foreign language as in their first language until they have reached a threshold level of competence in that foreign language. This conclusion would support the commonsense statement of Coady (1979) that 'It is obvious that the ESL student is going to be deficient in process strategies which involve substantial knowledge of the target language'.

It is, however, worth considering the caution that Cummins offers on the interpretation of the threshold hypothesis. He points out that the threshold cannot be defined in absolute terms, but that it is actually likely to vary depending upon the demands being placed upon the learner by any given task: the more demanding the task, the higher the threshold is likely to have to be. The threshold is also likely to vary with the stage of cognitive development of the learner, and, we might add, with his level of relevant and available background knowledge. If he has a relatively high level of what Ulijn calls conceptual knowledge, he is presumably likely to require a lower threshold, or language competence ceiling, than someone with a lower level of conceptual knowledge, other things being equal (which, of course, they are unlikely to be). An interesting question is whether a high language competence can compensate for a low conceptual level or a lack of relevant background knowledge. The experience of native speaker students, with a presumed perfect language competence, but lacking knowledge as they attempt to *learn* a subject matter at, say, university level, suggests that such compensation may not be as simple as is perhaps being suggested here. The point is, however, that some threshold does, on the face of the evidence presented, appear to be necessary before other abilities, like one's first-language reading ability, can be brought to bear upon the task of reading in a foreign language.

Summary

In summary, then, we have examined some evidence relating to the question of whether poor reading in a foreign language is due to problems with the foreign language, or to problems with reading as a set of strategies. The first hypothesis examined was that reading problems in a foreign language were due to poor reading ability in the first language. Despite some evidence of transfer of reading ability from one language to another, from studies of bilinguals, only moderate to low correlations have so far been established between reading ability in first language and reading ability in the foreign language when the *same* individuals are studied in both languages. Some evidence, however tentative, suggests that proficiency in the foreign language may be more closely associated with foreign-language reading ability. This constitutes a measure of support for the second hypothesis proposed, namely that reading problems were due to language problems. Differences between native and non-native speakers were established in the ability to utilize contextual constraints, presumably a language-related ability. It was found that even non-natives of low levels of proficiency were able to use syntactic constraints, and other evidence was cited to suggest that syntax as such, even those syntactic patterns not occurring in the learner's mother tongue which might be expected to cause problems when reading in the foreign language, could not be conclusively shown to present problems, although no information was available on whether the learners concerned 'knew' the structures concerned, or on their level of foreign language competence. The weight of evidence seems to support the second hypothesis, at least at relatively low levels of competence. We have little or no evidence, however, about the role of foreign language competence at higher levels of proficiency. If syntax proves to be a relatively unimportant problem, then the hypothesis that the foreign language will require its own processing strategies because of its structural differences from the first language, receives little support. More plausible, but elusive, is the notion that problems in foreign language reading which are due to language have to do with semantic and discourse processing, and are related to problems of conceptualization and, to put it crudely, word meaning. Although differences were observed between native speaker readers and advanced non-native speaker readers, no clear explanations were offered to account for the differences. The question of whether, at more advanced levels, foreign language reading might become a reading problem has not been investigated, and remains open. Considerable support was found for the modified second hypothesis, namely that some sort of threshold or language competence ceiling has to be attained before existing abilities in the first language can begin to transfer. However, many questions remain to be answered within the scope of this hypothesis, for example, what the nature of this threshold is: to what extent is it syntactic, semantic, conceptual, discoursal? Does the level of the threshold vary for different learners, and for different tasks? Is it conceivable that good first-language readers will require a lower threshold before being in a position to utilize their good reading strategies? Will the attainment of a higher level of competence compensate a poor first-language reader?

The way forward

One of the problems of studies to date is that relatively few of them were designed to investigate the questions this paper has attempted to raise. What is needed at present is a series of studies which are directed to the problems of reading in a foreign language and its relation with language competence and first-language reading ability, and conceivably also other cognitive abilities in the area of what Cummins has called the cognitive/academic language proficiency. Such studies should benefit from an awareness of previous research, but in particular from a knowledge of the limitations of such research.

Perhaps the major problem in the design of many studies has been that they have failed to gather sufficient relevant information: what is needed is at least information on reading ability in the first language, ideally where the sample of subjects contained both 'good' and 'poor' first-language readers; information of the reading ability in the foreign language; and information about the level and, importantly, the nature, of the foreign language proficiency *of the same individual*. It is worth re-emphasizing at this point the warning of Cummins, mentioned above, of the dangers of comparing results of different studies whose subjects have had different levels of foreign language proficiency. In order to make such a comparison, it is necessary to know in considerable detail the nature of the subjects' proficiencies in both languages, their attitudes (and the attitudes of their society) to the foreign language, the role of that foreign language in their society, and a host of other social, cultural, economic, educational and political variables that may have a bearing on learning and processing language.

The second major limitation of much research is that it focused upon the product of reading — the comprehension of text — rather than the *process* of reading, the comprehending. Data collected was frequently in the form of test results, be they multiple choice or cloze tests. Such information provides no insight into how the reader has arrived at his interpretation, be it at the level of detail, main idea, inferred meaning, or evaluative judgement. Clarke's research marks the beginning of an attempt to gather information on the process of reading, through miscue analysis, but we need to develop a range of new techniques for process research. The thinking-aloud technique of Hosenfeld is one such possibility (Hosenfeld 1979 and this volume); immediate retrospections are another. The techniques suggested by Harri-Augstein and Thomas (this volume) are also possibilities. A technique worthy of investigation is the letter-crossing technique suggested by Hatch (1973), which attempts to gather information indirectly on the sorts of information that foreign-language readers are processing. Another possibility is the use of gap-filling procedures (not pseudo-random cloze tests), where the gaps have been produced according to a theory of processing, or contextual constraint. Such gap-filling exercises could be accompanied by introspections *à la* Hosenfeld, and the nature of the restorations might be first analysed and then explored with the subject. The important point to note is that we need to experiment with a range of different techniques that will give insight into reading behaviour, into the reading process, in both languages. The same is true of measures of language proficiency: where possible (and such measures are barely developed at present),we need to gain more insight not simply into the level of proficiency as indexed by some test score, but into the nature of that proficiency, if possible relating the language measure to the language of the texts to be processed. Another variable that needs to be investigated is the state of the learner's knowledge, particularly with regard to the subject matter of the texts he is asked to read during the study. Many studies have shown the text variable to have produced unexpected results, and this is almost certainly a result of topic knowledge and associated linguistic/conceptualization problems.

The third major limitation of virtually all the studies referred to in this paper is that they have been quantitative in nature, rather than qualitative. For adequate, illuminating research to be carried out in this area of foreign language reading, a range of information is required about individuals. If only because of the usual constraints of time and money, this would argue for in-depth qualitative studies, rather than extensive quantitative research. Quantitative research has tended to obscure important individual differences and individual factors. The problem with studies using test data and correlational techniques, analysis of variance and similar statistical treatments, is not merely that the interpretation of results can be problematic, but particularly that grouping data tends to reduce the effects of individual differences in favour of the similarities across individuals. Frequently, as we have seen, this involves *ignoring* important variables in order to concentrate on one or two only, or hoping that the effect of these other variables will be removed by *grouping* data. There is an increasingly strong case to be made, however, for deliberately maximizing differences by looking at individuals. What we seem to require, at least at this stage, is rich, varied information about individuals, selected for their characteristics on relevant variables: good or poor first-language reading, high or low general foreign language proficiency, different levels and qualities of topic information, and so on.

It would seem to make sense deliberately to select extreme cases for investigation rather than examining average or normal cases, since if studies of markedly different cases do not reveal expected results, grouping data or studying more normal cases is even less likely to be revealing. Thus a useful starting point would be to select clearly good and clearly poor first-language readers who happen to be learning a foreign language, and compare their reading ability in that language. Such a study would ideally be longitudinal, in order to examine the effect of increasing foreign language competence on the transfer of first-language reading ability. A longitudinal study of this nature would allow the investigation, if desired, of the effect of particular teaching techniques which might be aimed at facilitating transfer. What we are advocating, in effect, is a case study approach, longitudinal in nature, which would involve subjects carefully selected and matched for the purpose of comparisons and contrasts. One might, for example, select subjects who were good readers in their first language, but who varied in terms of their foreign language competence, but who had approximately the same level of relevant topic knowledge, and compare them with individuals who were similar in topic knowledge and foreign language proficiency but who were poor readers in their first language.

In short, it is becoming increasingly clear that future research will have to focus upon individuals, and be specifically designed to allow a detailed examination of the nature of their abilities, strategies, knowledges, attitudes and motivations, and any other variables that appear to be of relevance. Such research will also need to take account of the dynamic nature of learning, the interactive nature of reading and the importance of trying to characterize the process of reading. In addition it will have to take account of the difficulties of doing so by taking cross sections (snapshots as it were) of the state of a person's ability (often through test data) rather than by making longitudinal in-depth studies (slow motion films, perhaps) of the ongoing development of the ability and the variation in the deployment of strategies over time. This research might well include the use of techniques like protocol analysis, participant observation, and interactive, interventionist research.

To return to the question posed in the title: is foreign language reading a language problem or a reading problem? The answer, perhaps inevitably, is equivocal and tentative — it appears to be both a language problem and a reading problem, but with firmer evidence that it is a language problem, for low levels of foreign language competence, than a reading problem. As has been suggested, we do not *know* this yet, and the question needs further refinement and intense investigation. It is at least clear, perhaps frustratingly so, that there is a great need for further research into the relative contribution to foreign language reading performance of foreign language competence and first-language reading ability, on particular tasks, seen in relation to other factors like conceptual knowledge, to help us to define more closely the nature and level of the language competence ceiling or threshold for particular purposes.

Postscript on Alderson

EFL textbooks incorporating reading texts are somewhat ambivalent as to the function of these texts and their accompanying exercises. Often the texts seem to exist mainly to provide language data, so that the presence of a passive construction triggers an exercise on the passive, with no apparent aim of improving students' understanding of the text. Comprehension exercises, on the other hand, would seem to be aimed at practising reading skills. Although there may be nothing intrinsically wrong with using reading texts as language data, it might be beneficial if textbook writers and classroom teachers showed some awareness of this dual function.

The question which Alderson raises is thus a very pertinent one at the practical level. As Alderson makes clear, however, the area is fraught with complexities. Take, for example, the matter of transfer among bilinguals. Even if we leave aside the problem of defining bilingualism, we are hardly entitled to claim that a failure of transfer to take place in particular cases is evidence for the impossibility or difficulty of transfer in all cases. Take the example of an L1 speaker of Luo, a Kenyan language, highly literate in English (his L3) but barely literate in Luo. This is most easily explained, not by the impossibility of transfer, but by reference to his lack of need, or motivation, or opportunity to read Luo texts. Perhaps in this area we should eschew generalizations, and, as Alderson suggests, concentrate on well-defined, well-described individuals. When Cowan, for example, claims that English readers will be thrown by an ovs ordering in German, one is tempted to ask, 'Which English readers?' The reader who knows no German is unlikely to be able to start, and therefore the ordering is irrelevant; the highly fluent reader, on the other hand, is surely not likely to be thrown every time. The most one might claim about him is that he is likely to make more processing errors in this area than a German of comparable reading ability.

Having suggested that one should be remorselessly particular, we now propose to try to establish some general guidelines by describing some 'commonsense' positions. By commonsense positions, we mean generalizations which seem reasonable, but are not supported by experimental evidence, and may on occasion stand in opposition to such evidence.

a) There is a difference between language competence and reading skills. Many L1 speakers, presumably by definition competent in the spoken language, are at best only marginally literate. If one transfers this to the FL situation, then it seems reasonable to claim that there *could* be a distinction between learning English and learning to read in English.

b)   It seems unlikely that a poor L1 reader, however this term is defined, can, without tuition, move from this inadequate base to become a good FL reader. In other words, commonsense might lead us to believe that someone who is a poor reader in the L1 will also be a poor reader in the FL. As has been previously noted, however, this does not apply to readers who have attained their literacy primarily in an FL or L3.

c)   It is difficult to believe that a competent L1 reader will not in any circumstances be able to transfer his skills to the FL. Competence in reading is, of course, difficult to define, but one would wish to include in such a definition a predilection to treat a written text as carrying information, and a tendency to try to make sense of it by relating the information to background knowledge. More specifically, competence might include the ability to move about in a text, relating different parts, illustrations, captions, etc. It seems unlikely (although possible) that a fluent English reader will not attempt to do this when reading, say, French.

Such a position seems contrary to the experimental evidence cited in Alderson's paper. However, as Alderson himself suggests, the tests used (mainly cloze) do not necessarily measure high-level skills. Moreover, it is possible to envisage someone understanding the text but lacking the combined knowledge of syntax and lexis to come up with the required item, on a cloze test on that particular text.

d)   In spite of what has been said above, it seems obvious that the skilled L1 reader will, except in exceptional circumstances, require *some* knowledge of the FL before he can read in it with any facility.

If we put the above generalizations together, where do we arrive? From (d) we would have to assume the existence of some kind of threshold. From (b) and (c) we could suggest that once this threshold level is passed, a gap should develop in FL reading performance between the good and the poor L1 reader. This gap might be expected to become evident in higher level skills, though presumably after a suitable time factor one might expect to find it reflected in the lower level skills measured by cloze tests.

In other words, the good L1 reader might be expected to take off after reaching the threshold level, and reach satisfactory levels himself. This is not necessarily to say that any reading tuition will be useless. As we point out in the Introduction, it seems possible that all of us at any time can become more competent readers. The poor L1 reader, on the other hand, is not likely to improve by himself, if the position we have indicated in (a) is anything like the truth. He will need considerable tuition in reading skills. It would follow that in advance of, say, an EFL reading for study skills course, we would need to divide students on the basis of their reading ability in their L1.

As Alderson makes clear, however, the main questions remain to be answered. What is the nature of the threshold, if it exists? What types of language skills are involved in the learner reaching the threshold? We must be careful not to equate language skills with knowledge of what Widdowson (1979) has termed 'usage', i.e. formal descriptions of the language. It may well be that the FL reading skills of the good L1 reader cannot be satisfactorily correlated with his knowledge of, or even recognition of, say, the passive in English. It may be that there are communication skills not specific to a particular language, which the skilled reader is able to utilize. It is in this area that, as Alderson suggests, research into individuals can profitably be carried out.

2 Learning from the perspective of the comprehender

John D. Bransford, Barry S. Stein and Tommie Shelton

The purpose of this chapter is to explore some of the cognitive activities that people must engage in to comprehend and remember information that is communicated through language. We begin by illustrating how language comprehension depends on the activation of relevant knowledge; later we argue that people may differ in the degree to which they spontaneously activate knowledge that provides a basis for comprehension. This analysis has implications for understanding why some people learn more effectively than others and for creating programmes designed to help people learn to learn.

The active nature of comprehension

An effective procedure for illustrating how comprehension depends on the activation of relevant knowledge is to manipulate the availability of knowledge and assess the effects on comprehension and memory. Read the following passage and imagine that you will be asked to recall it later on:

> If the balloons popped, the sound would not be able to carry since everything would be too far away from the correct floor. A closed window would also prevent the sound from carrying since most buildings tend to be well insulated. Since the whole operation depends on a steady flow of electricity, a break in the middle of the wire would also cause problems. Of course the fellow could shout, but the human voice is not loud enough to carry that far. An additional problem is that a string could break on the instrument. Then there could be no accompaniment to the message. It is clear that the best situation would involve less distance. Then there would be fewer potential problems. With face to face contact, the least number of things could go wrong.

Bransford and Johnson (1972) read this passage to a group of

students (called the No Knowledge Context Group). After hearing
it, the group was asked to rate it for comprehensibility on a seven-
point scale (where 7 indicates highly comprehensible) and then to
attempt to recall it. As you might expect, people in this group
rated the passage as very incomprehensible (the average rating
was 2·3), and their recall scores were quite low (see Table 1).

Table 1   Comprehension and recall scores for the balloon passage

	no context	context before	context after	partial context	maximum score
Comprehension rating	2·30	6·10	3·30	3·70	7·00
Number of idea units recalled	3·60	8·00	3·60	4·00	14·00

The same passage becomes quite comprehensible if one is
supplied with an appropriate knowledge framework or context,
however. The picture in Figure 1 provides such a framework.
Look at the picture and then read the passage again.

People who first saw the appropriate picture and then heard the
passage (called the Appropriate Context Before Group) rated
the passage as very comprehensible (the average rating was 6·1).
Furthermore, their recall scores were over twice as high as
the first group's (see Table 1). However, the appropriate picture
had to be available while reading or hearing the passage. Bransford and Johnson presented another group with the picture *after*
hearing the passage; this did not significantly increase their
comprehension or memory scores relative to the No Knowledge
Context Group (see Table 1).

Why is the balloon passage so incomprehensible when presented
in isolation? How does it become comprehensible when one is first
provided with the information in Figure 1? An answer to these
questions requires an analysis of how the pictorial information
provides a basis for interpreting the words and phrases that the
passage contains. As an illustration, consider the first phrase which
states: 'If the balloons popped, the sound would not be able to
carry . . .'. What is the referent of the word 'sound'? With no
context, the obvious assumption is that 'sound' refers to the
balloons popping. Given this assumption, it is difficult to grasp the
relevance of additional information in the passage. For example,
what's the 'correct floor' that the sound could not reach? What's

Figure 1 Appropriate context for the balloon passage

the 'whole operation' that depends on a steady flow of electricity? Without additional information, it is difficult to determine the referents of many of the phrases and words.

When one reads the passage in the context of the appropriate picture in Figure 1, it becomes clear that the theme centres around a unique problem of communication between a 'modern day Romeo' and a woman. One therefore realizes that 'sound' refers

Figure 2 Partial context for the balloon passage

to the music from the loudspeaker rather than the balloons, and that the 'whole operation' refers to a particular method of communication that could break down in ways that the passage describes. The picture in Figure 1 provides concrete referents for words like 'balloons', 'wire', etc. but its most important function is to serve as a basis for specifying the goals of the Romeo and his method for solving a unique problem of communication. Note, for example, that the picture in Figure 2 contains the same concrete objects as Figure 1, but the method of communication is vastly different. Bransford and Johnson presented a group of students with this partial context picture (Figure 2) before hearing the passage and found that it did not significantly increase comprehension and memory scores relative to the No Knowledge Context Group (see Table 1).

Further illustrations of the role of activated knowledge

The balloon passage discussed a situation that is unique and unlikely to have been previously experienced. Are such unique contexts necessary in order to demonstrate the intricate relationships between general knowledge and the materials to be learned? Read the following passage. Once again, imagine that you will be asked to recall it after reading it once.

> Sally first tried setting loose a team of gophers. The plan backfired when a dog chased them away. She then entertained a group of teenagers and was delighted when they brought their motorcycles. Unfortunately, she failed to find a Peeping Tom listed in the Yellow Pages. Furthermore, her stereo system was not loud enough. The crab grass might have worked but she didn't have a fan that was sufficiently powerful. The obscene phone calls gave her hope until the number was changed. She thought about calling a door-to-door salesman but decided to hang up a clothesline instead. It was the installation of blinking neon lights across the street that did the trick. She eventually framed the ad from the classified section.

Stein and Albridge (1978) found that most people rated this passage as difficult to comprehend. Given prior exposure to a title like 'Attempts to get her neighbours to move', however, the passage makes much more sense. These differences in comprehensibility are also paralleled by people's ability to remember the information. Table 2 illustrates recall scores for three acquisition conditions in which students heard the passage with no title, heard the title before hearing the passage, or heard the title after hearing the passage. The recall test was given following an interval of 60 seconds of counting backwards. The scores are based on the number of key words recalled from the passage (i.e. nouns, verbs, adjectives and adverbs). As with the balloon passage, the title must be available at the time of acquisition in order to facilitate recall. Note further that people receiving the Sally passage presumably had a general understanding of the problem of getting one's neighbours to move before entering the experiment, yet they were still unable to comprehend and remember effectively unless explicitly prompted by receiving the story title. The availability of potential information is therefore not sufficient for comprehension; potential knowledge must be activated in order to facilitate people's abilities to understand and learn (see also Bransford 1979; Bransford and Johnson 1972, 1973; Dooling and Lachman 1971).

Table 2 Mean percentage of key words recalled from the Sally passage

no topic	topic after	topic before
31%	30%	40%

The role of general knowledge in everyday comprehension

The passages about the modern day Romeo and about Sally are specially designed to be incomprehensible without the activation of additional information. We rarely encounter anything as incomprehensible as these passages. One might therefore argue that these examples overemphasize the importance of activating relevant knowledge; perhaps 'normal' comprehension is much less dependent on people's general knowledge of the world.

Consider a simple statement such as 'The policeman held up his hand and the cars stopped'. People need no extra prompts or cues to understand this sentence, but this does not mean that they need not activate relevant knowledge in order to understand it. In particular, the ability to understand this statement seems to involve knowledge that cars usually have drivers and that drivers apply their brakes in order to stop. Collins and Quillian (1972) suggest the following thought-experiment regarding the policeman sentence. Assume there was an earthquake, which caused some parked cars to begin rolling down a hill. Now, given the sentence 'The policeman held up his hand and the cars stopped', one is forced to ask: how did he do that? The earthquake context rules out the possibility of assuming that drivers applied their brakes when viewing the policeman's hand signal. Under normal situations, however, assumptions about 'drivers who apply their brakes' seem to be made.

The policeman example requires that one make a connection between that outstretched hand and the cars stopping. The sentence doesn't specify how the outstretched hand 'caused' the cars to stop but it really doesn't need to; most people can supply this information on their own. Similarly, most people who attempt to understand a sentence such as 'The floor was dirty because Sally used the mop' make additional assumptions. Many assume that the mop was dirty before she began to clean the floor. If the sentence is changed to 'The floor was dirty so Sally used the mop', however, assumptions about the mop initially being dirty are less likely to be made. McCarrell, Johnson and Bransford (in Bransford and Johnson 1973) presented students with either *because* or *so* versions of sentences such as those listed above and then gave them recognition tests. Certain test items contained information that was congruent with inferences that students were expected to make during acquisition (e.g. Sally used a dirty mop to clean the floor). Students who originally heard the *because* version of each acquisition sentence were highly likely to think they had actually heard these test items during acquisition; those who received the *so* versions did not falsely recognize these test items. These data suggest that people do indeed actively make assumptions in order to fill in the gaps in messages and that they often think this inferred information was actually presented during the acquisition task.

Rumelhart and Ortony (1977) provide an additional example of the importance of activating knowledge that fills in the gaps in messages. Consider the following sentences:

1. Mary heard the ice cream man coming.
2. She remembered the pocket money.
3. She rushed into the house.

Rumelhart and Ortony note that these three sentences form a 'snippet' of a story which most people can interpret quite readily. Nevertheless, a number of assumptions are necessary in order to accomplish this feat:

> Presumably this interpretation is along the lines that Mary heard the ice cream man coming and wanted to buy some ice cream. Buying ice cream costs money, so she had to think of a quick source of funds. She remembered some pocket money she had not yet spent which, presumably, was in the house. So, Mary hurried into the house trying to get the money by the time the ice cream man arrived. (p. 113).

A similar example of assumptions necessary to connect sentences is provided by Schank and Abelson (1977):

1. John knew his wife's operation would be expensive.
2. There was always Uncle Harry.
3. John reached for the suburban telephone book.

Clearly, a great deal of information is involved in tying these sentences together; for example, assumptions about the need for money, that a relative might be likely to lend it, that the money could never be borrowed without contacting the uncle, that telephones can be used to make contact, and so on. Even children's stories require many assumptions to link sentences together to form coherent events (see Charniak 1972; Rumelhart 1975, 1977; Trabasso (in press)). If people lack the knowledge necessary to make appropriate assumptions or inferences, most passages would presumably seem as arbitrary as the balloon or Sally passages presented above.

Comprehension and the utilization of familiar concepts

An emphasis on the use of general knowledge to comprehend linguistic messages has important implications for understanding why some people are better able to understand and remember information than others. First, people may differ in the degree to which they have acquired appropriate knowledge that serves as a basis for filling in the gaps in messages. For example, if someone lacked knowledge about the steps involved in eating at a restaurant, it might be difficult to understand and remember statements such as 'Bill refused to leave a tip because the service was slow' (see Schank and Abelson 1977).

A second possible source of individual differences in learning involves differences in the degree to which people spontaneously activate knowledge that is potentially available. For example, consider sets of simple sentences such as the following:

'The tall man bought the crackers.'
'The fat man read the sign.'
'The old man purchased the paint.'

These sentences are by no means incomprehensible. Nevertheless, the relationship between each type of man and the actions performed seems arbitrary. It is therefore difficult to remember which man performed which action. Experiments by Stein and colleagues show that when students are read sets of sentences such as those above (we shall refer to these as base sentences), their memory for them is quite poor (e.g. Stein, Morris and Bransford 1978; Stein and Bransford 1979).

How can the information expressed by each base sentence be made more meaningful or less arbitrary? What must students do in order to remember which man did what? A number of theorists argue that people must elaborate to-be-learned information by relating it to previously acquired knowledge (e.g. Anderson and Reder 1978; Craik and Tulving 1975; Rohwer 1966). However, there is a need to specify the *kind* of knowledge that must be activated in order for people to understand and learn.

Some theorists (e.g. Craik and Tulving 1975) argue that the activation of additional knowledge will facilitate learning as long as this knowledge is semantically consistent or congruous with to-be-learned information. As an illustration, the base sentences presented earlier might be elaborated as follows:

'The tall man bought the crackers and then went home.'
'The fat man read the sign that was two feet high.'
'The old man purchased the paint from the clerk in the store.'

Each of the preceding examples illustrates an elaboration that is semantically congruous with its respective base sentence. However, recent research by Stein, Morris and Bransford (1978) and Stein and Bransford (1979) demonstrates that elaborations such as these actually *debilitate* retention relative to groups that receive the base sentences alone. For example, Stein *et al.* (1978, 1979) presented people with either the base sentences (e.g. 'The tall man bought the crackers') or the base sentences with elaborations (e.g. 'The tall man bought the crackers and then went home'). When subjects were tested with questions such as 'Which man bought the crackers?' performance was significantly better for the group that received the base sentences alone than for the group that received the elaborated base sentences.

Stein and colleagues argue that only certain types of elaborations facilitate understanding and learning. People must activate knowledge that clarifies the significance of to-be-learned information, that makes it less arbitrary. For example, imagine that each of the men described in the sentences above was chosen to perform each of the activities by a leader — a leader who was keenly aware of their unique characteristics. Why might each man have been selected to perform the particular activities described in the base sentences? Consider the following elaborations which appear to address this question:

'The tall man bought crackers that were on the top shelf.'
'The fat man read the sign warning about thin ice.'
'The old man purchased the paint to decorate his cane.'

Each of these elaborations renders the relationship between the type of man and the actions performed less arbitrary; for example, the fact that the crackers were on the top shelf helps people realize the significance or relevance of being tall. Stein and colleagues call these types of elaborations *precise* elaborations (the earlier set of elaborations are imprecise elaborations). When subjects were presented with precise elaborations they were excellent at remembering target adjectives (i.e. they were able to answer questions such as 'Which man bought the crackers?'). Memory data for the three groups we have discussed are presented in Table 3 (cf. Stein and Bransford 1979).

Table 3   Retention of target adjectives as a function of elaboration condition

base sentences alone	imprecise elaborations	precise elaborations
42%	22%	74%

The precision of elaborations also has powerful effects on retention when people generate their own elaborations. Stein and Bransford (1979) asked students to generate continuations of base sentences such as those presented earlier. Independent judges rated the precision of these self-generated elaborations and were able to agree with each other over 90% of the time. Elaborations rated precise resulted in a much greater ability to answer memory questions (e.g. 'Which man bought the crackers:') than did elaborations that were rated imprecise.

One way to characterize the processes that prompt precise elaborations is to focus on the types of questions people ask themselves while learning. Consider once again the base sentence 'The tall man bought the crackers'. Imprecise elaborations such as 'and then went home' or 'and ate them' seem to be possible answers to a question like 'What else might happen?' In contrast, a precise elaboration such as 'that were on the top shelf' is a possible answer to the question 'Why might this particular man do this particular thing?'. Stein and Bransford (1979) asked different groups of college students to generate their own continuations of base sentences in response to either the first or second question noted above; they were then asked memory questions such as 'Which man bought the crackers?'. Memory scores for the second group were superior to the first group. Furthermore, independent judges rated more of the elaborations of students in the second group as precise.

Activities that clarify the significance of unfamiliar concepts

Activating knowledge that clarifies the significance of facts can also be important for acquiring new concepts or schemata. As an illustration of the importance of using previously acquired knowledge to learn new information, imagine being presented with a passage describing the similarities and differences between veins and arteries. The passage might state that arteries are thick, relatively elastic, and carry blood rich in oxygen from the heart. In contrast, veins are thin, less elastic, and carry blood rich in carbon dioxide. What types of activities are necessary in order for people to understand facts about veins and arteries and to remember this information so they can use it later on?

One approach to learning about veins and arteries is to use various mnemonic techniques. For example, the fact that arteries are thick could be remembered by forming an image of a thick, hollow tube that flashes 'artery'. The fact that arteries are elastic could be remembered by imagining that the tube is suspended by a rubber band which stretches and contracts, thereby causing the tube to move up and down. We could embellish the image by having red liquid (blood) plus round (like an 'o') bubbles (oxygen) pouring out of the tube, and these could be moving in a direction away from an image of a Valentine-day heart. This composite image could serve as a basis for remembering that arteries are thick, elastic, and carry blood rich in oxygen away from the heart. An alternative technique is to use verbal elaborations; for example, '*Art*(ery) was *thick* around the middle so he wore pants with an *elastic* waistband . . .'

It is important to note, however, that the problem of learning frequently involves more than just remembering facts. In order to use information that may be accessible it is often necessary to understand why certain relationships exist and to understand the functions they serve. For example, imagine that people remember 'Arteries are elastic' either by thinking of a rubber band holding a tube or 'Art(ery) and his elastic waistband'. What if these people are confronted with the task of designing an artificial artery? Would it have to be elastic? What are the potential implications of hardening of the arteries? Would this have a serious impact on people's health? Learners who used the previously mentioned mnemonics to remember that arteries are elastic would have little basis for answering these questions. Indeed, the 'rubber band' and 'waistband' mnemonics could easily lead to misinterpretations:

perhaps hardening of the arteries affects people's abilities to stretch their arms and legs.

Mnemonic techniques are useful for many purposes, but one must take a very different approach to learning in order to develop an understanding of veins and arteries. Effective learners attend to factual content but they also seem to seek information about the *significance* or relevance of facts. For example, the passage about veins and arteries stated that arteries are elastic. What's the significance of elasticity? How does this property relate to the functions that arteries perform? An effective learner may seek information that can clarify this relationship. For example, our imaginary passage states that arteries carry blood from the heart — blood that is pumped in spurts. This provides one clue about the significance of elasticity — arteries may need to expand and contract to accommodate the pumping of blood. Some learners might then ask why veins do *not* need to be elastic. Since veins carry blood back to the heart, perhaps they have less of a need to accommodate the large changes in pressure resulting from the heart pumping blood in spurts.

Some learners may carry this process a step further. Since arteries carry blood *from* the heart there is a problem of directionality. Why doesn't the blood flow back into the heart? This will not be perceived as a problem if one assumes that arterial blood always flows downhill, but let's assume that our passage mentions that there are arteries in the neck and shoulder regions. Arterial blood must therefore flow uphill as well. This information might provide an additional clue about the significance of elasticity. If arteries expand from a spurt of blood and then contract, this might help the blood move in a particular direction. The elasticity of arteries might therefore serve the function of a one-way valve that enables blood to flow forward but not back. If one were to design an artificial artery it might therefore be possible to equip it with valves and hence make it non-elastic. However, this solution might work only if the spurts of blood did not cause too much pressure on the artificial artery. Our imaginary passage does not provide enough information about pressure requirements, so a learner would have to look elsewhere for this information. Note, however, that our learner realized the need to obtain additional information. The learner's activities are not unlike those employed by good detectives or researchers when they confront a new problem. Although their initial assumptions about the significance of various facts may ultimately be found to be incorrect, the act of seeking clarification is fundamental to the development of new expertise. In contrast, the person who simply concentrates on techniques for memorizing facts does not know whether there is something more to be understood.

Individual differences in learning

The preceding analysis suggests that people may differ in the degree to which they spontaneously activate knowledge that could clarify the significance of factual content. Research by Stein, Bransford, Owings and McCraw (in preparation) investigates this issue in more detail. They asked academically successful, average and less successful 5th grade students (ranked on the basis of teacher ratings and test scores) to learn new factual content and to elaborate this content in a way that would help them remember it. The children were presented with facts such as 'The hungry man got into the car', 'The tall man used the paintbrush' and were asked to write a continuing phrase that would help them remember which man did what. Independent judges rated the degree to which each elaboration clarified the significance of each to-be-learned fact. Results revealed large differences among the three groups of students, with the successful students producing the greatest number of precise elaborations and the less successful students producing the least. For example, successful students produced continuations such as 'The hungry man got into the car and drove to the restaurant' whereas less successful students produced ones similar to 'The hungry man got into the car and drove away.' Retention scores were affected by the precision of students' elaborations; statements that had been elaborated precisely resulted in better retention (e.g. 'Which man got into the car?') than those that had been elaborated in imprecise ways.

Why might the less successful students have been less likely to activate knowledge that precisely clarified the significance of the factual content that they were learning? One possibility is that these students lacked the knowledge necessary to elaborate precisely; an alternative explanation is that they failed to ask themselves relevant questions about the information they were trying to learn. In order to differentiate between these possibilities, Stein *et al.* worked with the less successful children in order to see whether they had the potential to elaborate precisely. The first step was to help the students experience the difficulty of remembering arbitrary sets of facts. The children were therefore asked to help the experimenters evaluate why some things were harder to remember than others. Children were read a new list of ten arbitrary base sentences (e.g., 'The kind man bought the milk'), with no instructions to elaborate. They were then asked questions such as 'Which man bought the milk?. As expected, their memory performance was very poor, averaging only one or two items correct. This was not upsetting to the children because they were evaluating the materials; they concluded that these materials were indeed hard to learn.

This experience set the stage for analysing why each base sentence was so difficult to remember. Given a statement such as 'The kind man bought the milk', for example, the students were prompted to ask themselves questions that would enable them to realize that the relationship was arbitrary. They might therefore be asked 'Is there any more reason to mention that a kind man bought milk than a tall man, a mean man?'. This set the stage for the next step which was to prompt students to activate knowledge that could make the relationship between 'kindness' and 'milk-buying' less arbitrary (e.g. 'Why might a kind man be buying milk?'). The third purpose of the intervention was to prompt students to evaluate their own continuations. For example, less successful students might write 'The kind man bought the milk because he was thirsty'. The experimenter would then ask, 'What does this have to do with being kind? Wouldn't a mean man be just as likely to do the same thing?' Given these explicit queries, all the children were eventually able to write continuations that clarified the significance of kindness, for example 'The kind man bought the milk to give to the hungry child'.

During the first few trials of the intervention the students had to be explicitly reminded to ask themselves relevant questions. For example, they were eventually able to activate information that clarified the significance of the first base sentence (e.g. kind man) yet rarely did this spontaneously for the base sentence presented on the second trial. After a few trials, however, the children began to internalize the process of question-asking and to evaluate whether their elaborations clarified the significance of the facts. For example, given the base sentence 'The rich man walked to the store', one student said 'to buy some candy'. She then remarked 'Wait, candy doesn't cost that much, I need something different', and after a brief pause said (smiling) 'and bought the whole store'. Many of the children's responses were quite creative, and they seemed to enjoy the task thoroughly.

After the children had elaborated the set of ten base sentences they were administered the same memory test that they had done so poorly on earlier. Nearly all of them did perfectly. The most interesting data involved their excitement and pleasure; a task that had initially been extremely difficult became very easy to perform. The children then received the initial set of base sentences used in the *original* study and were asked to write phrases that made the facts meaningful and non-arbitrary. Over 90% of these elaborations were precise (i.e. clarified the significance of the factual content). These students' initial failure to activate relevant knowledge had therefore not been due to a lack of potential knowledge nor to some inherent 'lack of verbal fluency'. They needed help finding ways to evaluate whether information seemed arbitrary, to use their knowledge to make it less arbitrary and to evaluate their attempts to meet this goal. By prompting the students to ask themselves relevant questions, the experimenters were able to observe a definite improvement in their performance on the experimental task plus a marked increase in their enthusiasm for the task.

Bransford, Stein, Shelton and Owings (in press) discuss additional data which suggest that less successful students often fail to activate relevant knowledge that could clarify the significance of factual content. When studying a passage about returning versus non-returning boomerangs, for example, less successful students studied by simply re-reading the passage. The successful students seemed to take a very different approach to the learning task. They appeared to ask themselves how the two types of boomerangs differed structurally (i.e. visually) and attempted to understand how particular structures were related to particular functions. For example, many realized the significance of the fact that non-returning boomerangs were heavier than returning boomerangs; the former were used to kill large game, the latter were not.

Summary and conclusions

To summarize, the ability to understand linguistic messages is not simply a function of 'knowledge of a language'; language comprehension depends on the availability of relevant knowledge to fill in the gaps in messages. However, even the availability of knowledge is not sufficient; it must be activated in order to facilitate people's abilities to learn. Research suggests that people may differ in the degree to which they spontaneously activate relevant knowledge that is potentially available. In particular, academically less successful students seem less likely to answer questions (of themselves and others) that could supply the information necessary to understand in more precise ways.

There are several possible implications of an approach to comprehension and learning such as the one we have outlined. First, the present approach emphasizes the importance of cognitive activities that enable one to *understand* as well as remember information. Next, a number of investigators have explored activities that facilitate memory (e.g. the use of various mnemonic techniques), but those techniques often fail to help people understand, and sometimes even detract from the comprehension process (see Stein and Bransford 1979). Thus, one can use various techniques to memorize statements such as 'Arteries are elastic' or 'The tall man bought the crackers' yet fail to ask oneself questions designed to clarify the significance of these facts. Similarly, imagine that college students with no chemistry background are told, 'Be sure you know that alcohols are organic compounds of the general formula (ROH) where R is an alkyl group'. One could use mnemonic techniques to remember the concept names (e.g. alkyl group) and formula (ROH) but this would not ensure a precise understanding of the statement. Effective learners would realize that they must do more than understand and remember the statement about alcohols at a linguistic level; they would assume that there is a reason for emphasizing particular concepts and that they had better understand these reasons. Thus even someone with little background in chemistry might infer that there are organic compounds other than alcohols, and that something about the general formula (ROH) is important for identifying alcohols. An additional inference is that there are different kinds of alcohols; all will probably have something in common yet will vary in their chemical composition. The use of general knowledge to generate and evaluate plausible assumptions therefore provides a plan for identifying additional information that must be specified. This comprehension-based approach to learning is very different from approaches that simply emphasize techniques for memorizing facts.

The preceding discussion also has implications for creating and evaluating programmes that are designed to help people learn about particular areas. In particular, there are important differences between programmes that help people learn particular

44   *John D. Bransford, Barry S. Stein and Tommie Shelton*

factual content and those that help them learn to learn. For
example, the memory performance of the academically less
successful students who were presented with statements such as
'The hungry man got into the car' could have been improved
considerably if the experiments had supplied the students with
precise elaborations. This would have helped the students learn
the factual content but it would not necessarily have helped them
learn to learn. In order to learn to learn students must become
able to evaluate the arbitrariness of factual content, to attempt to
activate knowledge that could make it less arbitrary and then evaluate their own attempts to meet this goal. The problem of understanding how people learn to learn represents an important
challenge for future theorizing and research.

Note

The research reported in this paper was supported in part by
grants BNS-7-077248, NIEG-79-0117 and by a University
Research Council Fellowship awarded to J. Bransford. The
passage about Sally used in the text was adapted from McCarrell
and Brooks (1975).

Postscript on Bransford *et al.*

The topics investigated by Bransford and his associates have recently become of increasing concern to workers from a variety of disciplines, e.g. ethnology, cognitive psychology and applied linguistics. In addition, however, their concentration on comprehension of linguistic information *and subsequent retention of the material comprehended* makes their work of immediate relevance to teachers of reading for learning.

The main features of the position they adopt towards comprehension may perhaps be summarized as follows:
1. no language text is ever 'complete in itself';
2. in order to be comprehended in a satisfactory manner, the text must be related to the reader's background knowledge;
3. the process of relating text and background knowledge, which some writers have referred to as 'making sense of texts', involves the reader in an active role. Hence reading is primarily a cognitive activity.

It will be recognized that much of this is not, strictly speaking, new. That reading is essentially a cognitive activity was stressed by Huey (1908) and Thorndike (1917). In fact Fries (1963) attacked much contemporary teaching of reading as, in fact, teaching of *thinking*. The need to relate text to existing knowledge has often been stressed in pedagogic advice to readers, e.g:

> By evaluating what you read and associating what you already know with information you are acquiring, you will read with more understanding and you will remember better what you read. (Parker 1959)

It must be admitted, however, that recently reading courses have tended to be very text-oriented, with minimal emphasis on the contribution of the reader.

The most exciting aspect of the work of Bransford and his associates is the manner in which it provides empirical evidence for what before was commonly expressed as pious but unsubstantiated advice to readers. Thus they demonstrate elegantly just how much readers' comprehension is affected by the activation or non-activation of background knowledge, and how cognitive activities are present in the interpretation of texts. Moreover, in an extremely interesting and relevant development, Stein *et al.* show that the ability to make sense of a text by relating it to background knowledge can be improved .

The implications of this view of comprehension, for which Bransford and his colleagues have provided empirical evidence, are clearly of major importance in the reading classroom. An extreme view would be that acceptance of the position would involve rejection of most forms of traditional teaching of reading. Such teaching often seems to consist of guiding students towards a set of 'correct' answers. However, if comprehension involves interpreting text in the light of one's background, and it is accepted that any individual's background knowledge is likely to be unique in at least some respects, then the status of such 'correct' answers is questionable. Moreover, if traditional teaching becomes suspect, testing of reading becomes much more so, since the questions and answers in a typical test might be regarded as expressing merely the tester's individual interpretation of the text. The controversy also affects *simplification*, since, as Bransford *et al.* demonstrate, what renders a text simple is not necessarily the language, but whether the information can be related to the readers' background knowledge. Again, since each reader's background knowledge is likely to be to some extent unique, any general form of simplification would seem to be impossible.

However, such views are extreme. From a theoretical point of view, adherence to these views would seem to involve a confusion between *comprehension* of a text and *what is done with that comprehension*. The fact that readers may interpret a text in different ways does not necessarily mean that their handling of a text-based task will be different. (The reverse also seems likely to be true: the fact that students may behave similarly on a test-task does not necessarily mean that their interpretations of the text are identical.) From an empirical point of view, one conclusion to be drawn from the work of Bransford *et al.* is that the background knowledge activated by different subjects appeared to be very similar. For example, the judges in the experiment by Stein *et al.* seemed quite capable of agreeing as to whether an elaboration was precise or not. Subjects' reaction to the Sally text appeared to have been very similar. Such presumed similarity of background knowledge is surely to be expected: normal communication between members of the same society would seem to depend on reference to shared background knowledge.

Thus it would seem that the effect of the work done by Bransford and others will be not to start a revolution in the teaching of reading but to help shift the emphasis away from a teacher-dominated, one-meaning approach to comprehension towards a more reader-oriented, interpretative approach.

There are two areas in which an emphasis on the importance of background knowledge would seem to cause particular problems.

The first is the general FL reading class. Here the class may be culturally very heterogeneous; alternatively the class may be homogeneous but belong to a different cultural group from the teacher and the material. The second area is language for special purposes (LSP). Here, apart from the cultural differences which often exist between student and student, and students and teacher, there is the major relevant difference of content-area knowledge between students and language teacher.

In the first case, the problems may be met if the teacher becomes more aware of the possible existence of a large number of different interpretations of a text rather than a single comprehension. One of the teacher's main jobs will then be to define learning goals, i.e. what it is that the students can expect to learn from a text, and to provide illustrative examples of how these goals are to be arrived at. The students should be encouraged to accept that there may well be many different, but valid interpretations arrived at on the way to these goals. In other words, there will be considerable emphasis on learning to learn.

In the case of the LSP reading class, the problems are similar but perhaps more extreme. The difficulties of language teachers faced with, say, science texts have long been discussed. If the view of comprehension held by Bransford and others is accepted, then it must be seen that the language teacher simply will not understand an unfamiliar text in the same way as content specialists. Thus with more advanced material, the role of the teacher or materials writer as setter of questions and evaluator of answers would seem to require modification. The reading teacher can emphasize learning to learn, but there appears to be a need for a content specialist to participate in some form of team teaching role.

It is sometimes implied that the view of reading as a problem-solving activity, allowing for a wide variety of valid interpretations, is impractical and out of touch with the realities of the classroom. The evidence produced by Bransford and his colleagues suggests strongly that this is not the case. When subjects activated background knowledge in comprehending texts, they not only judged the texts easier to understand, they also remembered them better. The students who proved good at providing precise elaborations were also academically the most successful. The teacher who adopts this view of reading may find that he has to sacrifice his dominant role as evaluator of interpretation, but he will have the consolation of taking part in a more practical and relevant learning activity.

3 Cultural knowledge and reading

Margaret S. Steffensen and Chitra Joag-Dev

Introduction

While foreign language teachers and theorists have been aware of
the fact that students from different cultures will bring different
systems of background knowledge to the comprehension process,
pedagogical methods and materials have not always reflected this
insight. This may be attributed to a number of factors. First, the
power and scope of this effect has probably been underestimated.
Second, foreign language pedagogy, until recently, has factored
out skills as productive or receptive, and oral or written. Within
a structuralist framework, emphasis has been placed on oral skills
and this focus has persisted in language teaching. Third, it is easier
to identify and teach specific features of the phonological and
grammatical systems of language in a methodical and concise way
than it is to teach features of culture. In this chapter, several
positions related to the influence of cultural knowledge on reading
a foreign language and two applied studies will be reviewed, and
an experiment designed to measure this effect will be described.

Fries (1945, 1963) was the first American linguist to incorporate
cultural background information into a description of meaning. In
his analysis, there are three levels of meaning: lexical, grammatical, and social-cultural. Comprehension of the total meaning of
a sentence occurs only when the linguistic meaning of the sentence
is fitted into 'a social framework of organized information'. He
illustrates the importance of the social-cultural level with a passage
from Washington Irving. The response to Rip Van Winkle's
'archaic' use of the term 'Tory' after an absence of twenty years
can be attributed to the fact that its cultural meaning had changed
from 'good citizen' to 'enemy of the new government'. Fries
argues that readers have missed the meaning of the story if they
do not understand the reaction of the group to Rip's words. For

mastery of a foreign language, he argues that 'one must find some substitute for the kind of background knowledge he has in his own language' (Fries 1945, p. 100). While these insights have influenced subsequent pedagogical writings directed to foreign language and EFL pedagogy, the position Fries advanced has been somewhat attenuated.

One position that has been adopted is that there will be cultural interference at the affective level, in the connotative values of words and in the attitudes expressed in, and underlying, the passage. A second is that there will be interference at the denotative level as well, and students must have a rather complete understanding of the background information if there is to be complete comprehension of a text. This position is close to that advocated by Fries but generally is not as rigorously stated. A third recognizes that complete mastery of a language is dependent upon knowledge of the culture but recommends the use of literature to achieve this goal. Each of these positions will be briefly considered.

Wilga M. Rivers is representative of the first viewpoint. In her book, *Teaching Foreign Language Skills* (1968), she describes methods for teaching both reading and culture within an audio-lingual framework.

Rivers identifies differences in values and attitudes (often expressed at the lexical level) as one of the main sources of problems in a foreign language and one area in which significant progress can be made in understanding a foreign culture. For example, she points out that a word such as 'mother' will have varying affective values depending upon the cultural context in which it is used. She makes the important point that any authentic use of literature will introduce cultural concomitants into the classroom, a point supported by cross-cultural research. However, she objects to 'civilization' courses which teach features of social life, such as marriage customs, leisure time activities, and festivals, because she feels that they do not throw much light on basic attitudes.

More recently, Rivers and Temperley (1978) emphasize providing background information, explaining high-frequency culturally-loaded terms, and supporting reading selections with illustrations as ways of adding new meaning to simple texts. However, social-cultural meaning is still described as an affective dimension and a great deal of reading performance is attributed to knowledge of vocabulary.

Paulston and Bruder's (1976) work exemplifies the second

position, which anticipates greater interference from cultural *knowledge*. Following Kenneth Goodman's thesis that the proficient reader must draw on his/her experiential conceptual background in order to supply a semantic component to the message, they conclude that learning to read is easier 'when the cultural background is familiar and students can draw on cultural information in the decoding process' (p. 160).

Robinett (1979) takes a similar position on reading. She says:

> Many things enter into comprehension: the students' grasp of the subject matter of the reading, *their understanding of the cultural content implicitly or explicitly expressed*, and their ability to cope with the grammatical structures in the passage. (ibid. p. 255; emphasis ours).

A variety of means is suggested for providing the background information needed for mastery of the foreign language, such as pictures, films, and descriptions of the teacher's own experiences in the target culture.

A third perspective focuses on literature as a means of teaching culture. William F. Marquardt (1967, 1969) views literature as a vehicle for creating cross-cultural empathy and appears to assume that at a certain point in their development students will possess the reading skills necessary for processing a passage, regardless of its content. He makes a number of general statements which are questionable in light of empirical research, e.g. 'The surest way to teach empathy for culturally different problems is through literature. Literature vivifies and highlights the ways people of a particular culture live. But more important, it enables the reader to experience how they feel' (Marquardt 1969, p. 133). Many practitioners use foreign literature or simplified reading materials based on the target culture in their classroom with this sort of expectation.

Like Marquardt, W. P. Allen (1956) is interested in using literature to teach culture. His goal, however, is in supplying substitute experiences in the target culture because '... language derives its meaning from the situations, or the contexts, in which it is used' (p. 1). He is, therefore, interested in literature as a means of furthering foreign students' acquisition of English. He presents an exhaustive checklist for American culture which he developed from those used for anthropological fieldwork. This list is to be used to analyse short stories and novels, which Allen considers the easiest forms of literature for the foreign learner. Once the cultural features that occur in the text have been identified, the lesson may be planned.

Another area in which the impact of cultural differences has been recognized is testing. In discussing the assessment of oral language proficiency and language dominance, Burt and Dulay (1978) point out that background information is a factor that must be considered:

> In order not to confound linguistic proficiency and knowledge of the world, the content of a language measure . . . must not be outside the experience of the students being tested, nor inconsistent with their cultural customs and values. (p. 188).

Unfortunately, this effect has not been widely recognized by test developers. While many tests have sections on reading, their developers seem to have been unconcerned about, or oblivious to, the possible cultural bias in the materials. To the best of our knowledge, the possible confounding of reading ability and cultural information in testing has not been studied experimentally, but an examination of test passages suggests that it may occur. For example, in *A Vocabulary and Reading Test for Students of English as a Second Language* (Harris and Palmer 1965), there are five separate paragraphs in the reading comprehension section. Two of these involve American and European history, two are from the natural sciences, and one is based on literature. Comprehension is tested by multiple choice questions. The following is from the literature selection:

> Johnnie, son of Scully, in a tone which defined his opinion of his ability as a card-player, challenged the old farmer of both grey and sandy whiskers to a game of High-Five. The farmer agreed with a contemptuous and bitter scoff.

The pertinent question on this passage reads as follows:

When Johnnie spoke he sounded
A. self-confident   C. very polite
B. quite rude   D. rather angry

Challenging an older person for anything would be considered 'quite rude' in many cultures. The right answer, however, is 'A. self-confident'.

Most proficiency tests provide guidelines for placement, and English language courses are recommended if students' scores are low. There are no tests that examine the students' need for pertinent background information. It therefore follows that there are no guidelines recommending a course in culture for the student with low scores on reading comprehension. However, the relevant cultural background as well as the command of language would be especially important in the social sciences and humanities.

Applied studies of cross-cultural reading performance

Two applied studies have been directed to the effect of cultural knowledge and values on reading comprehension. Gatbonton and Tucker (1971) conducted an experiment to determine whether cultural instruction would improve reading performance. An American control group, a Filipino control group and a Filipino experimental group read two stories and responded to items constructed to tap cultural differences. It was found that the two Filipino groups responded similarly and that both performed significantly differently from the American group. During the second phase of the study, the experimental group's teacher focused the subjects' attention on contrasting aspects of American culture which had been revealed by an analysis of the two texts. The Filipino control group discussed the two stories, but without a cultural orientation. Both groups were then tested again. In the final phase of the study, all subjects read two new stories to ascertain whether the experimental treatment had generalized.

The results of tests after the experimental manipulation suggest that even a brief treatment such as that provided to the experimental group will result in a change in reading performance. Post-test responses of the Filipino experimental group differed from their pre-test in the direction of those of American subjects, while post-test responses of the Filipino control group remained unchanged. Furthermore, on the basis of the experimental group's responses to new stories, there was some indication that the cultural orientation instruction resulted in a different approach to literature and a new awareness of certain signals in the texts.

A second applied study (Yousef 1968) evaluated an attempt to teach culture in a course specifically designed for that purpose after an attempt to use literature to accomplish that goal was judged ineffective. The subjects of the study were Middle Eastern males who had been working between four and twenty years for an American business organization.

All were participating in a training programme that was intended to instil in the students an understanding of the American people with whom they were working. Even though the subjects could speak, read and write English well, they did not seem to understand the literature they were studying. As the teachers observed their students' responses, it became clear they 'would never be able to reach an understanding of the people and the culture of the United States by studying American literature. Instead, the study of American literature actually seemed to increase misunderstanding and confusion' (Yousef 1968, p. 228). The teachers felt that cultural orientation was necessary *before* literature could be taught in a meaningful way, and two trimesters were devoted to a cultural orientation course. The values and patterns of behaviour in America were discussed, explained, and contrasted with the students' own cultural patterns. The meaning of behavioural patterns and social relations in different contexts was especially stressed.

During the course, quiz questions were of two types: those that involved a general and rather abstract understanding of American culture and those that directly reflected the everyday interaction of the American and Middle Eastern employees of the company. It was found that students were able correctly to answer the former, which were deliberately impersonal, but that in the case of the latter they continued to follow the dictates of their own cultural patterns. Their unconscious emotional reaction against certain aspects of American culture was so strong that it was only with intensive direct instruction that they were able to respond in ways that were more appropriate from an American point of view. The unstated but implied conclusion was that it is futile to expect students to absorb culture unconsciously from literature.

A cross-cultural study of reading comprehension

The fact that even highly proficient speakers of English often find it quite difficult to read English texts was the motivation for a study by Steffensen, Joag-Dev and Anderson (1979). Subjects from India and the United States were asked to read and recall two texts describing an Indian and an American wedding. The recall protocols were then analysed for amount recalled and error types.

The conceptual framework for the study was the schema theory of reading. Schemata are abstract cognitive structures which incorporate generalized knowledge about objects of events (Anderson, Spiro and Anderson 1978). These abstract structures contain 'slots' which are filled with specific information bits as a text or message is processed. For example, most adult Americans possess well-developed schemata relating to the wedding ceremony. Given a message about a wedding, an American reader would anticipate references to, and specific information about, an engagement ring, bridesmaids, a stag party, the wedding cake, etc. On the other hand, there is no reason to predict that a naïve Indian reader would expect this sort of information or would have the pre-existing conceptual framework necessary for integrating such bits of information.

Three functions of schemata have been identified (Anderson, Reynolds, Schallert and Goetz 1977). First, schemata provide the basis for 'filling the gaps' in a text: no message is ever completely explicit, and schemata permit a coherent interpretation through inferential elaboration. Second, schemata constrain a reader's interpretation of an ambiguous message: if readers possess background information and assumptions which differ from those of the author, they will re-interpret vague aspects of the passage to conform with their own schemata and will be unaware of other possible interpretations which in fact conform to the author's schemata. Third, it is by establishing a correspondence between things known, as represented by schemata, and the givens in a message that readers monitor their comprehension and know whether they have understood the text. This meta-comprehension function is extremely important in language-learning situations.

On the basis of schema theory, three predictions were made for the present experiment: (1) Subjects would recall more of the native text than the foreign text. (2) Subjects would produce more culturally-appropriate expansions of the native text than the foreign text, i.e. they would 'remember' things that were not specifically mentioned in the text but were consistent with it. (3) Subjects would produce more distortions of the foreign text than of the native text, e.g. they would assimilate events in the foreign wedding and produce an incorrect recall of those events. On the basis of anecdotal information, it was also predicted that it would take subjects longer to read the foreign passage than the native passage.

Two texts in English were prepared, both in the form of a personal letter. One described a traditional American wedding and the other described a typical Indian wedding. An attempt was made to control for syntactic complexity by making the number of words in a T-unit for each of the two texts essentially identical. A T-unit consists of a main clause and all its subordinate clauses, if any. (See Hunt (1965) for a discussion of this unit of measure.)

T-unit scores for the American and Indian letters were 12·6 and 12·56, respectively.

Each text was parsed into idea units. For ease of scoring, an effort was made to establish a unit in which there was only one bit of information expected to be significant for the analysis. In the American text, which was 677 words in length, there were 136 idea units; in the Indian text which was 702 words in length, 127 (see Table 1). These units were verified by two independent judges.

Table 1 Examples of Idea Units

American Text (Three Idea Units)
  The minister/who performed the ceremony/was an old family friend.
Indian Text (Three Idea Units)
  The auspicious time/told by the priest/was 9·38 in the morning.

Subjects were given the experimental texts in booklets which included pages for recording the time, blank pages for the recall procedure, and a personal data sheet. The order of the two passages was counterbalanced. Subjects read a warm-up passage, then one of the experimental passages. After a filler task, which was expected to inhibit short-term memory, they turned to a blank page and read instructions which directed them to recall the letter about the wedding. In order to avoid the impression that the study was a creative writing task, conformity to the form, wording, and order of the original letter was emphasized. Finally, subjects were asked a number of questions on the passage. The same sequence was repeated with the second wedding text, i.e. subjects read the passage, completed an interpolated task and the written recall task, and answered questions on the second passage.

Subjects were 20 Indians and 20 Americans who were matched on age, sex, marital status, highest year of education completed and area of academic specialization. One Indian subject misunderstood the directions and her protocol was not included in the analysis. The median age range for subjects was 26–30. 43% were married. 78% were engaged in graduate study or had completed a Ph.D., 18% had terminated their education with the bachelor's degree, and only 5% had not completed a bachelor's degree. In terms of academic specialization, 38% were in the physical sciences; 15%, the biological sciences; 43%, the social sciences; and 5%, the humanities. Since both groups of subjects were living in Illinois, all were asked how long they had been in the United States. Subjects were asked whether they had ever attended an

American or an Indian wedding and how familiar they were with
American and Indian wedding customs. No American subjects
had ever attended an Indian wedding, had ever visited India, or
presumed any familiarity with Indian marriage customs. A number
of Indians, however, rated themselves as familiar with American
wedding customs and one had even attended an American
wedding. They were, therefore, a less naïve population than the
American subjects. Since rated familiarity and number of years of
residence in the United States correlated ·58 and ·31, respectively,
with gist recalled, results might have been stronger if a more naïve
Indian population had been used.

All protocols were analysed for the number of idea units for
which the gist was recalled. As predicted, subjects accurately
recalled more of the native passage and less of the foreign. Americans recalled an average of 52·4 idea units from the American
text and only 37·9 from the Indian. Indian subjects recalled an
average of 37·6 idea units from the Indian and only 27·3 from the
American (see Table 2).

Errors were broken down into three groups. The first group
consisted of culturally appropriate elaborations. As expected,
each group elaborated their native text (see Table 2). For
example, a passage in the Indian text read:

> Prema's parents were very sad when she left. They were saying that
> now they know that everything that has been said over thousands of
> years about the sadness of giving a daughter away is true.

This was recalled by an Indian subject as:

> Her parents started weeping, along with her, but elders advised her
> parents that one day or the other she should go . . .

Table 2 Subjects' mean performance on various measures

| Measure | Nationality | | | |
	Americans		Indians	
	American passage	Indian passage	American passage	Indian passage
Time (seconds)*	168	213	304	276
Gist recall*	52·4	37·9	27·3	37·6
Elaborations*	5·7	·1	·2	5·4
Distortions*	·1	7·6	5·5	·3
Other overt errors	7·5	5·2	8·0	5·9
Omissions	76·2	76·6	95·5	83·3

* The interaction of nationality and passage was significant (p < ·01)

The information that the bride and her parents cried at the time of the departure was 'recalled' by another subject as well, but this was not explicitly mentioned in the text. Such expressions of grief are a fairly common occurrence at Indian weddings.

Differences in the connotative values of terms appeared to have a profound effect on recall. In the passage describing the dowry arrangements, there was a reference to the groom's parents which read, 'Prema's in-laws seem to be nice enough people'. Most Americans would consider this a very mild endorsement, but as the following protocols show, Indian subjects recalled it as very favourable:

> Her in-laws were really nice for they didn't make any fuss although he was their only son.

> Her in-laws seem to be very nice people. Though he is their only son they didn't give much trouble.

No such interpretation appeared in any of the American protocols. Such variation can probably be attributed to the much more negative value that the concept 'in-laws' has for Indians than Americans.

Similar elaborations of the American text occurred in American protocols. For example, the passage reading:

> They were talking about the exciting life that Pam will be leading as the wife of a man who does so much international traveling.

was recalled by an American subject as:

> Everyone is excited for Gloria in marrying a man with such a promising future and with the chance for so much international travel.

The information about 'a promising future' was inferred by the subject on the basis of her knowledge of American culture and expectations associated with foreign travel. For many Americans, this subject's recall would be considered an accurate paraphrase. However, Indian subjects' protocols show that expectations regarding a bright future are intruded from cultural information and are *not* contained in these words.

A rather extraordinary elaboration involved the fact that the American bride wore her grandmother's wedding dress and the statement from the text:

> That gave her something that was old and borrowed, too.

This was recalled by an American male as:

> So she had something blue and something borrowed too.

This subject obviously was familiar with the dictate that a bride must have 'something old, something new, something borrowed, and something blue'. In spite of the fact that essentially all adult Americans know that a traditional wedding gown is white and are aware of the symbolism involved (purity, virginity), this subject, influenced by the prescriptive jingle, intruded the wrong adjective in his reference to the dress.

A second set of errors were distortions that could be related to gaps in the subject's knowledge about the foreign wedding customs or intrusions of native customs and beliefs into the foreign text. This result was also highly significant (Table 2). An Indian subject recalled the passage about the American groom's travelling quoted above in a much more sombre vein:

> They were anxious as their daughter was going to get married and wondered at the fact that her husband would be an international traveller.

This is a clear case of a subject's distorting the foreign text in the direction of the native event. The fact that anxiety is a typical response of Indian families to the marriage of a daughter is supported by considerable evidence. First, other passages in the texts were recalled in ways that reflected an underlying concern (see above). Second, this was expressed in answer to the objective questions used in the study. One subject described the bride's parents as 'desperate and worried' about how the bride would adjust to her in-laws' household and another described them as 'scared' about the dowry arrangements. Third, in his massive study of Indian society, Mandelbaum (1970) gives a detailed description of marriage as a test of family status and refers to the tensions involved.

In the Indian text, reference to the two events which follow the Indian wedding (a wedding feast *and* a reception) was a rich source of errors for American readers. They collapsed these two events into one on the pattern of the American wedding reception. The passage involved read:

> There must have been about five hundred people at the wedding feast. Since only fifty people could be seated at one time, it went on for a long time. The first batch with the groom and important in-laws started at noon. Since we were the bride's party, and were close friends besides, we ate in the last batch with her parents. We barely had time to get dressed for the reception.

In one protocol, this event was remembered as having taken

place *before* the wedding. The process involved seemed to be that, first, the two foreign events were distorted and amalgamated into one event as they were assimilated to the generalized structure underlying the American reception. However, the subject remembered that the writer of the letter and her companions had to hurry to be on time for something. The coherence of the text was reduced as the cause-effect relationship (eating last at feast, rushing to reception) was destroyed but was re-established as events were re-sequenced to provide a new cause-effect relationship (eating last at reception, rushing to wedding). This 'successful' establishment of a logical relationship, of course, reflects a profound misunderstanding of the events recounted in the Indian passage.

There was one instance in which a subject was able to reproduce part of the text with some accuracy but indicated that he did not comprehend the message:

> And the husband and bride and the in-laws ate first and we ate last since we're such good friends of them (whaaat?).

This suggests this reader was not able to call upon the relevant schema, that he was monitoring his comprehension, and that he understood that he did not understand. It should be mentioned that he included the bride in the first batch with the groom. This is not necessarily the case and reflects incorrect cultural preconceptions, not what was present in the text.

The importance of schemata for providing a coherent interpretation of a passage was demonstrated by the problems that American subjects had with a rather long section (approximately 170 words) of the Indian text which described the gifts that the bride's family gave to the groom's, the gifts given to the bride, and the fact that there was no dowry. American subjects collapsed this passage to such terse and incorrect statements as:

> There were dowry gifts from both sides of the family — jewelry, saris. Something about a scooter also.

> Prema got a lot of gold as presents.

> For the dowry, everyone in the world got saris, and one person got pearls, which were white with something black in between them. It was pretty. There was some discussion about what the favors would be but they settled on silver cups for the men and saris for the ladies and toys for the children.

While it was conceivable that some readers did not know the meaning of the word 'dowry', far more than vocabulary interference or affective meaning must have been involved to produce such effects. American subjects were in the position of having to learn, from the text, not only all the details of these exchanges but also all the normative cultural behaviour, which was generalized background information for the Indian subjects.

There was one ambiguous statement in the description of the Indian wedding which read, '. . . the marriage was arranged only a month ago . . .'. This was intended by the author to mean that both sets of parents had decided that a match between their children was suitable, and the formal negotiations about the dowry and the wedding arrangements had been concluded. An American subject, operating under the dictates of his own cultural schemata, removed the ambiguity from this passage with a different interpretation when he wrote, 'The wedding was only arranged a month before the marriage'. This was a clear reference to the ceremony while the textual reference was to the union of the couple and their two families. One Indian clearly reflected this meaning when she referred to 'an arranged marriage'. Possessing the schemata underlying the text made it possible for her to remove the ambiguity from the sentence as the author intended.

A third set of errors was not obviously related to cultural backgrounds, such as recalling the colour of the bridesmaids' dresses incorrectly (Other overt errors, Table 2). Some of these might also have been culturally based, but that would simply increase the strength of the results.

Finally, subjects were able to read the passage based on their own culture more rapidly than the passage based on the foreign culture, i.e. Indian subjects read the Indian passage more rapidly than the American passage (276 seconds vs. 304) and American subjects read the American text more rapidly than the Indian (168 seconds vs. 213; see Table 2). There was also a significant main effect for nationality: American subjects read faster than Indian subjects. This was expected since Indian subjects were reading in a foreign language, English.

Conclusion

Cross-cultural experimentation demonstrates that reading comprehension is a function of cultural background knowledge. If readers possess the schemata assumed by the writer, they understand what is stated and effortlessly make the inferences intended. If they do not, they distort meaning as they attempt to accommodate even explicitly stated propositions to their own pre-existing knowledge structures.

Recent TESL and foreign-language pedagogy has moved away from the idea that comprehension involves abstracting meaning that is in some sense present on the page and is recognizing the creative contribution made by the reader. Interference is now understood as extending beyond the affective domain to the denotative values of words, and the propositional content at the sentence and text level.

While such an awareness is a major step forward, teachers, publishers and test developers can move beyond recognizing inter-ference to minimizing it and maximizing students' success in bridging to the target culture. For example, when students' responses to a text indicate that a described event is problematic, the teacher can probe to identify the scope of interference. Once this is determined, an appropriate interpretation can be encour-aged either by contrasting the event to a formally or functionally similar one in the native culture or by providing enough infor-mation about such events so that the student has some of the necessary cultural context. Text developers can perform an impor-tant service by employing writers with a detailed (or native) knowledge of the students' cultural background to produce reading materials and by using ethnic reviewers to screen out potential misunderstandings. Finally, evaluators must recognize that tests will more accurately reflect the reading ability of non-native groups *vis-à-vis* their native speaking peers if passages with heavy cultural loadings are avoided.

Note

The preparation of this manuscript was supported in part by the National Institute of Education under contract No. HEW NIE C–400–76–0116. An earlier version of this paper appeared in W. Diehl and C. W. Twyford (Eds.), *Reading English as a Second Language: Moving from Theory* (Bloomington, Indiana; University Monographs in Teaching and Learning, 1980).

Postscript on Steffensen and Joag-Dev

Although, as Steffensen and Joag-Dev point out, the idea that cultural knowledge plays a part in comprehension has been around for a long time, the experiment which they describe appears to have been the first to produce firm empirical evidence of this aspect of comprehension in operation. And in doing so, they provide, in an FL context, further evidence for the view that the meaning derived from a text cannot be confined to what appears on the printed page.

The parallels between this paper and that of Bransford *et al.* are at times close. Both groups of writers consider that texts are never totally explicit and therefore must be 'completed' by the reader. Bransford *et al.* refer to 'elaborations' which the reader can employ in order to make texts more meaningful (and hence easier to remember). Steffensen and Joag-Dev point out that, when reading texts relating to their own culture, readers produced 'elaborations' to supplement the explicit textual information.

As well as elaborations, however, Steffensen and Joag-Dev also refer to 'distortions'. This category is missing from Bransford *et al.* and marks an important difference between the two papers. There would seem to be two possible types of distortion, both found in the recall protocols referred to by Steffensen and Joag-Dev. The first involves an alteration of the explicit text, as, for example, when two separate events are telescoped or their order is reversed. The second involves the addition to the text of information which, in this case, is judged to be culturally inappropriate.

Writers who view the comprehension process as one in which a reader makes sense of a text in the light of his background knowledge would presumably see this second type of distortion merely as further 'elaborations'. From this point of view an Indian reader, faced with a North American text, is quite entitled to make sense of it by relating it to his own cultural background; in fact, he has no other choice. The fact that an American might judge the elaboration produced in this process as culturally inappropriate would seem either overly prescriptive or irrelevant to the reading process.

The problem, moreover, is not confined to instances where readers are faced with a text from an unfamiliar foreign culture. In the sense that one person's background knowledge is liable always to differ from another's any text can be a 'foreign' one, requiring 'elaborations' which another reader, or the writer, might judge to be 'distortions'. For those who view comprehension as a process of making sense of a text, there can be no single 'comprehension', only a large number of 'interpretations'. Steffensen and Joag-Dev refer to complete comprehension of a sentence. Some writers, notably in this volume Harri-Augstein and Thomas, would deny the possibility of achieving this.

There is no doubt, however, that most teaching materials, and perhaps a majority of teachers, are at least partially committed to the view that there are 'right' answers to comprehension questions. If questions are limited to examining information explicitly contained in the text, in the presence of the text, then this would not seem to present many problems. Even if questions are aimed at implicit information, say explanations for statements given, or writer's opinions, there might seem to be enough common background assumptions to justify expecting a wide measure of agreement as to the 'right' answer. It could be argued, however, that the now traditional practice of presenting students with multiple choice questions often tends to conceal differences of interpretation. The students are, as it were, directed down channels which present them with limited choices, none of which might have occurred to them in a free reading situation. One of the valuable aspects of Steffensen and Joag-Dev's methodology is that it allows readers to reveal their interpretations, and the processes underlying them, which would be concealed by traditional teaching practice, emphasizing as it does the *testing* aspect of reading.

In some areas of FL reading, the problems caused by different cultural backgrounds do not seem too severe. Widdowson, for example, has suggested that subjects such as physics constitute sub-cultures of their own, regardless of the L1 of the scientists concerned (Widdowson 1979). While there will obviously be differences of expertise and familiarity with some speciality, it seems reasonable to assume that the background assumptions contained in a physics text may well be recognized by a large number of physicists. Thus in general it might be claimed that the problem of differing cultures is likely to be less in learning language for specific purposes (LSP).

In more general areas of FL reading, the problems may be more severe. We are, however, doubtful of the value of stepping up the teaching of cultural information, though this may be useful in teaching contexts where it is possible to limit the scope of such information. The difficulty is that 'cultural' background knowledge would seem to be totally pervasive, and thus impossible to delimit and teach. After all, the socio-cultural level mentioned by Fries and cited by Steffensen and Joag-Dev encompasses not only the Rip Van Winkle situation but also the significance of statements like 'John Smith swam the 100 yards in 45 seconds'; that is, part of the meaning of this statement consists of a judgement as to whether this is a fast, slow or average time. The need to make sense of texts applies to all readers and all texts, and the problems faced by Steffensen and Joag-Dev's subjects in reading a 'foreign' text may be seen as simply an extreme case of a very general aspect of reading comprehension.

If, as seems likely, elaborations and distortions are an integral part of the normal comprehension process, then the best approach would be to tackle the learner's view of comprehension. If he believes in one correct interpretation of a text, then he is likely to be constantly held up by lack of knowledge, just as some learners refuse to proceed past an unknown lexical item. He should be encouraged to be tolerant of a number of interpretations, to examine his own interpretation and the knowledge involved in forming it, to compare his interpretation with others, both those of other learners and of L1 readers. The aim should always be to have the learner make sense of the text, and to use this provisional sense to move forward towards a more valid recognition of the writer's underlying assumptions.

4 Learning from text: methods of affecting reader intent

James M. Royer, John A. Bates and Clifford E. Konold

Most accounts of the reading comprehension process focus on three elements: the text being read, the background knowledge possessed by the reader, and contextual aspects (e.g. surrounding text and environment) relevant to interpreting the text. Another element that is important in a discussion of reading comprehension is the reader's intent. The importance of intent is apparent without much thought. When we have read a novel or short story for pleasure, we can report general details such as plot and gist with ease, but recalling with more detail may be difficult. If we attempt to recall what we have read in great detail, we quickly resort to fabrication, and our recall may be based more on general knowledge than on remembered fact. Compare this performance to what can be recalled after reading a professional article. Most researchers could report in great detail the logic, citations, specific procedures, outcomes, and conclusions of articles they have read with little difficulty.

These two examples refer to the fact that the level of detail learned from text will vary depending on what the reader wants to learn from text. We acquire gist and plot from fiction because that is primarily what we want. The researcher acquires detail from research reports because that is what he or she is reading for. But in addition to level of detail, reading intent can also affect the *nature* of the information that is acquired from text. Consider what happens when you read a text that, while not directly applicable to your area of interest, contains many relevant implications. A text concerned with the philosophy of science might be an appropriate example for many readers. Reading such a text involves many periods of mulling over ideas and translating information into a more familiar framework. What is acquired from the text is a richly interwoven structure consisting of material *generated* from the conscious interplay of the two. Thus, the very nature of the material acquired from the text has changed as a function of the reader's actions.

The suggestion that the level of detail and the nature of information learned from text will vary with reader intent seems to be obviously true. The question to be considered in this paper is whether the reader's intent can be brought under experimental control by manipulating task demands while reading. Specifically, is it possible to manipulate and control intent so that readers will either learn more from a text, or derive something from a text that is qualitatively different from what they would normally acquire? The analysis of the detail and nature of the material learned will serve as one of the focal points for the review of research to follow. Another focal point will be whether the techniques available in the literature are likely to be of any practical importance. The bulk of the research concerned with manipulating task demands while reading has been conducted in well-controlled laboratory environments. This leaves open the question of whether the techniques have any real-world utility.

In the pages to follow we will review three techniques for controlling a reader's intent while reading text. The three techniques include presenting readers with learning objectives that specify what is to be acquired from the text, inserting questions into the text, and asking readers questions that require more than the recall of specific information (i.e. 'higher-order questions').

Learning objectives

A common complaint among students in every academic area, especially at examination time, is that they frequently do not know what they are expected to learn. Learning objectives are designed to inform students of what they are to learn, while at the same time directing them to content deemed important by a teacher or experimenter. In the most complete form, a learning objective is a statement informing the student of (1) the specific information to be learned from text, (2) the procedure for assessing learning (e.g. oral presentation, multiple choice examination, written essay, etc.), and (3) the minimum level of acceptable performance.

The typical study of the effects of learning objectives involves presenting one group of subjects with a list of objectives prior to or concurrent with reading of text. After studying the objectives and text, generally at their own pace, the subjects are tested to determine their mastery of material specified in the objectives. Their performance is compared with that of another group of subjects who studied the same text, but did not receive learning objectives.

Logically, it would seem that learning objectives should consistently facilitate student performance. After all, if students know exactly how they will be tested, and what they are expected to learn, then they should be able to study more effectively for a test than other students who lack this information. However, the research evidence has not been so straightforward. In reviewing research that investigated only the effects of objectives on achievement, Duchastel and Merrill (1973) found that five studies demonstrated superior test performance for subjects who received learning objectives, but that five other studies demonstrated no effects, either positive or negative.

Despite such mixed results, the rationale for using learning objectives remains compelling. Other researchers have consequently attempted to specify both the conditions under which learning objectives may best facilitate achievement, and the qualities of to-be-learned information that are most affected by their presence.

One variable that may affect the usefulness of learning objectives is the degree to which the objectives direct student attention to information they might otherwise ignore. Duell (1974) provided college seniors in an educational psychology course with learning objectives derived from a new content area. Another group of seniors enrolled in the same course was not provided with objectives. Subjects in both groups then studied the same series of prose passages with the knowledge that they would be tested on their content. When subjects completed study of the passages, they were presented with a multiple choice test comprising items generated from the tasks specified in the learning objectives. Subjects were asked not only to answer the test questions, but also to judge whether each question did or did not reflect how well they had grasped the important principles contained in the passages.

Duell found that the two groups of subjects did not differ in performance on those test items judged to be important indicators of understanding (i.e. definitions of principles, and applications of principles to new situations). However, the learning objectives group significantly out-performed the group without objectives on those test items that had been judged by the subjects to be unimportant (i.e. names and dates associated with principles discussed in the passages). From these results, Duell concluded that the usefulness of learning objectives presented concurrent with the study of text may be dependent on how effectively the objectives direct attention to information that students might not consider to be important.

Another factor investigated in the learning objectives literature has been the number of sentences contained in a to-be-studied text that are directly related to a particular objective. Rothkopf and Kaplan (1972) defined a specific objective as being related to only one sentence in an experimental text passage, whereas a general objective was related to between two and five sentences. Subjects were presented with both specific and general objectives while studying text. As was the case in previous studies, subjects who received both specific and general objectives outperformed those who did not. In addition, subjects learned significantly more material covered by specific objectives. This effect has been replicated by Kaplan (1976) and by Kaplan and Rothkopf (1974). It should be noted that the superiority of specific objectives over general objectives *is not* an effect having to do with lower-order versus higher-order objectives (e.g. factual recall versus application). In general, specific objectives asked for the recall of a single factual piece of information, whereas subjects had to recall several pieces of factual information to satisfy general objectives. Unfortunately, the cognitive level of objectives has not received much attention in the learning objectives literature.

As indicated by the research reviewed thus far, objectives have been shown to enhance the amount learned from text when learning is measured by performance on test questions directly related to those objectives. Educators have frequently expressed a concern that although objectives may facilitate such *intentional* learning, their presence may direct student attention and effort away from other equally important content (cf. Atkin 1969; Popham 1969). Important information not specified by an objective may be ignored, possibly because the students do not believe they will be tested on that information. The relative effects of learning objectives on intentional and *incidental* learning have been investigated by a number of researchers. Rothkopf and Kaplan (1972), Kaplan and Rothkopf (1974), and Smith and Kulhavey (1974) have demonstrated that, generally, subjects given objectives learn more intentional material. Further, these researchers have not found a decrease in incidental learning for subjects given objectives relative to other subjects who have not received objectives. In fact, the evidence from the studies cited above has indicated superior incidental learning for subjects provided with objectives.

The finding that objectives produce beneficial effects on both incidental and intentional learning is not consistent throughout the research literature. For example, Duchastel (1972), Duchastel and Brown (1974) and Kaplan and Simmons (1974) have all reported studies in which incidental learning was significantly depressed for subjects receiving objectives. It is not obvious why the results of these studies should be at odds. It is possible, as Melton (1978) has suggested, that the instructions given to subjects may account for the differences. Subjects given specific instructions to learn only the material contained in the objectives may obey, resulting in depressed incidental learning. Subjects given more general instructions may study all of the material more diligently, enhancing incidental as well as intentional learning.

Other variables have also been manipulated in the learning objectives literature. Duchastel (1977) has suggested that objectives may have no effect unless students are convinced that studying the objectives is relevant to course evaluation. Dalis (1970) has noted that student test performance may vary as a function of the degree of ambiguity in objectives. Finally, Kueter (1970) has demonstrated that the presence of objectives may have little or no effect on the performance of students who are already highly motivated to master course material.

Overall, learning objectives have been found significantly to enhance at least intentional learning from text in several experimental environments, provided that (1) the objectives are clearly stated and are each related to only a few specific text sentences, (2) the students are convinced that studying the objectives is of academic value, (3) the students are not already highly motivated to master course material, and (4) the objectives direct student attention to information that may not be immediately seen as being important. Thus there is evidence from laboratory studies that providing students with objectives will increase the *amount* of information they acquire from text. It is unfortunate, however, that there has not been any research that has directly manipulated the cognitive level of objectives, and has thereby attempted to alter the *nature* of the information readers acquire from text. It would seem that providing readers with learning objectives would be an ideal way to direct them to generate knowledge not immediately available in the text.

A second issue is whether the use of learning objectives has any real-world utility. Most of the studies reviewed thus far were conducted in laboratory settings. There has not been an abundance of reported learning-objective research conducted in classrooms, using standard course materials. In their 1973 review, Duchastel and Merrill discussed 28 studies of learning objectives conducted between 1963 and 1971. Only 11 of these investigated the effects of objectives in classroom settings using textual materials. Of the 11, only 5 demonstrated a positive effect for students using objectives (although none demonstrated a clear negative effect).

It should also be pointed out that learning objectives may affect other, less tangible, aspects of learning from text that are not easily measured in either experimental or applied settings. For example, logically ordered objectives presented prior to new information may similarly order the student's inspection of the information, thereby maximizing the efficiency of study behaviours. However, the development of sufficiently non-ambiguous objectives, where none is currently available, may require a substantial investment of teacher time. Nevertheless, since research on learning objectives has frequently indicated that their use may enhance some aspects of text learning, many educators may consider the investment worthwhile.

Inserted questions

A second major class of task manipulations that has been found to affect text learning is the insertion, throughout the body of a text, of questions similar or identical to those that are used for examination purposes. Like learning objectives, inserted questions are intended to direct the student's attention to information in a text that will later be tested. In addition, inserted questions provide the student with the opportunity to make overt responses within a test-like situation while actively studying to-be-learned material.

A research design employed by Rothkopf (1966) has served as the model for most investigations of the effects of inserted questions. Six groups of subjects read the same twenty-page text, with the knowledge that they would later be tested on this material. Five of these groups were presented with a series of completion-type questions requiring rote recall of textual information. One group received all the questions and their correct answers before reading the text. For two groups, the questions were inserted in pairs into the body of the text shortly before the particular passage that contained the tested information (pre-questions). One of these groups was provided with the correct answers immediately following each question; the other group saw only the questions. Another two groups of subjects were presented with the inserted questions shortly after the relevant text sections (post-questions), one group receiving both questions and answers, the other group receiving only the questions. The last group of subjects was a control that read the text, but was not exposed to the inserted questions. As has been the case in most research on inserted questions, none of the subjects was permitted to review the text when answering the questions.

After all subjects had completed their study of the text, they were given a test that included both the complete set of inserted questions which some of them had already completed (intentional learning), and an additional set of questions covering previously unquestioned information (incidental learning). Rothkopf (1966) found that intentional learning was greater for all groups that had been provided with the inserted questions than it was for the control group. He also noted superior incidental learning for subjects presented with post-questions without answers; the other four experimental groups did not statistically differ from the control group in incidental learning. Rothkopf interpreted these results as demonstrating that (1) inserted questions, whether pre or post, facilitate the learning of question-specific information by directing attention to relevant parts of a text, (2) inserted post-questions have an additional facilitative effect on the acquisition of general skills related to the inspection of to-be-learned material, resulting in increased incidental learning, and (3) providing subjects with answers probably lessens the attention to the text during reading.

Rothkopf and Bisbicos (1967) expanded the investigation of inserted questions by asking whether such questions will direct students to learn particular types of information. Specifically, they wanted to determine if repeated exposure to questions calling for recall of a specific type of information would result in steadily increasing acquisition of that type of information. Rothkopf and Bisbicos replicated the finding that post-questions have a greater general facilitative effect (i.e. enhanced incidental learning) than do pre-questions. In addition, they found that exposure to post-questions calling for a specific class of information (e.g. names of important people) leads to greater learning of information in that class than of information in another class (e.g. technical names). Moreover, this facilitative effect increased with continued exposure to such post-questions. Additional support for the notion that inserted post-questions may have a specific effect on the acquisition of new material has been provided by Meyer (1975).

Since Rothkopf's (1966) initial paper on inserted questions, hundreds of research papers have been published and presented at conferences, and several articles or chapters have reviewed the literature (e.g. Anderson and Biddle 1975; Bull 1973; Faw and Waller 1976; Ladas 1973; Rickards 1979). The bulk of the research has focused on issues such as the position and frequency of questions, length of passages, knowledge of results, incentive effects, and whether inserted questions affect retention of text. In addition to these largely empirical issues, one theoretical issue has received a great deal of attention — whether the increased learning associated with the use of inserted questions can be attributed to increased attention or to a 'backward review' of recently read text. Rothkopf's early suggestion (1966) was that questions cause readers to read text more carefully than they would without questions. More recently, studies have appeared (McGaw and Grotelueschen 1972; Rothkopf and Billington 1974) which suggest that at least part of the enhanced learning associated with inserted questions could be attributed to a mental review of recently read information while searching for answers to questions. The evidence indicates that both of these effects are operating when subjects receive inserted questions while reading text (cf. Rickards 1979).

In summary, research on inserted questions has generally demonstrated that pre-questions may enhance intentional learning and that post-questions may facilitate both intentional and incidental learning. There is also evidence that frequent exposure to post-questions of a particular type will result in increased acquisition of that type of information. Rarely has the use of inserted questions been demonstrated to depress learning below the level of subjects not provided with questions.

Despite the bulk of experimental evidence indicating that inserted questions will affect the amount of information learned from text, there is considerable question as to whether inserted questions have practical utility. First, the size of the effect, while statistically reliable, is typically not very large. Under carefully controlled laboratory conditions, subjects receiving questions generally perform only a few percentage points higher than subjects who do not receive questions. Thus, the size of the effect may not be large enough to be of practical significance. Another aspect that is likely to limit the usefulness of inserted questions in real-world settings is the high degree of subject cooperation necessary to obtain the effect. In order for questions to be effective, subjects receiving them must read the text before examining the questions, and then construct complete answers to the questions. In a real-world setting it is likely that students may attempt shortcuts, and thereby lose the benefit of receiving questions.

Higher-order questions

The evidence discussed in the previous section was restricted to studies of inserted questions that have required verbatim factual responses, directly accessed from a text. Many important learning outcomes in the classroom, whatever the subject matter, are not directly related to the rote acquisition of facts, figures, names, or dates. Instead, higher-order outcomes such as comprehension and application of principles are frequently of greater concern to educators. This section is concerned with the issue of whether inserting questions calling for higher levels of cognitive functioning will alter the nature of the information learned from text.

It seems reasonable to assume that questions which focus student attention on relatively superficial aspects of some information should lead to a different kind of understanding than would questions directing attention to more complex aspects of the same information. As an example, consider the different cognitive activities needed to respond to the following questions:

1. What is the formula for computing the arithmetic mean?
2. Write down five different numbers that have an arithmetic mean of four.

Recently, students in an introductory statistics course at the University of Massachusetts were asked both these questions. These students had never before been asked to write down numbers which would have specified a mean, but they were well practised in calculating a mean when given a set of numbers. All of the students were able to answer the first question quickly, but most of them could not answer the second question immediately. Only after considerable thought were they able to provide an acceptable solution. In fact, several students could not solve the problem at all, nor did they have an idea of how to go about trying to solve it. Students need only recall a fact from memory to respond correctly to the first question. The second question requires not only that students recall the formula for computing the mean, but that they either perceive the relation between the mean and the sum, or apply the concept of the mean as a balance point in providing an answer. Simple knowledge of a formula is insufficient to answer the question.

The idea that the nature of the questions asked affects the level of learning has a long history. However, only recently have investigators attempted to document the idea empirically (cf. André 1979). In this section we will review this research, limiting our attention to studies that have investigated the effect of inserting different types of questions into text either during or immediately after a subject has read the text.

Studies investigating the effect of different question-types on text learning generally involve having students read several passages of less than 1,000 words each, and then answer inserted questions that are directed either at recall of factual material (knowledge or comprehension levels of Bloom *et al.*'s 1956 taxonomy), or at more complex cognitive abilities (application through evaluation levels of Bloom *et al.*'s taxonomy). A post-test also consisting of different question-types is then administered to determine if type of inserted question is related to performance on the post-test.

An experiment conducted by Watts and Anderson (1971) provides a good example of a typical study. Three hundred high school seniors were randomly divided into six groups. Each group read the same five passages that described different principles of psychology. The passages were similarly organized. First, an example (example 1) of the concept or principle was given, after which a verbal description or definition was provided. Then the name of a psychologist identified with the principle was mentioned, followed by a second example (example 2). The passages were approximately 450 words in length. Immediately after reading each passage, students in five of the groups answered one multiple choice question. In two of the groups, the question required that the student select the exact example (repeated example) given either in the first part of the passage (example 1) or in the second part (example 2). In two groups, the question required that students be able to identify a new instance (application) of either example 1 or example 2. One other group had to select the name of the psychologist associated with the psychological principle. The groups identifying the repeated examples and the psychologist's name were assumed to be operating at the knowledge level of Bloom *et al.*'s (1956) taxonomy, while the two groups choosing new examples of the principles were assumed to be operating at the application level. After completing the passages and questions, students were administered a 25-item post-test, which consisted of all the questions asked the students. Thus, each group had previously been exposed to five of the post-test items, while the other twenty were new. A control group was included in which students read the passages without answering any inserted questions, and then took the post-test.

Watts and Anderson found that the application groups performed better than the other groups on both old and new application questions on the post-test. Moreover, the application groups also performed as well as the other groups on repeated example and name questions. This is an important finding because it indicates that students receiving application questions not only learn factual content, but they also learn that content in a manner that allows them to apply it to instances they have never seen before.

The results of the Watts and Anderson (1971) study suggest that the nature of what has been learned from text can be altered as a function of the kinds of questions encountered while reading. Moreover, the indication is that this alteration in the nature of learning leads to differential performance on post-tests. If the above hypotheses are true, then assessment of the actual *nature of learning* should be related to a student's performance on test items varying in cognitive complexity. Readers who thoroughly understand what they have read should have integrated the material into their existing knowledge structure, and should also be able to answer both factual and application questions. In contrast, a reader who does not thoroughly understand what has been read may not have integrated the information in a meaningful way into cognitive structure. This reader might be able to answer questions calling for low-level factual recall, but should have difficulty with questions calling for higher levels of understanding.

Bates (1979) and Konold and Bates (1978) have recently reported studies that examine the above hypothesis. Students in introductory educational psychology courses were asked at the beginning of the semester and at the end of the semester to rate the similarity of pairs of psychological concepts. In addition, a group of subject matter experts (i.e. professors and graduate students) were asked to rate the same concepts. An index of cognitive structure was obtained by comparing each student's end-of-semester ratings with the ratings of the group of content experts. This index was then correlated with performance on lower-level (e.g. factual comprehension) and higher-level (e.g. application) test items. These researchers found that there was a much higher relationship between the cognitive structure index and higher-level test items than there was between the index and lower-level test items. These results are clearly consistent with the idea that the nature, as well as the amount of learned information can vary. Furthermore, information thoroughly integrated into cognitive structure can support performance not supportable by less thoroughly learned material.

Several studies have reported results that are similar to those reported by Watts and Anderson (1971). Hunkins (1969) had sixth-graders study social study materials containing either knowledge (low-level) or evaluative (high-level) questions for a four-week period. At the end of the period, the students took an examination consisting of questions at all six levels of Bloom *et al.*'s taxonomy. The finding of major interest was that the two groups did not differ on items from the lower taxonomic levels, but they did differ on new evaluative items. Subjects receiving higher-level items during the study phase performed significantly better on the evaluative questions on the post-test. McKenzie (1972) reported a long-term study in which eighth-grade students took weekly quizzes which required that facts be recalled (group 1), or inferences be drawn (group 2) about the political interests of groups discussed in the text. McKenzie found that the two groups of subjects did not differ on post-test items assessing recall of facts. However, group 2 significantly out-performed group 1 on items that required new inferences to be drawn.

In contrast to the research described above, there are a number of studies that have not found beneficial results as a function of exposing readers to higher-level inserted questions. Allen (1970), McConkie *et al.* (1973), and Shavelson *et al.* (1974) have reported studies in which subjects receiving higher-order questions did not differ from subjects receiving lower-order questions. Three studies reported by André (1979) make the situation even more complex. Using the Watts and Anderson (1971) passages, André found that students given factual questions out-performed students given application questions on two occasions, while no difference was observed in the third.

There are several potential explanations for these conflicting results. Although most studies of higher-order questions have been similar in basic design and intent, they have often differed to a great extent in methodology. The number of inserted questions used, relative to length of text, has varied, and in many cases is not clearly reported. Some studies have allowed students to refer back to the text in answering inserted questions, while others have not. Frequently, subjects have been provided with feedback concerning performance on inserted questions; sometimes, they have not. Another feature that has varied is subject performance on the inserted questions themselves. Some experimenters have not considered performance on the questions as being important enough to report. One of the major methodological problems with this literature is that the difficulty of inserted questions has rarely been considered or discussed. If application questions are more difficult than factual questions, and, in addition, if no feedback is given, it is entirely possible that students receiving factual questions would perform better on a post-test than students receiving application questions.

Of primary importance to this discussion, however, is whether higher-order questions can be used beneficially in real-world settings. This issue has not been explored in great depth. As was mentioned earlier, in order for inserted questions to have a positive impact, there must be a great deal of compliance on the part of the reader. The reader must answer questions only when it is appropriate to do so, and he or she must answer questions in a diligent and conscientious fashion. The question then becomes: how can one gain control of the readers' behaviour so that they approach the reading task in the appropriate manner? This question will be considered in the discussion section which follows.

Discussion

At the beginning of this paper we indicated that there were four elements to be considered in a discussion of text comprehension: the text, the background knowledge the reader uses in interpreting the text, contextual aspects present while reading, and the reader's intent while reading. This paper has discussed several ways in which intent can be brought under some degree of teacher or experimenter control.

Providing learning objectives and inserting lower-level questions in text have been shown to be moderately effective laboratory techniques for influencing the amount of information acquired from text. Readers who receive learning objectives or inserted questions typically acquire more of the factual information cued by the objectives or questions than do appropriate control readers and, further, they frequently acquire more of the non-cued (i.e. incidental) information than do controls. Thus it has not generally been found that the learning increase in cued information has been bought at the expense of a decrease in the learning of non-cued information.

The research on the use of higher-order questions has shown that under some circumstances readers receiving higher-order questions learn information in a qualitatively different manner than do readers not receiving questions. Readers receiving higher-order questions have been shown to be able to make use of the information they have learned, to respond to new higher-order application and evaluation questions, in addition to being able to respond to lower-level factual recall and comprehension questions. In contrast, individuals not receiving questions, or receiving only lower-order questions, may perform adequately on new lower-level questions, but poorly on higher-order questions.

As the research review indicates, objectives and questions do not always lead to improvement in the amount of information learned, nor do higher-order questions always result in increased higher-order learning. Furthermore, there is a considerable likelihood that the effects that have been found are largely laboratory effects, and if the treatment were presented in the same way in real-world settings, the results would not be reproduced. One reason for this is that the effects have not been very large in the laboratory studies, thereby raising the possibility that they would be swamped in the greater variability associated with real-world settings. A second reason is that the beneficial effects are reliant upon a considerable degree of reader compliance. It is not likely that readers in real-world settings will conform to task instructions as well as subjects in controlled laboratory experiments. What is needed is some way to gain control of the reader's task-compliance motivation in real-life settings, in addition to manipulating cognitive and inspection behaviours through the use of objectives and inserted questions.

The literature on learning objectives, inserted questions, and higher-order questions contains very little research which has as its focus task-compliance motivation of readers. There is only one study by Frase, Patrick and Schumer (1970), in which subjects were paid varying amounts of money for correct response to questions, but there is no research that examines procedures which would be realistic under classroom conditions. However, there is a considerable body of literature investigating what is known as the personalized system of instruction, which has direct implications for the issue of influencing a reader's task-compliance motivation.

The personalized system of instruction (PSI) is a technique of individualized instruction introduced by Keller (1968). Keller identified five features that distinguish PSI from other instructional methods:

1. The instructional material is organized and sequenced into smaller components or units, and students are required to 'demonstrate mastery' by performing at or above some minimum achievement level before proceeding to subsequent units.
2. The material consists almost entirely of written, textual information.
3. Lectures or demonstrations are not used explicitly for instructional purposes, but as techniques to stimulate student interest further.
4. Students are ideally allowed to proceed through instructional units at their own pace, going as fast or as slow as their abilities or special needs dictate. They are, however, usually expected to have finished by the regularly scheduled completion date of the course.
5. Because of the added burden on the teachers' time of supervising and repeatedly testing students over course materials, student proctors are employed to assist in the management and running of the course. Their most important task is that of providing students with immediate feedback and necessary tutoring at the completion of each unit quiz.

There is an additional practice, not usually included in a list of critical PSI features, that also seems to have become an integral component of PSI. This is the use of classically-stated behavioural objectives (cf. Mager 1962) and/or study questions designed to focus student attention on the most important aspects of an instructional unit. Several other variations on this basic methodology have been introduced, which include giving oral rather than written exams (e.g. Ferster 1968) or group rather than individual-administered quizzes (e.g. Malott and Suinicki 1969) and attempts to allow the students to choose from a wider variety of course activities and objectives (e.g. Lloyd 1971).

The interesting aspect of PSI, from the perspective of this paper, is that it incorporates several of the techniques discussed earlier (i.e. learning objectives, and study questions which may function in a manner similar to inserted questions) in actual instructional settings. Moreover, the research on this technique suggests that PSI is highly effective. Robin (1976) reviewed 39 studies that compared achievement in PSI courses to achievement in comparable lecture discussion classes. In the typical study, students are enrolled in either a PSI or a traditional section by either administrative or random assignment. The different sections use the same text, cover the same material, and then take the same comprehensive final exam at the end of the semester. Performance of the groups is then compared. Of the studies reviewed by Robin, 30 of the 39 comparisons showed better performance for students in the PSI sections. PSI student achievement was, on the average, approximately 10% higher than traditional student achievement on the final exams. Seven of the studies also compared retention after several months and found that the PSI students retained, on the average, 13% more of the information than the other students.

The bulk of the research reported above has been conducted with lower-level questions. As an instance, Chase, Johnson and Keenan (1977) examined over 1,200 study and exam questions from twenty-one different PSI study guides. 87% of these items called for the recall of names, definitions or specific facts. Thus, to this point at least, very little, if any, of the PSI research has been conducted with higher-level questions.

There are a number of problems with the PSI research literature that prevent unconditional acceptance of the benefits of the technique (cf. Kulik, Jaska, and Kulik 1978; Wodarski and Buckholdt 1975). For example, the drop-out rates in PSI courses are typically 40% higher than they are in traditional courses (Robin 1976). In the fourteen studies reviewed by Robin that provided drop-out data, PSI courses had an average drop-out rate of 14%, whereas lecture/discussion courses had an average drop-out rate of 10%. The higher drop-out rate can probably be attributed to the heavier work load in PSI courses, which means that the poorer students are more likely to drop out. In addition, course instructors frequently teach both the PSI course and the traditional course in comparative studies. This raises the possibility of experimenter bias (Rosenthal 1969) affecting the outcome of the comparison.

Despite these qualifications, the preponderance of evidence indicates that PSI is a more effective technique than traditional instruction when achievement is measured by examinations assessing lower-level factual knowledge. The likely reason for this effectiveness is that PSI requires that students take frequent quizzes, and re-take quizzes over information they have not mastered. The net effect of these two techniques is to motivate students to spend more time studying course materials. In fact, students consistently report that they spend more time studying in PSI than in traditional courses (Robin 1976). The importance of the PSI approach is that it demonstrates that the task-compliance motivation of readers can be brought under control by manipulating classroom contingencies. Students in PSI courses study more carefully and work harder because they encounter frequent quizzes that they must pass at mastery level before they can proceed to new material.

PSI is certainly not the only technique that could be used to influence the motivation of readers. But PSI has received substantial documentation as an effective technique, and as such, it illustrates that the task-compliance motivation of readers can be brought under experimenter or teacher control. This raises the possibility that a technique designed to influence motivation could be combined with the presentation of learning objectives and inserted questions at varying levels to maximize the amount and the quality of information readers acquire from text.

82   *James M. Royer, John A. Bates and Clifford E. Konold*

Postscript on Royer *et al.*

Classroom teachers are sometimes dismissive of the types of psychological experiments described by Royer *et al.* The tasks set the subjects often seem trivial, the conclusions obvious, and the laboratory conditions impossible to equate with those of the average classroom. In fact, Royer *et al.* themselves express doubts on the applicability of some experimental findings to the classroom.

It would, however, be a mistake to dismiss such work. Although some experimental tasks may seem trivial compared to those faced by the real-life student, the *principles* being tested are relevant and important. It is also the case that some of the hypotheses tested in laboratories seem, in a more general and diffuse form, to be accepted as unexamined fact by classroom teachers. Thus some of the experiments described in this paper relate to classroom practice, but in a far more explicit, and hence vulnerable form.

There are obvious similarities between the experiments and the classroom, apart from those pointed out by Royer *et al.* in connection with the PSI reading scheme. As far as *learning objectives* are concerned, for example, the work done on giving specific information to be learned from the text relates closely to classroom practice in 'scanning' texts in order to answer previously given questions. The possible role of learning objectives in directing students to generate 'knowledge not immediately available in the text' (p. 70) can be equated with the practice of starting the lesson with a general discussion of the topic dealt with in the text to be read. As far as *inserted questions* are concerned, they have already appeared in EFL teaching materials, notably in the *Focus* series and in *Reading and Thinking in English*.

In general, Royer *et al.*'s paper has wide implications for the reading classroom. In effect, they show that the purpose that a reader has in reading text will affect the outcome of his understanding — the product of comprehension. We might ask ourselves what purpose the foreign language learner has, in contrast to a native speaker user of a given text, and in particular when reading in the so-called intensive reading class. Such readers' purposes may well relate much more to learning the language, to treating the text as an example of the target language, to be exploited for all it offers in terms of vocabulary, word associations and semantic fields, grammatical structures, style or whatever. In such classes, the text might well be read slowly and carefully. Contrast this with the real-world purposes that readers might have: reading for pleasure, to while away the odd hour, to learn new information, to gain status by having read a particular book or author, and so on. If readers could be encouraged to develop their own purposes in reading, as is suggested by Harri-Augstein and Thomas in this volume, and if teachers could be encouraged to tolerate different purposes, then perhaps more meaningful lessons might take place. Teachers and materials designers will need to remember that different purposes will lead to different products; if purposes are to be left at least partly to the reader to determine, then outcomes become less predictable than has been thought to be the case.

The experimental evidence reviewed in this paper relates to some deep assumptions underlying much teaching of reading. In particular, it relates to the notion, whether overtly expressed or not, that it is possible to *train* someone in desirable reading habits, and to the part assigned in this training to different kinds of questions. It is often remarked that a great deal of testing of reading goes on, but little teaching. The use of questions in *tests* would seem unexceptional; if, however, one seriously advocates their use in teaching, one must presumably argue, for example, that:

1. the questions direct the students' attention to information in the text that they would not otherwise have noticed,
2. the answers to the questions constitute the relevant information which the students should extract from the text,
3. practice with such questions improves the students' ability to extract similar information from other texts.

The experiments discussed in this paper relate to all these claims.

It has frequently been suggested that an essential part of the reading *process* is the creation of hypotheses about what the text is about, and about which ideas or language are to come (a process sometimes known as *predicting*). Such hypothesis creation is said to be followed by a selective search in samples of text for confirmation. It could be that inserted questions of the type suggested by Royer *et al.* might be a useful first step on the way to encouraging the reader to formulate his *own* questions whilst reading, questions about what he has just read and importantly about what he is about to read. If this is the case, then the use of inserted *test* questions about *product* might be a useful attempt to influence the *process* of reading.

Thus Royer *et al.* suggest an important role for tests in reading instruction, which is somewhat counter to the mainstream of thinking in EFL, which tends to downgrade the usefulness of tests in favour of exercises. Royer *et al.* claim that the frequent occurrence of tests ('quizzes') in PSI has a positive effect — or at least that students study more carefully and work harder. Since questions interposed in text can enhance both intentional and incidental learning, if formulated appropriately and placed correctly, then a testing approach to the teaching of reading would still be justified. The authors rightly emphasize the importance of higher-order questions in guiding readers to higher-order comprehension products. However, if the learner is not able to answer the inserted question correctly, a testing approach is unlikely to help him arrive at a correct answer. In other words, a testing approach may affect the product of reading in favourable circumstances, but is unlikely to influence the process.

Most of the experiments described here do not necessarily commit their authors to the belief that training effected by questions will continue once the questions are withdrawn. It could be argued that inserted questions should be included in all learning texts, not so much as a training device but as a regular study aid. Thus the experiments would seem to be neutral as to whether one should attempt to improve the *reader* or the *text*.

The experiments also raise the important issue of *control*. They belong to a tradition in which the experimenter attempts to bring subjects' behaviour under control. Royer *et al.* lay stress on this aspect of learning experiments. Though teacher control of this kind is perhaps not so explicitly asserted, much teaching practice and material seem to assume that the teacher or the material should control reading behaviour, by setting the goals and evaluating how well the students have achieved them. Training implies control.

Not all the writers in this volume would subscribe to the desirability or even the possibility of such control. Fransson, for example, thinks that the way a reader processes a text depends on his motivation, level of interest and so on, and is not subject to outside manipulation. Harri-Augstein and Thomas explicitly reject experimenter control, and see the reading teacher as a guide, rather than trainer.

A major problem, clearly pointed out in the experimental context by Royer *et al.* and forcibly encountered by Fransson, is the difficulty of *establishing* control. Thus Royer *et al.* point out that many of the experimental results depend on the compliance of the subjects, a compliance which cannot be assumed by either experimenter or teacher. Paradoxically, it may be easier to gain this compliance in the classroom if the student does not feel himself deeply involved. This presents the teacher with an awkward dilemma. It may be that as long as the student considers the material to be irrelevant, he will accept the teacher's formulation of the goals. In the absence of strong sanctions, however, he will be unlikely to take the process very seriously, and the training is unlikely to have lasting effects. On the other hand, if the material is seen as relevant by the student, he may well bring to the reading task his own, self-formulated reading objectives, and either dismiss or ignore those set by the teacher or materials writer. If the above account is at all accurate then, at the very least, control must be modified by negotiation between teacher and students.

5 Cramming or understanding? Effects of intrinsic and extrinsic motivation on approach to learning and test performance

Anders Fransson

For a hundred years learning psychologists have focused on quantities rather than qualities. Experimenters have manipulated different conditions of learning and tried to 'measure' effects by counting numbers of correct answers on performance tests. The performance of each subject has been neatly summarized by a single score. The approach of the subjects to the experimental tasks (very often nonsense syllables, mazes and other tasks of little relevance to ordinary life) has seldom been reported, and failures to give the right answers to test questions have been regarded simply as failures.

The research programme of a group working at the Institute of Education at the University of Göteborg has been developed in reaction to this dominant tradition.

'Both for instructional purposes and for the understanding of "what it takes to learn" a description of *what* the students learn is preferable to the description of *how much* they learn', Marton and Säljö (1976) declared in an article presenting the research approach of the group. Another important feature of work of the group has been the effort to study learning of meaningful material. In all of our experiments we have used texts taken from regular academic textbooks or similar material written by ourselves. Most of the time our subjects have been students.

My own specific interests concern effects of extrinsic and intrinsic motivation on learning and in the second part of the paper I will present some results from an experiment where I have tried to study different effects of these two kinds of motivation on approach to learning and on recall. To give a background to the experiment I will first discuss some of the main variables of our work and present some results.

Extrinsic and intrinsic motivation

A highly motivated student works hard and learns more than a less motivated one. This is a common view among teachers. The problem of how to get and maintain a high level of motivation in all students is often solved by using different kinds of rewards and threats. By announcing a test the teacher can use both kinds of incentives at the same time; promise of rewards for good performance and threat of disapproval and other punishments for bad performance. It is well known by people working in schools that intensity of work usually rises remarkably in the days immediately preceding an important exam. It is also well known that most students devote little time to chapters that will not be covered by a test. Intensive work is supposed to lead to good learning. By 'good learning' is often meant a high score on a test.

Since the beginning of this century psychologists and educational researchers have reported a large number of experiments on the relation between motivation and learning performance, and tried to summarize their findings in theories. It is an intellectual challenge to try to reconcile the contrasting findings. Sometimes a moderate positive relation is reported, sometimes a negative one and very often almost no relation at all. The confusing findings contrast markedly with the importance ascribed to motivation in the classroom. The teacher turning to experimental research on motivation to get help in his daily work will surely be disappointed. Of course researchers have tried to help him to find some pattern in the confusing mass of results, but these patterns are not easy to apply in practice.

The Yerkes–Dodson law, named after two researchers working at the beginning of this century, is regarded by many to be the best attempt to summarize the experimental findings on the relation between intensity of motivation and level of learning performance. This law in its general form is presented in Figure 1.

As can be seen in Figure 1, up to an optimal point an increase in level of motivation is accompanied by a rise in learning performance. An increase beyond that point seems to have negative effects. The position of the optimal point depends on the difficulty of the learning task. The easier the task the higher the optimal level of motivation. The Yerkes–Dodson law summarizes a number of empirical observations but it offers no explanations.

The teacher trying to use the Yerkes–Dodson law in his practical work in the classroom will have to find out and try to create the optimal level of motivation for each kind of learning task.

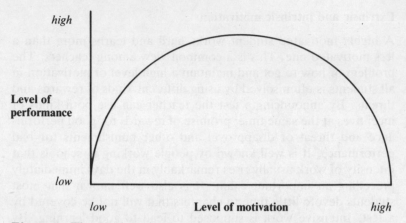

Figure 1: The Yerkes–Dodson Law

Recently Biggs (1971) and Saltz (1971) have made some very important critical remarks on the Yerkes–Dodson law. Biggs makes the distinction between intrinsic and extrinsic motivation and argues that the law describes only the relation between *extrinsic* motivation and learning. Extrinsic motivation for learning is a state where the reasons for the learning effort have nothing to do with the content of the learning material. A good learning performance serves merely as a means for achieving some desired end result.

Almost without exception learning researchers have tried to manipulate level of motivation by varying the amount of reward for success and the threat of punishment for failure. Level of anxiety in the learning situation has often been regarded as a proper expression of level of motivation.

Intrinsic motivation has a quite different quality and is charac-terized among other things by total involvement of self and lack of anxiety. It is a state where the relevance for the learner of the content of the learning material is the main reason for learning. There is no reason to expect disruptive effects of intense intrinsic motivation, Biggs argues.

Saltz presents some evidence to prove that the anxiety that often accompanies extrinsic motivation has disruptive effects on thinking, problem-solving and other cognitive activities. The curvilinear relation between level of motivation and learning performance described by Yerkes and Dodson might be regarded as the combined effect of increased efforts and disruptive effects of anxiety, according to Saltz. If Saltz is right the task for the teacher working with extrinsically motivated students would not be to find the optimal level of motivation but to reduce anxiety as much as possible.

An important point made by Biggs and Saltz is that the experimental research on the relation between learning and motivation has been limited to situations where the learning performance is instrumental to reach some external goal (money, praise, points on a test), or avoid some kind of punishment (blame, electric shock, etc.). The competence acquired has not been an end in itself. The learning tasks have been presented to the subjects irrespective of their relevance to the interests and the life of the subjects.

Several researchers and educational reformers from Dewey onwards have underlined the importance of making a distinction between intrinsic and extrinsic motivation. They have argued that intrinsic motivation causes distinctly different *kinds of learning*. Koch (1956) describes the experience of intrinsic motivation dramatically: 'you do not merely "work at" or "on" a task; you have committed yourself to the task and in some sense you *are* the task, or vice versa.'

My twelve-year-old son has been very interested in aeroplanes since he was six. He has built hundreds of models and read lots of books on the history of aeroplanes. When he was about eight years old he had learnt enough English (almost without help) to be able to read building instructions and technical data. Sitting in his room for hours building a new model he clearly demonstrates the effects of intense intrinsic motivation. He is totally absorbed, he forgets his meals and he works with very high precision. He seems happy but I do not think he is aware of that himself.

Dewey (1913) coined the term 'unified activity' to denote intrinsically motivated activity and contrasted it to 'diverted activity' where the attention of the subject alternates between the task itself and possible consequences of the end product. The intrinsically motivated subject forgets himself and the external situation. All his energies are devoted to the task and he feels free to explore and experiment for the sake of satisfying his curiosity and increasing his competence to deal with the environment. The extrinsically motivated subject tries to find out the demands of his teacher or parents. 'Young children in school expend extraordinary time and effort working out what it is that the teacher wants — and usually come to the conclusion that she wants tidiness or remembering or doing things at a certain time in a certain way', Bruner (1974) writes.

Recently Deci (1975) and others have presented some support for the hypothesis that the addition of external rewards to the intrinsically motivated student may reduce task motivation rather than enhance it. Deci argues that the rewards cause the student to subordinate his spontaneous interest to the demands of the rewarder. 'The introduction of pay into play makes it work', as DeCharms (1968) summarized the results from some early experiments. Rewards will have this negative effect on intrinsic motivation unless they are given in such a way as to provide guidelines for further training or explorations. When amount or intensity of work is rewarded the student is tempted to concentrate his efforts on task areas where he can easily impress the rewarder. He cannot afford to spend too much time on the tasks that excite him most.

In spite of these very important theoretical considerations there seem to be few, if any, experimental studies simultaneously demonstrating the effects of intrinsic and extrinsic motivation. The reason for this is not hard to find. Intrinsic motivation is not open to experimental manipulation. The experimenter has to find subjects with real differences in intrinsic motivation for studying the learning material he has prepared for his experiment. In the experiment reported later in this paper I have tried to overcome these difficulties. I have tried to find out whether extrinsic and intrinsic motivation lead to different *kinds of learning* and what the nature of this difference might be.

Approaches to learning

The main research method used in our group has been experiments where the process and outcome of learning of small numbers of subjects has been intensively studied. Subjects have been asked to read one or more passages of academic prose, taken from ordinary textbooks in economics, education and so on, and have then been asked questions about the passages and about how they approached the text.

Two different ways of approaching the experimental texts have repeatedly been identified. The classification of learning approach was based on what the subjects said in interviews.

Some of the subjects directed their attention toward learning the text itself. They tried to remember the exact wording of central passages. They counted the number of arguments and memorized cue terms. Because their attention was focused on the surface of the text in contrast to its meaning in a deeper sense this approach was called 'surface-level learning'. It could also have been called 'reproduction-oriented learning'. Other students directed their attention toward the meaning of the text and tried to understand that meaning. While the former students often reported that they did not remember some parts of the text, the latter reported that they did not understand or did not see the point in some parts. These meaning-oriented or 'deep-level learners' regarded the text as an instrument to help them understand better some aspect of the world. The exact wording was unimportant to them. They related the ideas of the text to their own previous knowledge and experiences and they often reacted emotionally and evaluatively.

It was not surprising to note that surface-level learners as a rule tried to remember and reproduce the text as a whole when they were asked to summarize what they had read while the deep-level learners often commented on the most important conclusions and on their personal reactions to the contents of the text. More surprising is the fact that deep-level learners scored higher on factual knowledge tests on the text on a test given two months after the experiment whereas surface-learners had performed slightly better on a test immediately after the experiment (Säljö 1975).

These results led to a number of experiments where we tried to induce a deep-level approach in different ways. Marton (1974, 1976) reports two experiments where the subjects of the experimental group were given descriptions of a deep-level approach and asked to try to read a text that way. In the first experiment the experimental subjects were given a general instruction before reading the text. Subjects in a control group were asked to read the text as usual. The experimental group performed slightly better on a retention test. In the second experiment the efforts to influence the learning approach of the experimental subjects were intensified. Besides the initial instruction the subjects were asked the following questions after each section of the text. (The experimental sessions were run individually with only one subject and the experimenter in the room.)

— What sub-sections do you think there are in this section? (Say where they start and finish.)
— Can you summarize the content of each of these sub-sections in one or two sentences?
— What is the relationship between the various sub-sections?

— What is the relationship between each of the sub-sections and the section as a whole?
— Why do they come in this order?
— Can you summarize the content of the whole section in one or two sentences?
— What is the relationship between this section and the chapter as a whole?

The subjects of the control group were just asked to read the chapter thoroughly and be prepared to answer questions on the content. The text to be read was the first chapter in an introductory book *How to Study Politics* and consisted of 4,320 words, divided into five sections.

All subjects were given a retention test at the end of the experimental session and after two months' delay. To our great surprise the control group was clearly superior both on the immediate test and after two months' delay. The number of correct items was about 50% higher in the control group on both occasions.

In reflecting upon this depressing result Marton (1975) writes that the experimental group's decidedly weaker result could be explained by an effort to learn economically and effectively; the subjects possibly developed a strategy for picking up information that was necessary for answering the (inserted) questions which they knew they were going to be asked. A fixation on the specific questions may have resulted in their no longer proceeding via the text but rather around it.

Two excerpts from interviews with the subjects in the experimental group clearly demonstrate this. They also demonstrate the attitude of extrinsically motivated students.

EXPERIMENTER: How did you read the chapter?
SUBJECT (9): You said at the beginning what you were going to ask questions about . . . so of course I read the key sentences and then just skimmed through the rest of the piece, wrote a heading to it and put a mark in the margin . . . the next piece . . . did it the same way.
EXPERIMENTER: Did you think it was difficult today?
SUBJECT: No, I wasn't trying to learn it.

EXPERIMENTER: How did you read the chapter?
SUBJECT (11): After you had asked the questions the first time, I tried to remember what you asked, you know, roughly, and I then wrote some of those ridicu-

EXPERIMENTER: lous notes in the margin, which weren't any use afterwards even so.

Did you stop at any point in your reading?

SUBJECT: . . . I didn't. I just read on without really thinking of what I was reading at all, I'm afraid.

In later experiments Säljö (1975) tried to induce deep-level processing by test questions that required understanding, and Dahlgren (1975) by inserting content-oriented guidance in the text. Neither of them was altogether successful and Säljö describes a number of subjects in his experimental group as demonstrating the same kind of narrow test-oriented learning as Marton's subjects.

After a careful analysis of this series of failures to induce deep-level processing Edfeldt (1976) concluded that every form of disruption of the continuous contact between the reader and the content of the text has negative effects on the outcome of learning. *There is no shortcut to deep-level processing*.

Types of recall

Levels of Understanding
Säljö (1975) summarizes an attempt to describe qualitative differences in outcome of learning in the following way:

> On questions which were constructed with the aim of testing the subject's comprehension of certain fundamental concepts and arguments in the text it was found that the answers could be divided into a few — three to five — distinctive categories or levels denoting basically different conceptions of what was in the text regarding a specific phenomenon, principle etc. The difference between these levels could in most cases be described in terms of the amount of information they contained; the higher the level the more of the intended content the answers contained and the lower the level the more fragmentary the answers.

To illustrate this I would like to cite one of Säljö's analyses. The subjects in the experiment referred to read a text by Coombs on the world educational crisis. One of the problems discussed by Coombs is the disproportion between the number of professionals and sub-professionals in many countries. The shortage of persons who can serve as assistants to highly qualified specialists means that the latter cannot make full use of their very expensive training. Instead they are forced to spend a lot of time on duties which could have been done by people with lower education. For society this means that a great proportion of the resources invested in the education of the specialists is wasted since the professionals could, in fact, have carried out most of their job with a less advanced training.

The subjects were asked the following question: 'How can the proportion of, on the one hand, highly qualified university graduates to, on the other, technicians and assistants respectively, affect the effectiveness of the educational system in relation to the needs of society?'

Säljö discerned three types of answers with the basic structures:

A. Professionals end up doing the job that should have been handled by sub-professionals.

B. Professionals need a suitable number of sub-professionals as assistants if the former are to be able to work effectively.

C. There should be a balance in the number of professionals and the number of sub-professionals educated.

The three types of answers thus represent three levels with gradually less informative answers as we go from type A to type C. Type A indicates a higher level of understanding than type C.

In this case none of the answers is incorrect. Very often, however, the lower levels in the hierarchy of answers represent misconceptions of the ideas and principles of the text.

Säljö's analysis of a follow-up question illustrates this. Säljö asked 'In what way has one tried to master this problem in certain countries?' (The problem of disproportion between professionals and sub-professionals.)

According to Coombs the measures taken to deal with the disproportion include the introduction of multipurpose comprehensive schools and the strengthening and modernization of secondary level mathematics and science courses. The idea behind these measures has been to make students better prepared for their future careers irrespective of whether they go to university or start working immediately after their secondary education.

This proved to be a very difficult question for most subjects. Säljö classified the answers into six different categories:

A. The establishment of a secondary education which aims at preparing students for university studies as well as for work.

B. Secondary education has been changed.

C. An attempt has been made to achieve balance in the number of professionals and sub-professionals educated.

D. Increase recruitment or import assistants by offering better salaries and benefits, etc.
E. Cut down admission to higher education.
F. No answer.

Only answers at the A-level indicate a clear understanding of the point of Coombs's argument. The B-level answers represent a vaguer variant of the A-level answers. They talk about a change of secondary education but do not explain the nature of that change. The C-level answers are still vaguer and just talk about 'attempts', not even localizing these attempts to secondary education. D-level answers suggest a solution not discussed by Coombs. Importing assistants might be a plausible solution to the disproportion, however. The E-level answers are examples of direct misconceptions of the problem and the measures taken to solve it. The subjects giving E-level answers presuppose that there is an overproduction of highly qualified people in an *absolute* sense, while Coombs refers to the *relative* proportions between two categories of personnel.

About two months after the experiment Säljö reinterviewed his subjects about Coombs's text. Although the individual subjects in many cases gave different answers it was possible to use the categories developed immediately after the experiment to classify practically all answers. Now an interesting pattern was found. Almost all subjects who answered in a different way on the second occasion had moved to a lower level category. This supports the hypothesis of a hierarchical relation between the different categories.

The kind of qualitative analysis of learning illustrated here has been performed in a great number of studies in the last five years. It has proved useful both directly for evaluation of lectures and textbooks and for research on learning.

Types of Free Recall
In his analysis of free recall reports of his subjects Säljö (1975) found three distinctively different ways of treating the content of the text:

> The most superficial treatment of the content consisted of a mere *mentioning* of the fact that the author discussed a certain problem or concept in the text. At the next level there are more or less extensive *descriptions* of what was said in the text and at the highest level, finally, there are treatments of the content, which are *conclusion-oriented* in

the sense that subjects in those parts of their recalls which related to a specific problem or concept discussed in the text included some kind of conclusion.

The three types of treatments can be illustrated by excerpts from Säljö's interviews with his subjects immediately after they had finished reading. The experimenter started the interview by saying 'I would like to begin by asking you to relate the main points of this chapter'.

All excerpts refer to the passage discussing the disproportion between professionals and sub-professionals.

Subject 17 just *mentioned* that this passage was included:

> . . . and then he talks about how they train too many doctors in relation to nurses in, for example, the developing countries . . .

Subject 22 gave a *description* of the disproportion and presented some of the content of the text:

> . . . and then there was the example taken from . . . there was an American expert who had calculated that the number of technicians in relation to university graduates ought to be approximately between 3–1 and 5–1. At best, this relation in developing countries was 2–1 and at worst 1–2. And then there was an example from Chile which showed that there were three doctors for every nurse. In Sweden there are five nurses to two doctors and in the USA it was 7–2 . . .

The description-type recalls summarized the content, often extensively, but did not abstract the main points of the author's argument. That was the case in the third type of recalls, called *conclusion-oriented*, here illustrated by an excerpt from Subject 20:

> And then we have the problem of the different areas . . . that is to say, the rate of training university graduates in one area must be in relation to . . . have a certain relationship to the training of less qualified manpower in the same area. That is to say, a university graduate must have a fairly large number of technicians at his disposal, otherwise he will have to do their work and that means . . . the whole thing is wrong.

These types of free recall presentations have been found in other experiments also, and, as will be shown later, they are systematically related to different approaches to a text.

The mentioning-type of recall presentation is common among subjects who obviously have tried to satisfy external demands and have treated the text as some kind of catalogue where they looked for correct answers. They have not tried to understand the meaning of the text but have just stayed on the surface and looked for the right cues. It might be that many of the fill-in exercises that are common in textbooks today lead to this kind of disciplined and restricted reading.

The description-type of recall presentation is the most common type among surface-level reading subjects reading with only a general idea of the demands of an expected test. They seem to organize the different parts of the text as a sequence of separate pieces of information.

The conclusion-oriented type of recall is found almost exclusively among deep-level readers. It reflects the search for meaning characterizing this type of learning.

Surface-level and deep-level readers have been found to perform about the same on regular quantitatively scored tests for factual knowledge. When questions demand understanding of arguments or principles deep-level readers have been shown to perform better (Marton and Säljö 1979). Because of their approach to the text surface-level readers often seem to learn examples illustrating a principle as separate parts of information instead of using them for understanding the principle better. They also often fail to see conclusions as consequences of arguments presented. Their surface orientation sometimes makes them make absurd mistakes when they fail to remember factual details or instructions correctly. The surface-level reader may report that 60,000 were killed in a Nazi concentration camp when the correct figure in the text book was 600,000. A deep-level reader not remembering the exact figure would probably guess that about half a million people were killed.

As already mentioned Säljö (1975) found long term memory for factual information of deep-level readers to be better than that of the surface-level readers even when the deep-level readers had not focused their interest on factual information.

Svensson (1976) found deep-level reading to be strongly related to academic achievement in a number of subjects.

An experiment on effects of intrinsic and extrinsic motivation on learning

Hypotheses
Stimulated by the ideas put forward by Dewey (1913) and others that intrinsic motivation may cause different kinds of learning to extrinsic motivation I planned the experiment presented below.

Some of the hypotheses providing the starting point for the design of the study were:

1. When learning a text is made instrumental to reaching important goals or to avoiding aversive consequences with no relation to the content of the text, the student will try to memorize the text in order to be able to repeat the whole passage. He will make his greatest efforts on the points that he thinks the examiner will question him about. If there are no hints as to probable questions he will follow the outline of the text. The greater his extrinsic motivation the more effort he will put into his reading.

2. In contrast, when learning a text is not instrumental to reaching goals or avoiding aversive consequences, the student will approach the text in a personal way. He will not try to memorize the text but rather use it for his personal needs, which means that he will read selectively and focus on the meaning of those aspects of the text that he finds interesting.

3. If most of the content is irrelevant to his interests and needs, his intrinsic motivation for reading the text will be very low and he will have little to say about the text other than that it was not interesting. If he is asked to answer test questions on the contents of the text he will perform very badly. If on the other hand the content of the text meets important needs for information, his intrinsic motivation will make him absorbed in the text and he will learn effectively even without a conscious intention to do so.

4. Students with strong intrinsic motivation for reading a text will be put into a conflict between different learning strategies if learning the text is made instrumental to reaching some goal irrelevant to the content of the text. This conflict will cause them to learn less than extrinsically motivated subjects with low intrinsic motivation.

Method

As choice of learning material and choice of subjects are closely related, I sought a solution to this problem in the following way.

A text containing a description of the examination system at the Institute of Education, University of Göteborg, was written in close co-operation between myself and the course leaders. The design of all tests in the basic course was described in detail. The text contained 3,160 words. Students assumed to have a high intrinsic motivation for reading the text were recruited from students registered for Education. Students assumed to have low intrinsic motivation for reading the text were recruited from those registered for Sociology, who had not earlier taken Education.

As level of test anxiety has been found to be an important factor in studies on the relation between extrinsic motivation and learning, the subjects were asked to rate their level of test anxiety in regular test situations. This rating was made a couple of weeks before the experimental sessions started.

Four experimental groups with supposedly different levels of intrinsic motivation and different levels of test anxiety were formed.

Table 1   Number of Subjects in the Four Experimental Groups

	Strong intrinsic motivation	Weak intrinsic motivation
Low test anxiety	13	20
High test anxiety	25	30

The subjects of each sub-group were randomly assigned to one of two experimental conditions. One of the experimental conditions was designed to eliminate as many features as possible that could create extrinsic motivation. The other condition was designed to induce rather strong extrinsic motivation. The experiment was conducted with groups of 3–5 subjects at a time. In the strong extrinsic motivation condition the subjects were told that after the reading session one of the students was to be asked to report what he had gathered from the text to the rest of the group. The report was to be tape recorded for later detailed analysis. A large tape recorder was placed in front of the subjects and prepared for immediate use. The performance session was to be finished by a group discussion on the merits of the text as information material. It was believed that these arrangements should make learning instrumental, threatening the self-confidence and self-esteem of the subjects.

In the weak extrinsic motivation condition, measures were taken to create a friendly, relaxed atmosphere. The students were instructed that after the reading session they would be asked to write down what they recalled from the text. As in the other group the session was to be finished by a general discussion on the merits of the text as information material. In reality all subjects were treated in the same way during the performance phase. Immediately after the reading session all subjects were first asked to write summaries of the most important information of the text. The question was phrased as follows: 'Summarize below the most important information on the information sheet you have just read'. This question was followed by an empty page. When they had completed their summaries the subjects were asked to answer a fifteen item short answer test of factual knowledge based on the content of the text. Finally each subject was interviewed individually about his way of approaching the text and his experiences while reading. The interviews were recorded and transcribed.

Results
The presentation of results is divided into three sections. In the first section an analysis of ways in which subjects approached and processed the learning material is presented. This section also includes analyses of outcomes of learning. In the second section effects of different types of motivation on process and outcome of learning are studied with subjects divided into the four experimental groups. In the third section effects of different types of motivation are studied with subjects divided according to their reports of how they actually perceived the experimental conditions.

1   APPROACHES TO LEARNING AND RECALL

1.1 *Qualitative differences in the process of learning*

In spite of the fact that the learning material used in the present experiment was somewhat different from the text used in the previous studies of the Göteborg group (Marton 1975; Säljö 1975, Dahlgren 1975; Svensson 1976, 1977) the same two levels of processing were found when the transcribed interviews were analysed and categorized. In addition to the two levels of processing, two levels of attention were identified. Within each level of processing some subjects were working very intensively while others seemed to be satisfied by forming a general impression. The deep-level processors working with a high level of attention tried to go behind the information given in great detail. Deep-level processors working with a low level of attention tried to form a general impression of the information material in order to be able to return to the text when their need for this special information became more pressing. Surface-level processors working with a high level of attention tried to press the text into their minds, while low level of attention at this level of processing meant a kind of lazy reading hoping that at least some information might slip into the memory. (For technical details of methods of analysis and reliability checks, interested readers are referred to the summary in English in Fransson 1978.) The four categories are illustrated by excerpts from the transcribed interviews:

a) *Deep-level processing, high level of attention. Subject 47:*

INTERVIEWER: What were you thinking of while reading this? Were you thinking of the situation, were you thinking of the text as such or were you thinking of what the text was about, the phenomena behind it?

STUDENT: I was primarily thinking of what it was about. I made comparisons with our own Sociology course and I concluded that there were great similarities between the two courses. That was the first thing I was thinking of. Then I started to think of how it would have been if I had taken Education instead of my present course.

b) *Deep-level processing, low level of attention. Subject 24:*

INTERVIEWER: What did you think of this material you have just read?

STUDENT: Well, I found it most interesting because I don't know very much about Education, you know. I didn't know anything about the instructional methods used . . . the design of the courses and their contents. It was very useful to get information about all these things.

INTERVIEWER: What did you expect when you came here? About the material, about the situation and so on?

STUDENT: I wasn't nervous or anything like that. Maybe I became a bit nervous during the tests because I read the information sheet as I would have done at home. I know that I can read it once more if I am wondering about some detail. I just scanned the material to see what kind of information it contained.

c)   *Surface-level processing, high level of attention. Subject 43:*

INTERVIEWER: Were you able to concentrate on the contents?

SUBJECT: As I knew that you had to try to remember the whole thing it was very difficult to concentrate on the content — I mean in a deeper sense — what it meant. I just thought: now I must remember this and that. I tried to pick out some facts.

d)   *Surface-level processing, low level of attention. Subject 82:*

INTERVIEWER: If I have understood what you have said you were not thinking of what the text was about, the courses described, but of memorizing the details?

SUBJECT: Yes, I did.

INTERVIEWER: Would you like to tell me something about how you read? Did you read it as you read a newspaper, as you read a good book or as you read course material?

SUBJECT: In the beginning I read very carefully but after that I hurried through it. I lost interest, I didn't think about what I was reading.

To summarize: the two subjects classified as deep-level processors were both thinking about the conditions and demands described in the text and relating the information to their personal situations while the two subjects classified as surface-level processors tried to memorize the text itself.

The two subjects classified as reading with a high level of attention read the whole text carefully, they put effort into their reading while the low attention level readers felt satisfied with a quick look. Level of attention is thus an alternative term for level of effort.

1.2   *Qualitative differences in free recall presentations*

As already mentioned Säljö's analysis (Säljö 1975) of answers to free recall questions identified three recall strategies: mentioning, describing and conclusion-oriented answers.

The text used as learning material in the present experiment differed in important respects from Säljö's texts. The authors of our text were not trying to present theoretical concepts or a set of arguments. They were just trying to give a neutral description of the system of examination of the basic course at the Institute of Education. Nevertheless the categories of answers identified by an analysis of answers to the open question of the first test turned out to be very similar to the categories identified by Säljö.

The similarities are so striking that it has been natural to adopt Säljö's terminology. When the analyses presented below were carried out, however, Säljö's results were not known to this author. Four categories were identified:

a) *Conclusion-oriented, content*
   The student summarizes his main conclusions from reading the text. He explains his thoughts and reflections while reading the text, and summarizes the parts of information that he has found most interesting.

b) *Conclusion-oriented, mentioning*
   The student reports that he has found certain parts of the information sheet interesting, but he does not summarize the contents of these parts.

c) *Description, content*
   The student has tried to give a neutral and complete summary of the content of the text.

d) *Description, mentioning*
   The student has intended to write a complete list of kinds of content of the text, saying for example that the text was about 'examination procedures' and 'examination demands' without describing these 'procedures' and 'demands' as the students in category C have. The answers categorized as 'mentioning' by Säljö belong to this category.

The relation between levels of processing and categories of outcome is presented in Table 2:

Table 2 Level of Processing in Relation to Type of Free Recall Summary

Type of free recall	Deep-level processing	Surface-level processing	Sub-totals
Conclusion content	15	3	18
Conclusion mentioning	6	3	9
Description content	18	24	42
Description mentioning	7	5	12
Sub-totals	46	35	81

($chi^2 = 8.98$ d.f. = 3 $p < .05$)

A clear majority of the surface processors gave descriptive summaries of the whole experimental text. Very few who had approached the text in this way presented conclusions or personal reactions to the conditions described. Conclusion-type recalls were more common among deep-level processors and almost half of this group presented or listed conclusions they had drawn during or after reading the text. Descriptive recall was the most common response type also among deep-level processors, however, and this was surprising. A possible explanation of the pattern of results might be that deep-level processing made it possible to choose a response strategy according to the student's perception of the demands of the test situation, while surface-level processing prepared the student for one type of performance only.

Results presented by Säljö (1975) and Fransson and Rovio-Johansson (1973) support such an explanation. Table 3 presents clear evidence that there was no conflict between deep-level orientation and acquisition of facts. Because there are good reasons to expect level of attention to be related to factual knowledge learning, the subjects are divided both according to level of processing and level of attention.

Table 3 Level of Processing and Level of Attention in Relation to Performance on a Factual Knowledge Test

	Approach to learning			
	Deep-level high attention	Deep-level low attention	Surface-level high attention	Surface-level low attention
Mean	12·1	7·3	8·8	7·2
S.D.	3·2	2·7	3·1	1·7
N.	18	28	30	5

It was reasonable to expect the factual knowledge test to be adapted to the learning approach of surface-level learners reading the text at a high level of attention. The best results were not achieved by this sub-group, however, but by deep-level learners reading at a high level of attention ($t = 3·46$, $p < ·01$). Surface level learners reading at a high level of attention performed only slightly better than deep-level learners reading at a low level of attention ($t = 1·93$, $p < ·10$).

As the reader might remember, subjects in the latter group limited their reading to the main points of the text and postponed a more careful reading to a later occasion when they might need this kind of information. It is hard to understand why subjects trying to memorize the details did not perform significantly better than this group. Svensson (1976) studying the relation between level of processing and results in examinations among students in a number of university subjects also found deep-level processors to achieve better in factual knowledge examinations than surface-level processors but not in initial examinations after a few weeks of study. The difference appeared first after some months and it was suggested by Svensson that this was because memorizing is a more tiresome and less effective way of organizing and storing large amounts of information than deep-level processing, under-standing and relating to previous knowledge. As noted earlier Säljö (1975) also found deep-level processors to perform better on a delayed test but not on an immediate retention test. Svensson and Säljö did not take level of attention into account. If they had made this distinction deep-level processors working at a high level of attention might have proved to perform best on immediate tests also in their studies.

Of course, deep-level processing might not always be expected to lead to good results on a factual knowledge test. Sufficient background knowledge and mastering of the terminology of the text are necessary prerequisites for reaching an understanding of the content. Entwistle, Hanley and Hounsell (1979) have recently discussed this point in an article summarizing research on the relationship between study strategies and academic performance.

2 EFFECTS OF INTRINSIC AND EXTRINSIC MOTIVATION: AN ANALYSIS PERFORMED FROM THE EXPERIMENTER'S PERSPECTIVE

In analysing experimental data it is usually taken for granted that experimental manipulations were effective and that assumptions concerning the attitudes of the subjects were correct. In the ana-lyses presented in this section I have followed this practice by assuming that subjects were indeed extrinsically or intrinsically motivated as intended by the experiment.

Students registered for Education were expected to be strongly intrinsically motivated to read the experimental text, whereas students registered for Sociology were expected to have a low or non-existent intrinsic motivation. Students given the instruction that the performance phase of the experiment would involve close inspection and assessment of their recall under socially demanding conditions were expected to be strongly extrinsically motivated for learning the text while subjects given an instruction intended to reduce ego-involvement during learning were expected to be weak in extrinsic motivation.

The results were perplexing. The experimental manipulations seemed to have had effects only among subjects weak in intrinsic motivation. Within this group strong extrinsic motivation was strongly related to surface-level reading, a high level of attention, and neutral descriptive recall strategies. The results are presented in Tables 4–6.

Table 4 Intrinsic and Extrinsic Motivation in Relation to Level of Processing

Extrinsic motivation	Level of processing	Intrinsic motivation strong	weak	Sub-totals
Weak (supportive)	Deep-level	12	16	28
	Surface-level	8	7	15
Strong (threatening)	Deep-level	12	6	18
	Surface-level	6	14	20
	Sub-totals	38	43	81

Whereas strong extrinsic motivation was clearly related to surface-level processing among subjects weak in intrinsic motivation, deep-level processing dominated in both conditions among subjects strong in intrinsic motivation.

Table 5 Intrinsic and Extrinsic Motivation in Relation to Level of Attention

Extrinsic motivation	Level of attention	Intrinsic motivation strong	weak	Sub-totals
Weak	High	12	9	21
	Low	8	14	22
Strong	High	12	15	27
	Low	6	5	11
Sub-totals		38	43	81

The pattern of results was exactly the same as in Table 4. Most subjects strong in intrinsic motivation reported a high level of attention regardless of experimental conditions. The experimental manipulation has effects only among subjects weak in intrinsic motivation where strong extrinsic motivation was rather closely related to high attention.

Table 6 Intrinsic and Extrinsic Motivation in Relation to Type of Free Recall Summary

Extrinsic motivation	Type of summary	Intrinsic motivation		
		Strong	Weak	Sub-totals
Weak	Conclusion	11	8	19
	Description	9	15	24
Strong	Conclusion	7	1	8
	Description	11	19	30
Sub-totals		38	43	81

Again the experimental manipulations seemed to have had an effect mainly among subjects weak in intrinsic motivation, although there was a tendency to more descriptive summaries also among subjects strong in intrinsic motivation.

I expected that subjects strong in intrinsic motivation would be distracted by the threatening conditions intended to create strong extrinsic motivation and learn less than under supportive conditions. This expectation was not confirmed.

Both extrinsic and intrinsic motivation were positively related to results on the factual knowledge test, so that the stronger the motivation (be it extrinsic *or* intrinsic) the better the score. In other words, there would appear to be no Yerkes–Dodson effect.

A detailed analysis indicated that the lack of experimental effects among subjects strong in intrinsic motivation was at least partly caused by the paradoxical behaviour of subjects high in trait anxiety. Trait anxiety is the characteristic of people who are *habitually* anxious, whereas state anxiety is the term used to characterize those people who are *actually* anxious in a given situation, regardless of their habitual anxiety. Thus, state anxiety subjects may include subjects with high or low trait anxiety.

Some of the subjects high in trait anxiety seemed to have misinterpreted the experimental conditions and expected threats that were never intended by the experimenter.

State anxiety during the learning session turned out to be strongly related to performance on the factual knowledge test. When the level of extrinsic motivation is replaced by level of state anxiety the expected results appear, however. State anxiety was measured by a self-rating questionnaire immediately after the test was taken. There was a strong interaction of level of anxiety during learning and level of intrinsic motivation.

The pattern of results can be inspected in Table 7 and Figure 2.

Table 7 Mean Scores on a Test of Factual Knowledge in Relation to Levels of Intrinsic Motivation and to Levels of State Anxiety

	Intrinsic motivation	
State anxiety	strong	weak
Weak	10·3	7·2
(N)	(19)	(20)
Strong	8·5	9·5
(N)	(19)	(23)

Strong state anxiety seems to have had a disruptive effect among subjects with strong intrinsic motivation but not among subjects weak in intrinsic motivation, where the relation is reversed. The difference between the regressions in Figure 2 is highly significant ($F = 8·5$ p. < ·001).

The relation between state anxiety and learning is further analysed in the next section.

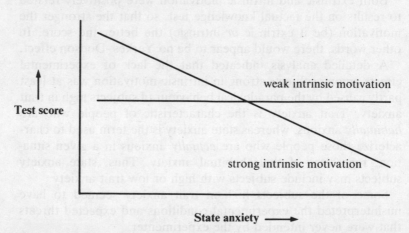

Figure 2: Regressions of Scores on a Factual Knowledge Test on State Anxiety While Reading the Experimental Text among Subjects with Different Levels of Intrinsic Motivation

3 EFFECTS OF INTRINSIC AND EXTRINSIC MOTIVATION: AN ANALYSIS
PERFORMED FROM THE SUBJECTS' PERSPECTIVE

The interviews concluding the experimental sessions revealed that
the basic assumptions used in defining the experimental groups
were true only to a limited extent. Some of the Sociology students
whom we had expected to have low levels of intrinsic motivation
found the learning material of the experiment very interesting and
were thus clearly intrinsically motivated. On the other hand some
of the Education students found the text of limited relevance. The
efforts to manipulate the level of extrinsic motivation also turned
out to have been only moderately successful. Level of trait anxiety
seemed to have been an important factor influencing how the
subjects actually perceived the experimental situation. The anoma-
lous reactions of a sub-group of Education students with a high
level of trait anxiety became more intelligible on closer examination of their definitions of the situation. Fourteen students from
this group participated in the experimental conditions designed to
reduce extrinsic motivation. In spite of the attempt to create a
supportive climate, nine of these students perceived the experimental situation as demanding and adapted their way of reading
to an expected, but not announced, factual knowledge test. Seven
of these nine students were classified as surface-level learners.
Only five out of the fourteen students experienced the experimental conditions as the experimenter intended and, of these, four
were classified as deep-level learners.

These observations formed the starting point for a second analysis based on the reports of the subjects on how they actually
perceived the experimental conditions and how interesting they
really found the learning material.

'Level of real intrinsic motivation' will be henceforth paraphrased as 'level of interest' in this section, and 'level of real
extrinsic motivation' will be paraphrased as 'adaptation to
expected test demands' to avoid confusion with Section II which
dealt with motivations expected by the experimenter, rather than
'real' motivation (as reported by the subjects in the interviews).

The perplexing results of Section II are not found when the analysis starts from the subjects' reported experiences.

Lack of interest in the text, efforts to adapt to expected test
demands and high trait anxiety all increased the tendency towards
surface-level processing. The results support hypotheses 1 and 2
which are here repeated:

1. When learning a text is made instrumental to reaching important goals or to avoiding aversive consequences with no relation to the content of the text, the student will try to memorize the text in order to be able to repeat the whole passage. He will make his greatest efforts on the points that he thinks that the examiner will question him about. If there are no hints as to probable questions he will follow the outline of the text. The greater his extrinsic motivation the more effort he will put into his reading.

2. In contrast, when learning a text is not instrumental to reaching goals or avoiding aversive consequences, the student will approach the text in a personal way. He will not try to memorize the text but rather use it for his personal needs, which means that he will read selectively and focus on the meaning of those aspects of the text that he finds interesting.

Raw results simultaneously relating level of interest in the text, trait test anxiety and adaptation to expected test demands to level of processing are presented in Table 8. The relation between these variables and level of processing can be more easily seen in the conflated Tables 8a, b and c and the reader is recommended to proceed directly to these tables.

There was a clear relation between adaptation to expected test demands and level of processing. Very few subjects reading with no intention to adapt to expected test demands reported surface-level processing. As can be seen in Table 8, the three subjects who deviated were all weakly interested in the content of the text. Among subjects adapting to expected text demands a majority reported surface-level processing. As can be seen in Table 8b, below, level of interest in the content of the text was also clearly related to level of processing.

A close inspection of Table 8 shows that all eight strongly interested subjects reporting surface-level processing were adapting to expected test demands. All strongly interested subjects not distracted by expected test demands chose deep-level processing, although the choice might not have been consciously made.

Table 8c shows the relation between level of trait anxiety and level of processing.

There was a weak association between level of trait anxiety and level of processing. The most important effect of trait anxiety was the low susceptibility of highly trait anxious subjects to experimental manipulations, however. This effect was discussed in the previous section.

Table 8 Reported Level of Interested Adaptation to Expected Test Demands in Relation to Level of Processing.

Adaptation to expected test demands	Level of processing	Low (trait) test anxiety		High (trait) test anxiety		Sub-totals
		strong interest	weak interest	strong interest	weak interest	
Non-adaptive	Deep-level	5	5	6	3	19
	Surface-level	—	1	—	2	3
Adaptive	Deep-level	8	5	8	6	27
	Surface-level	2	7	6	17	32
Sub-totals		15	18	20	28	81

Table 8a Adaptation to Expected Test Demands in Relation to Level of Processing

Level of processing	No adaptation	Adaptation
Deep	19	27
Surface	3	32

$chi^2 = 10.76$ $p < .01$

Table 8b Level of Interest in Relation to Level of Processing

Level of processing	Strong interest	Weak interest
Deep	27	19
Surface	8	27

$chi^2 = 10.40$ $p < .01$

Table 8c Level of Trait Anxiety in Relation to Level of Processing

Level of processing	Low trait anxiety	High trait anxiety
Deep	23	23
Surface	10	25

$chi^2 = 3.78$ $p < .10$

The relation between *state* anxiety and level of processing was on the contrary considerable. ($r_{pbi} = .41$ $p < .001$). Highly state anxious subjects were generally surface-processors.

The last line of hypothesis 1 runs 'The greater his extrinsic motivation the more effort he will put into his reading'. High extrinsic motivation in this section corresponds to 'adaptation to expected test demands'. As can be seen in Table 9, there was a strong relation between adaptation to expected test demands and intensity of reading.

Table 9 Adaptation to Expected Test Demands in Relation to Intensity of Reading

Level of intensity	No adaptation	Adaptation
High	6	42
Low	16	17

chi^2 = 12·79   p < ·001

Most subjects not expecting a test evidently did not find the text worth too much effort. Nevertheless most subjects read intensively if they had reason to expect a test. Quite a few subjects reported that they had prepared for a test not announced by the experimenter.

Level of interest had no relation to intensity of reading.

The combined effect of adaptation to expected test demands and level of state anxiety while reading on approach to learning and on intensity of reading is very interesting. The patterns of Figure 3 concerning intensity of reading, and Figure 4 concerning level of processing should be compared.

The two figures summarize the effects of adaptation to expected test demands on intensity of reading and on level of processing and they show how these effects are enhanced by level of state anxiety.

Experimental conditions provoking adaptation to expected test demands and high state anxiety are closely related to surface-level processing and high intensity of reading. In contrast *all subjects* not adapting to an expected test and low in state anxiety reported deep-level processing and in most cases a low intensity of reading.

School teachers normally wish their students to read intensively and often use tests to achieve this effect. They also prefer deep-level processing to surface-level processing. These results can be taken as a warning that a higher intensity of reading before a test might be achieved at the price of a shift from deep-level to surface-level processing.

Table 10 shows an analysis of the relation between reported level of interest in the text and type of free-recall summary.

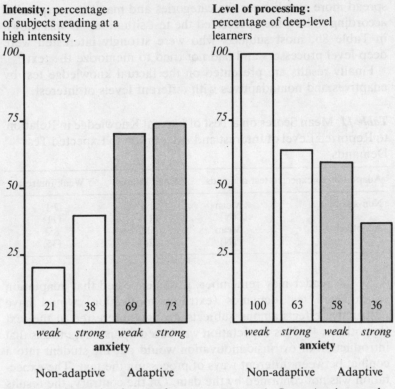

Intensity: percentage of subjects reading at a high intensity

21	38	69	73
weak	*strong*	*weak*	*strong*
	anxiety		

Non-adaptive   Adaptive

Figure 3: State Anxiety and Adaptation to Expected Test Demands in Relation to Intensity of Reading

Level of processing: percentage of deep-level learners

100	63	58	36
weak	*strong*	*weak*	*strong*
	anxiety		

Non-adaptive   Adaptive

Figure 4: State Anxiety and Adaptation to Expected Test Demands in Relation to a Level of Processing

Table 10 Reported Level of Interest in Relation to Type of Free Recall Summary

Type of summary	Strong interest	Weak interest
Conclusion content	9	9
Conclusion mentioning	8	1
Description content	11	31
Description mentioning	7	5

Most subjects with a weak level of interest in the text gave descriptive summaries. The majority of those who did so reported that they had prepared for a test. Strongly interested subjects spread more evenly over the categories and may have responded according to how they perceived the test situation. As was shown in Table 8b, most subjects who were strongly interested were deep-level processors and had not tried to memorize the text.

Finally results are presented on the factual knowledge test by adaptives and non-adaptives with different levels of interest.

Table 11 Mean Scores on a Test of Factual Knowledge in Relation to Reported Level of Interest and Adaptation to Expected Test Demands

Adaptation to expected test demands		Strong interest	Weak interest
Non-adaptive	Mean	8·6	7·1
	(N)	(11)	(11)
Adaptive	Mean	10·5	8·3
	(N)	(24)	(35)

As the reader may remember, it was expected that adaptation to expected test demands (extrinsic motivation) would have destructive effects among subjects strongly interested in the text (hypothesis 4). This expectation was based upon a hypothesis that introduction of extrinsic motivation would put the student into a conflict between different ways of processing the text. The expectation was not confirmed by the data. On the contrary, the results indicate positive effects of adaptation to expected test demands irrespective of level of interest. The results presented in the previous section pointed in the same direction. Strong state anxiety but not adaptation to test demands was negatively related to factual knowledge among strongly interested subjects.

To sum up: adaptation to expected test demands was related to level of processing. Non-adapting subjects were with few exceptions deep-level processors, while a majority of the adaptors were surface-level processors. Level of processing was also clearly related to level of interest in the text. Strongly interested subjects were deep-level processors while most of the weakly interested were surface-processors. These relations were presented in Tables 8a and 8b. Trait anxiety had only a weak relation to level of processing but state anxiety was rather closely related. Highly state anxious subjects were generally surface-processors.

Intensity of reading was related to adaptation to test demands but not to level of interest (Table 9).

Most subjects with a weak level of interest in the text, especially if they had adapted to an expected test, tried to give a neutral description of the whole text when asked to recall it, while strongly interested subjects gave different types of summaries depending upon how they perceived the request for a recall (Table 10).

Strong level of interest in the text and adaptation to expected test demands were both related to performance on a factual knowledge test (Table 11). Strong state anxiety but not adaptation to expected test demands seemed to impair learning among strongly interested subjects (Figure 2).

Conclusions

Once more it has been possible to differentiate between the qualitative levels of processing and outcome identified previously. But it has also been possible to show that the type of motivation for reading a particular text is an important factor influencing the choice of approach to learning, and thus also determining likely levels of outcome.

A subject motivated by expected test demands to read a text for which he has very limited interest is likely to adopt a surface-learning strategy, while deep-level learning seems to be the normal strategy chosen by a student motivated only by the relevance of the content of the text to his personal needs and interests.

Level of trait anxiety has been shown to be an important variable influencing the receptivity of the subject to situational cues. Expectations built up by previous experiences might sometimes be a more important factor determining the perception of the learning situation of the highly trait anxious student than the situation as it is defined by the experimenter.

The results support the arguments by Edfeldt (1976) and Dewey (1913) that the natural impulse of the intrinsically motivated learner, unthreatened by expectations of a factual knowledge test, is deep-level processing — a state of undisturbed contact between the author and his reader.

The conclusion to be drawn for teaching is that if deep-level processing is valued, every effort must be made to avoid threatening conditions, which rely mainly on extrinsic motivation. This is especially important when the initial level of interest of the students in the learning task is low.

Postscript on Fransson

In what we might think of as the 'typical' reading class, students
are presented with a text accompanied by a number of questions.
They read the text, answer the questions, and are then given the
'right' answers. It is usual for the teacher to discuss these answers,
pointing out why they are correct.

There are, of course, many possible variations inside this
pattern. However, these do not alter the basic pattern, consisting
of READ/RESPOND/CHECK RESPONSE FOR CORRECTNESS.

A major weakness of this type of activity is that it does not
provide the teacher with much information about what the student
is doing when he reads a text. In general, the teacher knows only
what answer the student has selected, with little indication as to
why. If the student's answer is the correct one, his reading behaviour is to that extent judged satisfactory; if not, it is hoped that
an explanation will help him avoid similar mistakes in future.

One of the most interesting aspects of the work of the Swedish
group described in the first section of this paper is their concentration on how a student approaches a text, and the type of answer
he produces. There is still, of course, a strong prescriptive
element: Säljö's 'levels of understanding' are hierarchically
ordered, as are Fransson's types of recall. Both types of analysis,
however, provided they are sufficiently reliable, can provide
valuable insights into the type of information students extract from
texts, and the way in which they structure it.

In a sense, the Swedish group may be placed somewhere
between the American workers referred to by Royer *et al.*, and
the position of Harri-Augstein and Thomas as set out in their
paper. Like the Americans, the Swedes utilize conventional experimental techniques. But they incorporate interviews as a form of
eliciting information in a manner similar to Harri-Augstein and
Thomas's conversational methods. In fact, Fransson's experiment
in one respect provides a bridge between the two positions.
Having at first classified subjects as either intrinsically or extrinsically motivated on the basis of their academic field of study, i.e.
a placing directed by the experimenter, Fransson had to re-
allocate subjects to categories on the basis of what they reported
about their own approach to the text (p. 109).

The distinction between deep and surface processing appears
fundamental in the Swedish work, and one is perhaps led to look
for parallels in the American studies of high and low levels of

comprehension. It is tempting, for example, to equate Fransson's deep processors with Watts and Anderson's 'application' group, or Hunkin's 'evaluative' group (Royer *et al.*, p. 76). The resemblance might seem to be strengthened by the findings that Hunkin's high-level group did as well as the low-level group on factual questions, while in Säljö's (1975) experiment, and in Fransson's experiment, deep processors did better on factual questions.

Such parallels, however, must be treated with caution. In the Swedish work, deep and surface processors are distinguished according to their reports on how they approached the text. The difference in behaviour is not induced by different training or different instructions. Once subjects are placed in one or other category, relationships between type of processing and, say, level of outcome can be examined. However, there is no *necessary* relationship between depth of processing and 'height' of recall. As Table 2 shows, more than 50% of Fransson's deep processors produced description–content summaries, a 'lower' level of recall. It is, in fact, the complex relationships between motivation, processing level and type of outcome which makes Fransson's findings initially difficult to interpret.

Thus we cannot assume, for example, that deep processors will do better at 'high-level' comprehension tasks, though we might hypothesize that they will. Conversely, we cannot assume that Watts and Anderson's 'application' group approached their texts as deep processors. In fact, given Fransson's finding that adaptation to test demands tended to result in surface processing, we might assume that they did not.

The most important variables in Fransson's experiment seem to be level of processing, type of recall, and intrinsic/extrinsic motivation, later referred to as level of interest and adaptation to expected test demands. We shall comment briefly on certain aspects of the first two of these before discussing the pedagogical relevance of Fransson's findings.

Level of processing: As Fransson says, most teachers would prefer students to approach the text as deep processors rather than to attempt verbal memorization. Advice on how to read, such as given by the SQ3R technique, stresses the importance of asking questions, and relating text information to background knowledge and interests. Bransford *et al.*'s efficient learner (pp. 39–40) is clearly a deep processor. It is perhaps worth noting, however, that there may be degrees of depth of processing; as Table 2 (p. 103) shows, three of Fransson's surface processors produced conclusion–content results.

Fransson's subjects were university students, and can be assumed to have been competent readers. With respect to such subjects, Dewey's point (p. 115) that deep processing is the 'natural' approach is probably valid. The educator's task in this case is to remove as many as possible of the factors which inhibit deep processing. There do, however, seem to be learners, in both L1 and FL, who, faced with written texts, fail to apply their 'natural' ability to be deep processors of language. Many of Cooper's subjects seem to fit this category. So, perhaps, do some of Hosenfeld's. For such learners, Stein's success in helping learners activate an aspect of deep processing (Bransford *et al.*, p. 40 ff) is encouraging, and a counter to Fransson's assumption that deep processing is not possible to 'teach'.

Levels of recall: If the list on p. 103 of recall types is hierarchically ordered, then not all teachers would agree that type (b), conclusion–mentioning, is superior to type (c), description–content, as the types are described there. In this respect, Säljö's three-part classification (p. 195) is clearer and less controversial. The problem of which recall type is 'superior' is made more obscure by the fact that Fransson does not provide any *quantitative* assessment of recalls, in terms of accuracy and completeness of the information contained. Clearly, there is scope here for further research.

A second point concerns the nature of description–content recalls. Säljö's descriptive type is said to summarize 'the content ... but not...the main points of the author's argument' (p. 96). Fransson's type (c), however, attempts to provide 'a neutral and complete summary of the content' (p. 103). While this formulation certainly excludes the student's own opinions, it does not necessarily exclude the main points of the author's argument.

A third point again concerns the nature and pedagogical desirability of type (c) recalls. Table 2 shows that nearly 70% of surface processors produced this type. It will be remembered that surface processors are said to aim at remembering the words of the text, rather than the meaning. However, a neutral and complete summary of a text of 3,160 words would seem to involve a degree of selection quite different from a naïve attempt at text reproduction. It could be argued, then, that some of Fransson's subjects, rather than blindly attempting to memorize, were submitting to authorial control, in the manner described by Widdowson (p. 222).

If this is accepted, then the question of the status of type (c) recalls is raised again, this time in relation to type (a). It could be argued that a beginner, faced with non-controversial, 'received' information to learn, would be advised to aim at a description–content form of recall.

There is, however, little doubt that the conclusion–content type of recall best represents the response to text of the mature learner in a 'normal' learning situation. No matter how marks are allotted for summaries done in the reading class, or for examination answers on received information, as mature learners we take from texts what we want, ignoring or quickly forgetting information we judge irrelevant to our aims. Hence the importance of the finding (Table 2) that very few surface processors produced this type of recall.

Applications: Given that we would like students to be deep processors, retrieving from texts something like Fransson's conclusion–content recalls, what potential applications do Fransson's findings have to the reading class? We suggest the following:

1. The first point derives from Fransson's accidental finding concerning the motivation of his subjects. It will be remembered that he first assumed that Education students would want to learn from a text relating to education, and would thus be classed as intrinsically motivated. Sociology students were classed as extrinsically motivated on similar grounds. As Fransson discovered (p. 109), these reasonable assumptions were invalid, and subjects had to be redistributed according to levels of 'interest' (intrinsic) and 'adaptation to test demands' (extrinsic).

   The relevance of this to the classroom arises from the fact that it is extremely difficult, if not impossible, for the teacher, like the experimenter, to predict what texts will interest individuals in a reading class. Even predictions for groups can be very unreliable; some Physics students, for example, may find any non-physics text irrelevant, hence uninteresting, while another group may claim that they handle physics every day, and want a change.

   This is important since, according to Fransson, interested subjects tend to be deep processors, and vice versa (Table 8b), and uninterested subjects are highly likely to produce description–content recalls (Table 10).

2. Fransson found a close relationship between adapting to expected test demands and level of processing. Subjects who did not adapt were overwhelmingly deep processors. On the other hand, subjects anticipating and hence adapting to a test set by the experimenter were far more inclined to be surface processors (Table 8a and Figure 4). But as we have already noted, it is a feature of the typical reading class that the students read in order to answer a comprehension test. Hence this type of classroom practice can be expected to induce surface processing. One of the editors had a student remark to him after such a practice, 'I got 100% on the questions, but I didn't understand the passage'.

3. State anxiety, that is anxiety induced by the experiment, tended to make subjects surface processors. Of subjects reading with interest and without anxiety, 100% were deep processors. For interested but anxious subjects, the figure dropped to 63% (Figure 4). Yet it can reasonably be argued that the typical class situation is likely to induce anxiety; the student knows that he faces a form of test, and that his score may well be publicly compared with other students'.

All these factors might seem to operate against the sort of reading behaviour we like to think we are aiming at. Indeed, Edfeldt concluded that everything coming between the reader and the content of the text has negative effects on the outcome of learning. Such intervention might include the kinds of 'high level' questions used by Marton (p. 91), remarkably similar as they are to the kinds of questions that appear in some reading books and in many reading classrooms.

Why then, do we continue in this way? One clue is perhaps supplied by Table 9; only 6 non-adaptors (27%) read with a high level of intensity. On the other hand, 71% of the adaptors did so. In other words, the traditional lesson gives the teacher the satisfaction of seeing his class work. Not only that, but as far as factual questions are concerned, this work brings success, as Table 11 shows.

Clearly, remedies for the problem are far too complex for a postscript of this size. We would suggest, however, that improvements could be brought about if (a) students were more free to choose their own reading material, perhaps to bring it into the classroom from outside; (b) if more realistic *learning* objectives were set in the reading class. Who ever needs to answer ten questions on a text, then promptly dismiss the content from his mind, except the student in the reading class? Perhaps if the student was encouraged to examine what he had learned over a fairly extended period of time from texts which interested him, he might learn more about his reading, and improve his ability to read to learn. In other words, we should concentrate less on answers, and more on learning to learn.

6 Linguistic competence of practised and unpractised non-native readers of English

Malcolm Cooper

This paper examines the problems of non-native readers of English who enter tertiary education and find that most or all of their subject textbooks are written in English. Two types of reader are considered. The first type has pursued a large part of his previous education through the medium of English and may be expected to cope adequately with the demands of his university textbooks. We will call him the *practised* reader. The second type has pursued his previous education through the medium of his *first* language, and has studied English as a foreign language. He may be expected to be at a considerable disadvantage compared with the practised reader when confronted with university-level textbooks. We will call him the *unpractised* reader. Whatever their *medium* of instruction, both kinds of reader will have studied English as a subject up to the fifth form level of secondary school.

In the investigation reported here (see also *ELT Documents* 107, 1980), the first language of practised and unpractised readers was Malay, and the medium of instruction at the university level, with the exception of textbooks, was either Malay, or in the process of changing from English to Malay. All students who had previously had a Malay-medium education pursued courses in English on entering the university, concentrating on developing reading skills. Practised readers, on the other hand, were automatically exempted from such a course.

Reading competence: desirable and actual levels

In principle, reading is important at the university level where the system normally places a high premium upon the students' ability to extend their knowledge independently of their teachers. In theory, then, all students should be efficient readers, and if the reading is not in their first language, they require a level of reading competence that is akin to the level of an educated native reader. At the very least, the unpractised non-native reader needs to be able to read as well as the practised non-native reader. To what extent is this level of competence realized?

A reading proficiency test was designed to discover the difference in reading competence between practised and unpractised readers. Four passages were selected from the introductory chapters of university textbooks and each text was accompanied by ten traditional multiple choice questions. The test was administered to a one third sample of all entrants to the University of Malaya in 1975. The mean scores were as follows (Chitravelu 1975):

Mean score — unpractised readers	8·95
Mean score — practised readers	22·5
Maximum possible score	40

There was thus a wide disparity between the performance of practised and unpractised readers.

This result, which in itself was not surprising, is illuminated by the results of a study by Criper (personal communication) of the comprehension levels of students in the same country at the secondary level of education. Students from Forms I to V were asked to complete a set of cloze tests based on passages graded according to their vocabulary level, from level A (500 words) to level G (2,000 words). The passages were taken from Longman readers simplified according to Michael West's *A General Service List of English Words* (Longman, 1953). Results showed that between Forms II and V there was virtually no improvement in reading level among unpractised readers. Students in Forms IV and V could, in fact, barely read at level G (the 2,000 word level) without teacher assistance. It was evident that considerably before students reached the university, their comprehension had reached a plateau that was inadequate for coping with university-level texts.

At this point, then, we had some idea of the comprehension gap that needed to be bridged by a reading programme. But we needed, if possible, more specific information about the students, their attitudes to English (as well as the attitudes of staff), and the kinds of linguistic competence which differentiated practised from unpractised readers.

Attitudes

A series of discussion questionnaires, interviews, studies of past examination results, and observations of teaching and learning enabled us to form a number of conclusions that would be helpful later in creating the optimum conditions for successful teaching and learning:

1. Unpractised readers were poorly motivated to spend further time on improving their English; they had a history of failure in English language examinations, and they saw little immediate need for English since their main medium of communication in social and educational settings was Malay.

2. Unpractised readers, as well as staff, considered in principle that reading was important to academic study. But in practice, several teachers thought that students could achieve a pass degree with little or no reading beyond lecture handouts (in Malay); and students soon gave up trying to read in English when they found the texts were too difficult for them.

3. Students and staff were accustomed to a classroom situation in which the teacher was the authority and the students recipients of knowledge. Students were thus conditioned to a more passive, dependent role than to one in which they took greater responsibility for their own learning — both on their own and in cooperation with their peers.

4. In their actual reading, unpractised readers showed excessive veneration for each word, and treated a passage in the English classroom as a quarry for vocabulary. They were not wrong, of course, in regarding a rich vocabulary as vital to successful reading, but they were blinded by words to other vital aspects of reading: for example, the importance of reading and understanding only that which is relevant to a reading purpose; and the importance of developing the ability to use the wider context to interpret what one does not know and what one needs to know. Hosenfeld (1977b) found that reading texts in very small chunks was a characteristic of unsuccessful language learners. By concentrating on words, and on word-by-word reading, our students were perpetuating their problems.

From this evidence we deduced that unpractised readers might respond more favourably to a reading programme in English if the following conditions were created:

1. They should experience immediate and frequent success in learning.
2. They should have copious opportunity to solve problems on their own and with their peers.
3. They should follow a variety of learning procedures which would be intrinsically interesting and of relevance to all their studies and not simply to the English lesson. In particular, as well as building their vocabularies, they should learn to use texts to hypothesize, predict and infer meaning.

Linguistic competence: the rhetorical hypothesis

Our first hypothesis was that the comprehension gap between practised and unpractised readers might in part be due to the unfamiliarity of unpractised readers with typical patterns of rhetorical organization and argument in English texts. We decided therefore to test the comprehension of both groups of readers on passages of Malay text which exhibited similar patterns of rhetoric to those found in academic textbooks in English. We predicted that if unpractised readers were indeed unfamiliar with such patterns, they would comprehend less well than practised readers when they encountered the patterns in their first language.

To test this hypothesis, thirty extracts of two or three sentences were chosen from the introductory chapters of university textbooks in English and translated by specialists into Malay, with instructions to preserve as far as possible the organization of the originals. Students were given the first part of each extract as context, and asked to select from three alternatives the one that would complete the 'paragraph' in the most sensible and coherent way. In twenty items an explicit sentence connector (equivalent to *however, moreover*) was given. In the remaining ten items there was no sentence connector. (For English examples, see below, Tests 4A and 4B.).

The test was administered to practised and unpractised readers entering pre-science courses in the university. Scores indicated that there was no significant difference between the two groups: the mean scores of both were 13. Thus, while it might be suggested that the scores of practised readers were depressed by the unfamiliar experience of reading academic texts in their own language, we concluded that we had not found support for our hypothesis, i.e. that the unpractised readers were handicapped by their inadequate knowledge of underlying rhetorical patterns. It seemed much more plausible that the problem lay in inadequate knowledge of English, and the ways in which English realized patterns of organization. The question now was: what aspects of English cause difficulty? Investigation thus turned to discovering areas of linguistic competence which might differentiate practised from unpractised readers.

Tests of linguistic competence

For this exercise it was necessary to select, and we decided to concentrate on a broad span of groups of features. The following were chosen: common affixes in academic texts; word meaning in context; syntactic features; grammatical and lexical cohesion; and inter-sentential connections. These features mark a progression from morpheme to sequences of sentences. We hoped to discover the following:
1. Whether performance on each group of features correlated with performance on a test of general comprehension;
2. Whether any group discriminated more highly than others between practised and unpractised readers.

The General Comprehension Test

This test consisted of three passages, each with ten traditional multiple choice questions. The passages were roughly graded in difficulty. Thus, passage I was taken from a Longman Simplified Reader written within a 1,000 word level; passage 2 came from a Form III English subject textbook; and passage 3 came from an introductory chapter of a university textbook. The test was administered to groups of practised and unpractised readers, and the scores on each passage were summed.

Results

Mean score: unpractised readers	12
Mean score: practised readers	19·7
Maximum possible score	30

Test 1A: The Meaning of Affixes

Students were given ten words consisting of prefix + root or root + suffix. Beside each word was a parallel item with the same affix but a different, invented root. Beside this list was a random list of definitions which included some distractors. Using the first list as analogies, students had to select an appropriate definition for each invented word.

Example

	root + affix	invented word		definition
1.	hopeless	contless	a.	not cont
2.	simplify	contify	b.	without cont
			c.	make cont
			d.	cont again

The scores on this test were not correlated with general comprehension but were combined with scores on Test 1B. A study of performance on individual items indicated that both practised and unpractised readers were uncertain about affix meaning. Unpractised readers were very insecure on all but two items (un- as in 'unable', and -ology, as in 'geology'). Discrimination between the two groups on five items was less than ·2. The other discriminations ranged from ·25 to ·6. The evidence thus pointed to a definite deficiency at this morphemic level, but the difference in performance of the two groups was not great enough for us to identify this linguistic area as a major distinguishing feature.

Test 1B: Word Meaning in Context

This test consisted of ten short texts of one to three sentences in length. Each text contained an underlined word whose meaning had to be identified from the context. It was accompanied by four alternatives from which an appropriate synonym could be chosen. Five of the words were invented, and five were words with different meanings in different contexts. Each context exhibited one of the following semantic relationships: particularization, contrast, affirmation, addition, reason. In addition, or combined with these relationships, contexts exhibited the lexical relationships of hyponymy, synonymy or antonymy.

Examples

1. Contrast and antonymy

Whereas glucose is absorbed rapidly into the bloodstream, the digestion of fat is a process of *flerg*.

a.	longer duration	b.	shorter duration
c.	the same duration	d.	great interest

2.   Hyponymy
Emily Brontë was skilled in painting, poetry and novel-writing, but she used her favourite *medium*, poetry, least of all.
a.   mode of expression   b.   average
c.   poetry   d.   language of instruction

Results of Tests 1A and 1B

Mean score — unpractised readers 8·0
Mean score — practised readers   15·2
Maximum possible score   20·0
Correlation of scores on these
tests with general comprehension   ·88

Scores on these tests correlated highly with scores on general comprehension. The results of Test 1B showed that all items except one involving *addition* produced discriminations ranging from ·54 to ·75. Smith (1978) has emphasized the role of previous knowledge in competent reading; in the present case, unpractised readers showed a tendency to use previous knowledge that was *irrelevant* to the context. For example, they displayed a preference for *language of instruction* as a synonym for *medium* in example 2 above. Moreover, they were influenced by the power of known collocations regardless of the meaning carried by the larger context. Practised readers, on the other hand, performed much more capably than they had on the meaning of affixes. One might speculate that the more context they were offered, the better they were able to perform. But this was not true of unpractised readers.

We concluded from 1B that unpractised readers were so preoccupied with the unknown word and its immediate context that they were blinded to the meaning potential of the whole context offered. It was not that they did not possess the strategy of searching the larger context for clues; they could evidently bring it to bear on texts in their first language. It was rather a question of reactivating the strategy in the relatively unfamiliar territory of English.

In sum, there was strong evidence for proposing that practised readers are distinguished from unpractised readers by their ability to use the whole context to decode the meaning of unfamiliar words, and that this ability involves an understanding of semantic relationships created by subordinators, sentence connectors and lexis.

Test 2: Syntactic Meaning

Pilot Study

This test was preceded by an informal study in order to assess the understanding of the following syntactic features (cf. Coleman 1965; Eskey 1975):

tense	passivization	non-finite clauses
aspect	complementation	conditional clauses
modality	cleft constructions	

Students were given thirty short texts of one or two sentences, each accompanied by three sentences which could or could not be derived from it. One or two of these sentences could be so derived.

Examples

1. Hypothetical conditional
   If the water had been pure, the animal life would have continued breeding in it.
   a. The water was not pure.
   b. The animal life continued breeding in the water.
   c. Animal life does not breed in the water now.

2. Cleft construction
   It is to solar energy rather than fossil fuel that scientists must now give their attention.
   a. Scientists must now give their attention to fossil fuels.
   b. Scientists must now give their attention to solar energy.
   c. It is necessary for scientists now to give their attention to solar energy.

The results suggested that both groups were insecure and inconsistent in their understanding of meaning carried by tense, aspect, modality, and non-finite participial clauses. Unpractised readers in addition had difficulty with hypothetical conditions, passivization, and participial relative clauses. The only feature which discriminated sharply between the two groups was hypothetical conditions. Complementation and passivization did not emerge as significant problems for either group.

Main test

In order to correlate performance on syntactic features with general comprehension, a shortened test was administered to another group of practised and unpractised readers. The test consisted of twenty-six items and concentrated upon tense, aspect and modality, which had previously been problematic for both groups, and hypothetical conditions which had discriminated sharply between them.

Results

Mean score — unpractised readers   10·2
Mean score — practised readers   15·0
Maximum score possible   26·0
Correlation of scores with
general comprehension   ·65

The results confirmed that neither group was secure in understanding tense, aspect or modality and the mean score of practised readers was rather low. Only hypothetical conditions again discriminated clearly between the two groups. The correlation with general comprehension of ·65 was quite high, but was the lowest recorded on all the tests. We concluded that, at least on the evidence of these features and these tests, practised readers are not distinguished clearly from unpractised readers by their ability to understand the meaning carried by syntax. It is an area in which both groups are weak, and unpractised readers especially so.

Test 3: The Meaning of Grammatical and Lexical Cohesion

This test sampled the students' understanding of the following features (see Halliday and Hasan 1976):
reference   ellipsis   synonymy
substitution   repetition   hyponymy (superordination)

Students were given twenty-eight items, each consisting of a short text of two or three sentences with a gap, and four alternatives from which to choose an appropriate word to fill the gap.

Examples

1. Locative reference
   I am leaving London to go to Paris next week for the first time. When I get _____, I shall find a hotel near the Eiffel Tower.
   a. to the Eiffel Tower b. there c. here d. to London

2. Hyponymy
   The square was filled with cars, taxis, buses, lorries, and tractors. None of the _____ had any lights on, not even the buses.
   a. cars b. tractors c. vehicles d. taxis

Results

Mean score — unpractised readers	13·2
Mean score — practised readers	21·6
Maximum possible score	28·0
Correlation of scores with general comprehension	·84

The correlation between performances on this test and general comprehension was high. The features which discriminated most clearly between practised and unpractised readers were lexical cohesion (in particular hyponymy, as in (2) above) and cataphoric reference; but both groups were insecure with synonyms. Grammatical cohesion achieved by anaphoric reference (e.g. locative reference as in (1) above), substitution and ellipsis did not appear to present much difficulty to either group. We concluded again that practised readers are distinguished from unpractised readers by their relatively superior lexical competence. Practised readers not only have larger vocabularies, but have greater knowledge of lexical relationships. In particular, they have a better grasp of the ways in which writers use words to create and maintain textual relationships by exploiting features like hyponymy and synonymy.

Test 4: Intersentential Relationships

This test was designed to assess the students' ability to understand the meaning relationships between sentences, both where the relationship is made explicit by a sentence connector (Test 4A) and where it is not realized by such a connector (Test 4B). The relationships tested were as follows (cf. Winter 1977):

Matching relationships, where the second sentence provides a reformulation, an addition, or a particularization;

Contrast relationships, where the second sentence provides a contrast, a correction, or an alternative;

Logical sequence relationships, where the second sentence provides a conclusion, an effect or a cause.

Examples

1. Contrast, with sentence connector:

In ancient times, when man needed more food, he cleared and planted new land which had never been planted before. Today, *however*, . . .

a. great areas of forest are being cleared to make room for food and other crops.

b.   new land is very scarce and even where large areas of unused land exist, they are very difficult to develop.

c.   countries like Malaysia also have large-scale programmes for clearing the land to make room for food production.

2.   Correction, without sentence connector:

It is mistaken to say that heavy industry is an essential basis for economic development.

a.   Most developed nations are heavily industrialized.

b.   The prosperity of New Zealand is based on agriculture, not on heavy industry.

c.   Japan and Germany are advanced countries with complex heavy industries.

Students were asked to choose from the three alternatives the sentence that completed the text in the most meaningful way. Test 4A consisted of twenty items, and Test 4B of ten.

Results	4A	4B
Mean score — unpractised readers	6·7	4·7
Mean score — practised readers	15·5	8·3
Maximum possible score	20·0	10·0
Correlations of scores with general comprehension	·88	·78

The correlation of scores with performance on general comprehension was high in the case of Test 4B and very high in the case of 4A. All items on both tests discriminated sharply or very sharply between practised and unpractised readers; nineteen of the thirty items produced discriminations between ·5 and ·88. The mean score of unpractised readers was especially low on Test 4A, indicating that the explicit sentence connectors did not help them to grasp the meaning relationships. Put another way, unpractised readers are very uncertain of the *meanings* of sentence connectors. The only relationship that they seemed fairly sure of was *addition*, typically signalled by *moreover*, *furthermore*, etc.

We concluded that practised readers are distinguished from unpractised readers by a far greater ability to understand meaning relationships above the sentence level, and that this ability includes an understanding of sentence connectors, as well as other cohesive relationships that we have previously examined.

The problem of inadequate vocabulary

A theme which has recurred in this study so far has been the fact that unpractised readers are severely handicapped by poor vocabularies. In order to get a clearer picture of the nature of this deficit, unpractised readers undergoing a pilot reading programme were asked to look through all the text including rubrics, lesson by lesson, and list the unfamiliar words. A study of these lists yielded much information, of which the following two points were particularly significant: (1) a high proportion of words were those which are common across subject areas and which have often been called 'sub-technical', for example, *contrast, similarity, function, characterize, depend on*; (2) also listed were a number of sentence connectors such as *despite, nevertheless, consequently*. These kinds of words are particularly important, because they not only signal the relationship of what is to come in the text with what went before (e.g. *similarly, in contrast, nevertheless* signal relationships of comparison and contrast), but they are often used to show what the writer is going to do or what he has done (e.g. to describe the *function* of something, to make a *contrast*). If readers do not understand the jobs that such words perform in relating and organizing meanings above the sentence level, their reading is indeed severely handicapped. And such was clearly the case with our unpractised readers.

General conclusions

1. All the test scores correlated highly or very highly with scores on general comprehension.
2. Unpractised readers differed primarily from practised readers in their inability to use the linguistic clues in the larger context to determine meaning. They found it especially difficult to deduce word meaning from context, to understand lexical cohesion, and to understand the meaning relationships between sentences.
3. Unpractised readers were severely disadvantaged by their poor knowledge of vocabulary. In particular, they were deficient in their understanding of the semantic relationships between words — relationships which writers exploit and create in order to make sentences cohere; they were unsure of the meanings of common sentence connectors; and their sub-technical vocabularies were generally very poor.
4. Unpractised readers displayed weaknesses in all the other main areas investigated, especially in understanding affixation and a range of syntactic features. But such features did not

so clearly differentiate unpractised from practised readers, who also displayed weaknesses.

5. In general, the higher one goes up the levels of grammar and liscourse, the wider the comprehension gap between practised and unpractised readers becomes.

Implications for a reading programme

The linguistic, attitudinal and other factors examined in this paper are just a selection of the variables that will influence programme design. What are their implications?

Perhaps the first point to make is that in view of the students' long record of unsuccessful language learning, any new programme must give them ample opportunity to succeed and thereby build their confidence and change their attitude to English from a negative to a positive one. Next, the evidence showed that students in their actual reading paid undue attention to the word level and failed to use the larger context to infer meaning at all levels. But it was also clear that their vocabularies were so poor that the 'whole' was often as unintelligible as its parts. If *successful* learning was to be initiated, it was important to make sure that texts contained enough known information for students to use it to interpret the unknown. It was also important to find a proper balance between building vocabulary and developing strategies for interpreting meaning at all levels. Smith (1978) observes that competent readers break out of the constraints of unfamiliar text by being prepared to 'take chances'. In her study of reading in second-language learners, Hosenfeld (1977b) has characterized 'taking chances' as the readiness to skip words that the reader views as unimportant to total phrase meaning, and, in the case of unknown but potentially important words, to skip them and use subsequent context as a clue to their meaning. Johns (1979) warns that materials which emphasize small points of linguistic and factual detail and encourage reference to the glossary may train students in exactly those strategies which Hosenfeld has shown to be associated with unsuccessful language learning. We should also emphasize a *purpose* for reading, because if readers do not know what they are reading for, then they are more likely to try to understand everything; and unpractised readers tend to do this word by word.

A reading programme, therefore, should give unpractised readers massive assistance in building up their lexical competence as we have discussed it in this paper, but this endeavour should place its emphasis on training students to take advantage of the larger context: the clues in the *co-text* and the *purpose* for reading. In this way, students might be weaned away from their obsession with words and encouraged to exploit their innate powers of inference and prediction from linguistic evidence (cf. Chitravelu 1980).

Finally, practised readers showed rather clearly that, although they had their weaknesses at lower grammatical levels, this did not prevent them from grasping larger meaning relationships between sentences, and by implication, larger chunks of text. Training and elicitation techniques, therefore, should focus on helping unpractised readers to understand and 'create' large coherent text relationships. The examples of Tests 4A and 4B provide a possible model for such creativity (see University of Malaya English for Special Purposes Project 1980 and forthcoming). By such means, unpractised readers might rise to the reading competence levels of practised non-native readers, and perhaps even exceed them.

Postscript on Cooper

At first sight, the series of tests forming the central part of Cooper's paper appears to exemplify the linguistic approach to reading problems. Thus, having established that the unpractised group were quite competent readers in Malay, and concluded that the problem lay in 'inadequate knowledge of English', Cooper proceeds to adopt linguistically defined areas of English syntax and semantics, test these, and correlate the results with reading scores. A simplistic conclusion to be drawn from studies like this, which Cooper does not make, is that, for example, unpractised readers need much more work on cohesion or sentence connectors.

In fact, Cooper's work does not conform neatly to the linguistic approach. This is partly because he attaches considerable importance to attitudinal factors, to which we shall return. The second reason is that some of Cooper's tests relate more to strategies than to linguistic 'knowledge'. For example, Test 1B appears at least in part to have tested the strategy of using context to arrive at the meaning of an unknown (because nonsensical) vocabulary item, rather than, say, the size and accuracy of students' vocabulary in English. It is perhaps revealing that the two tests which appear to concentrate more on linguistic knowledge, Tests 1 and 2, were the least successful in differentiating between the two groups.

Cooper's tests succeed in two ways: firstly, they establish a generally high correlation between success in the different tests and success in reading; secondly, they differentiate between the two groups of readers across quite a wide range of activities. Correlation studies of this sort do, however, suffer from certain limitations. It is, for example, well known that a high correlation does not imply a causal relationship. Thus a high correlation between size of vocabulary and reading ability would not justify us in advocating the teaching of large numbers of lexical items to poor readers. This limits the use of such correlations as a basis for action. In studies like Cooper's, this problem is compounded by the fact that the tests themselves necessarily involve reading; Test 4, for example, requires the subjects to read quite extended chunks of English. This being the case, a high correlation is perhaps not surprising.

It might seem, then, that *low* correlations, or test results which failed to differentiate between groups, would be of more immediate practical value, even though of a negative kind. Let us examine for a moment the results of Test 2, syntax. The correlation figure, 0·65, is relatively high, but it is the lowest correlation Cooper obtained, and the test furthermore failed to discriminate between the two groups (p. 130) It is interesting that in a study rather similar to Cooper's, conducted by Alderson and Richards (1977), syntax again gave the lowest correlation with reading ability.

From the finding that students who were competent readers of English were weak on syntax, and in fact not much better than subjects whose reading ability was poor, we might be tempted to conclude that syntax, or perhaps training in English syntax, was not necessary for students needing to read English.Such a conclusion might well be right, even though it would probably disturb many EFL teachers. However, it is sufficiently startling to stimulate us into examining the test more closely.

Two possible explanations are offered here for Cooper's results. Firstly, it may have been the case that the practised group were better able to handle syntactic meaning in context. That is, faced with an extended text, they were better able to use contextual clues in order to assign provisional meanings to difficult constructions. This explanation, which is in line with Cooper's general conclusions, might lead us to try to correlate scores on grammatical items encountered in isolation, and on the *same* items in an extended text.

The second explanation is that the comparatively low correlation and discrimination comes about as a result of the test design. It will be noted that, with the exception of hypothetical conditions, the grammatical structures tested were all items which a pilot test had found to give difficulty to *both* groups. Hence the fact that the test detected syntactic weaknesses among most of the students is not, perhaps, surprising. This might lead us to try to differentiate between two groups like Cooper's by using a much broader, much more general syntactic test, which would concentrate more on those items which the top group might be assumed to have mastered.

If we turn now to the unpractised readers, it seems clear that they conform in many ways to Hosenfeld's description of the poor language learner, fixated by individual word meanings, and unwilling to guess, Yet Hosenfeld's analysis was done in terms of individuals; it is disconcerting to find a large group of students all displaying the same characteristics. This is particularly so when we remember that these students were quite competent readers in their first language, yet appeared to be unable, or unwilling, to transfer these reading skills to the foreign language. (For an account of the problems of transfer of reading ability, we refer the reader to Alderson's paper.) That the tactics Cooper's subjects adopted were inefficient in their own terms can be seen by the fact that, even though they treated English texts as 'quarries for vocabulary', (p. 124), their subsequent vocabulary level was low (p. 133).

Hosenfeld suggests that poor readers have been exposed to written texts before they acquired sufficient oral vocabulary to reach take-off point. This may be the case with some learners; to consider it generally true, however, would seem to assume the truth of the 'oral language before written language' position, and there is no evidence this is valid for all learners. Cooper (p. 124) suggests a history of failure in English as an explanation. This seems reasonable, but leaves unexplained the initial *cause* of the failure.

Cooper lays stress on lack of motivation, and certainly with this particular group of students, he seems justified in this. Thus Cooper's study, while laying considerable stress on language features, would seem to share with Fransson's paper a common interest in psychological variables, such as motivation. And, in fact, Cooper's unpractised group could be viewed as extreme cases of Fransson's surface processors.

Given the situation described, Cooper's proposals for a revised reading programme seem eminently sensible. Yet when one considers his students' lack of *extrinsic*, as well as intrinsic, motivation, one wonders whether the damage can be repaired.

7 Syntactic components of the foreign language reading process

Ruth A. Berman

This paper is concerned with the nature and role of syntactic problems encountered by advanced-level students in reading foreign
language texts. In trying to investigate the effect of 'syntax' on FL
readers, we are aware that the aim of teaching reading is to reach
a point where students understand both the meaning of words *and*
how they interrelate within a given text; for it is clear that in
reading, as in auditory comprehension, syntactic decoding does
not proceed in isolation from semantic factors. The hypothesis
which motivated our study is, nonetheless, that syntactic factors
as such warrant attention in both the research and teaching of FL
reading, for the unravelling of parts of sentences and correct
perception of their grammatical and rhetorical interrelations
are important components of reading fluency in general. In section 1 we review different potential sources and types of syn-
tactically-based text difficulty, and make claims which we attempt
to substantiate in Section 2 by reference to experimental evidence of our own and of other researchers working with Hebrew-
speaking students of EFL. Finally, in Section 3 we review these
and other methods of research for pinpointing areas of text difficulty in general.

1. Assumptions concerning syntax-based difficulty

Our central claim is that efficient FL readers must rely — in part,
though not exclusively — on syntactic devices to get at text
meaning. To illustrate, consider the following sentence (from
Frank Davies 1973, p. 156).

1.   So widespread had the habit of reading the Bible in English
     become that official steps were taken to combat it.

The reader will not be able to work out the relationship between the parts of this sentence if he is not aware, say, that the first phrase is a syntactic re-ordering of 'the habit of reading (the Bible in English) had become *so* widespread *that* + CONSEQUENCE'; he must be aware that in this context the word 'official' functions as a modifier of the noun 'steps' and not as the head of a noun phrase, possibly with the word 'steps' as a verb predicate; that the passive verb phrase 'were taken' implies some agent(s) that took steps; and that 'it' has as its antecedent 'the habit of reading the Bible in English' rather than any part of this noun phrase or any other nominal in the sentence.

A second claim relates to the fact that successful reading, like all linguistic decoding, requires the reader to extract the semantic gist of the language material confronting him. In order to get at the basic *propositional content* of a sentence, readers must be able to manipulate the following interrelated components of sentence structure: constituent structure — what the parts of a sentence are, and how they interrelate hierarchically; structural items — function words and affixes which serve as markers of grammatical relations and of constituent and rhetorical structure; and dependencies — relations expressed between discontinuous elements such as *so* and *that* in (1) above.

Moreover, handling of constituent structure, structural items, and discontinuous yet interdependent elements in the sentence may be complicated by perceptual factors such as 'heaviness' — as noted in 1.3 below, and 'opacity', for instance, with regard to pronominal reference, such as the question of the antecedent of the pronoun *it* at the end of the sentence in (1). Below we expand on the nature and role of the factors of constituent structure, transparency/opacity, and heaviness respectively.

1.1 In terms of constituent structure, it would seem that a reader must first and foremost recognize the basic parts of a sentence — what constitutes its main and subordinate clauses, what their predicate and arguments are in propositional terms, the SVO of surface syntax, the NVN actor–action–patient semantic relations, which Bever (1970) argues are crucial in language perception and decoding. It follows that where there is a conflict between the more basic ordering of semantic and syntactic relations and the surface form of sentences, as in passives, or where material is preposed before the surface subject, or where adverbial clauses precede rather than follow the main clause, readers might be expected to encounter difficulty. That is, FL readers' comprehension is liable to be impaired by shifts in svo ordering; for where the typical expectations of the reader, certainly in a foreign language, are violated, his fluency may be disrupted and hence comprehension hindered.

This is evidently what happened in the experiment described in 2.4 below, where students reported having misinterpreted or 'not having understood at all' the core propositional relation 'It is necessary to do something in order to do something else' in the following sentence (from Frank Smith 1971, pp. 90–91):

2. To understand the research that has provided information about many aspects of vision relevant to the reading process, it is necessary to acquire some familiarity with a venerable piece of psychological instrumentation and with a rather precise way of talking about very small units of time.

Basically, then, we are suggesting that successful readers somehow manage to get at the core or 'kernel' of more complicated sentences, sentences of the kind that are quite common in the readings assigned to college students.

Moreover, appreciation of constituent structure is relevant not only at major boundaries, but within secondary constituents, too. Consider the following extract from a sentence — from the same source as (2) above — which was analysed with EFL students as described in 2.4 below.

3. ... *we* see/no spatial discontinuity
    at the point where
    the separate visual experiences
        from the two halves of our field of view
    are brought together

The string is represented in (3) in a graphic form adapted from Wood (1974), who presented 3rd and 5th grade children with sentences that were graphically 'parsed in segments that conformed to the phrase structure . . . and in segments that violated that structure' (1974, p. 21). She found that 'parsing sentences into their natural surface structure constituents clearly facilitates the speed at which sentences can be processed regardless of the grade level or the skill of the reader'. Similar findings are reported for other experiments conducted with native speakers (Clark and Clark 1977). With regard to the sentence in (3) above, if a reader fails to perceive *what* 'point' is referred to, *what* is 'separate' and from what, and *what* entities 'are brought together', he will not be able to process the sentence, and hence to understand it. Moreover, as the string in (3) is itself nested inside another set of dependencies — it begins with the words 'just as we see . . .' and is followed by a clause beginning 'so we are unaware of . . .' — getting at the meaning of the sentence as a whole would seem to require that constituent structure be hierarchically broken down and then re-synthesized.

1.2 We suggest, next, that the FL reader needs maximal 'transparency' in marking the relations between one part of the text and another. That is, certain kinds of cohesive devices (as discussed in Halliday and Hasan, 1976) may render a text opaque to the FL reader. These may take the form of *deletion* — for instance, by means of gapping, lack of relative pronouns in English relative clauses, *wh+be* deletion in post-nominal modifiers, etc. — or of *substitution* of, say, nominal *one* or verbal *do* as grammatical substitutes for repeated lexical material, as well as of lexical substitution. For instance, with respect to the sentence in (2) above, during the experiment described in 2.4 below, one student asked whether the opening phrase 'to understand' in fact 'means the same as "*in order* to understand"'; on being answered affirmatively, both she and other members of the class came out with remarks like: 'Oh, *now* I understand!'.

Thus, while the style approved in English rhetorical tradition and widely observed in discursive prose might encourage the dual mechanism of truncation and alternation, these may run counter to the requirements of maximal transparency from the point of view of the foreign language learner: and this opacity might be particularly acute in the case of EFL readers whose mother tongue not only tolerates but approves of lexical and grammatical repetition as a preferred rhetorical device — as is the case with Hebrew and Arabic.

1.3 We noted earlier the factor of 'heaviness' as a potential source of difficulty. By this we refer to constructions which extend the basic NV(N) structure so that one or more of the sentence constituents is 'heavy', containing many sub-parts of embedding or modification, as illustrated by the sentences in (2) and (3) above. Note that the notion of 'heaviness' is not a straightforward function of linear *length* in any simple terms. Rather, the problem seems to concern the amount and depth of information which the reader must store in memory in moving from one constituent to the next, and how hard the transition becomes as a result. And in fact, in the experiment reported in 2.4 below, students said things like: 'I was so busy working on this part of the sentence, I forgot it was connected with something else'.

Heaviness may also occur where the basic NVN or 'kernel' structure is violated by a process such as nominalization — there are grounds for believing that nominalizations are often more complex than corresponding sentences with simple verbs or adjectives (Stockwell 1977, p. 156). Thus, with respect to one of the sentences discussed in Section 2.4 below, the string 'X is no indication that Y' was much clearer to students when they realized that this meant, 'X does not indicate that Y'. The kind of texts encountered by EFL college students in their specialized reading often contain sentences which are not only long in number of words, but are also heavy and relatively opaque, in the sense in which these terms are used here.

1.4 In 1.2 above we noted the opacity entailed by deletion of relational markers as illustrated below (from the text by Frank Smith):

4. a.   Visual information (which/that) we may be exposed to
   b.   . . . many aspects of vision (which are) relevant to the reading process
   c.   . . . the amount of time (that) the shutter of a camera requires to be open (in order) to get a reasonable image on film

and we suggested this as a source of potential difficulty. A related issue is that in English, as in other languages, a single grammatical formative may perform various functions. Thus, its occurrence is no guarantee of a given type of constituent to follow. This is true, for example, of *that* as a relative marker and as a noun clause subordinator; of *one* as pronominal substitute and as quantifier; of *it* as a personal, anaphoric pronoun and as an empty pro-subject in clefts or with extraposed sentential complements; of *there* in its existential and adverbial uses, etc. That this kind of functional ambiguity may cause difficulties for language learners is suggested by the following two pieces of anecdotal evidence. Two consecutive paragraphs of a high-school English text for Israeli students begin with the word *since*, once marking a time clause and once an explanatory reason clause. A teacher using this material remarked that her students interpret them both as 'from the time that' — evidently because they are drilled in this sense of the word *since* when studying the present perfect in the intermediate stages of their high-school English; in Hebrew the two occurrences of 'since' are translated by totally different words. Similarly, when students participating in the experiment reported in 2.4 below were asked to give the Hebrew for the word *while* in the sentence numbered (17) in this paper, many students gave the appropriate equivalent of the duration marker 'at the same time that', but several others translated it as the concessive 'whereas', thus failing to understand the relation between the two clauses of the sentence in question.

This suggests the prevalence of what seems to be a typical FL reader strategy: the tendency to select one function for any given grammatical formative, so that when it marks some other function in the text, expectancies are not met and comprehension is impeded. Thus, words like *since, while,* and *then* may always be perceived in terms of time relations rather than of reason, concession, and result respectively; some students always take *just* to mean 'only a moment ago' in all its occurrences, others preferring to interpret it as 'exactly' in all cases. The problem of functional overloading of a small set of very common grammatical formatives thus seems to warrant special attention in foreign language methodology. For, while much important work has been done on these 'little' words' in studies of sentence processing, and FL methodologists do recognize their relevance, it seems that the latter focus largely on how students use these functors in production, e.g. distinguishing *who* from *which,* using *than* and not *from* in comparatives, assigning the right preposition to the governing verb, and using *in* and *at* correctly in expressions of place and time, etc. We suggest that special attention — both for research and teaching purposes — be given to these words in terms of how students perceive and utilize them in their reading, too.

2.   Types of experimental evidence

Against this background, we report below on some studies done with Hebrew-speaking college students at Tel Aviv University for whom English is a foreign language.

2.1 We conducted a pilot study with some 20 Hebrew-speaking college students, all of whom had had at least six years of compulsory English at school, and who were enrolled in an intensive course in reading English to help them gain access to specialized texts at the university. Subjects were divided into two groups, roughly equated for level of English; the control group was given a text of a little over 300 words which they had not previously seen, while the experimental group was given a reworked version of the same text. In the adaptation, vocabulary items were left as far as possible intact, and syntactic structures were simplified to eliminate the kind of difficulties noted in Section 1 above. The simplification undertaken was consistent with the idea that 'no one-to-one correspondence obtains between syntactic complexity and (sentence) length' (Schlesinger 1968, p. 72). Thus, while the 100 or so words of the simplified version were distributed in 4 sentences, as against the 3 sentences of the original version (83 words), at least one sentence of the simpler version was *longer* than the original. This added length, in number of words *and* number of sentences, seemed necessary to achieve simpler syntax, in view of the claims outlined in Section 1, for instance that repetition of the same lexical material within and across sentences may be important for greater referential clarity and transparency, even though it might go against the dictates of approved English style in composition. Thus, the simplified version deliberately reduced or modified cases of ellipsis, pronominalization, and substitution.

A single set of 30 questions was constructed and given to both groups of students, after first being tried out on two native speakers to make sure that the questions were clear. The questions were divided up as follows: 20 multiple choice items — 10 on factual details, 5 on pronominal reference, and 5 on overall content; and 10 open-ended questions relating to more general ideas, which students were free to answer in Hebrew. Here, the notion of 'overall content' or 'general ideas' as compared with 'factual details' corresponds to the distinction made by Cohen *et al.* (1978) between 'macro' questions 'which require some integration or generalization from specific sentences' and 'micro' questions which 'focus directly on specific sentences or parts of sentences'.

'Specific' or 'micro' questions were given in the order in which the relevant sentences appeared in the text. An example of such a question is given below:

5   According to this passage (sentence no. 1),
    a.   The simple family is always the most important unit in society.
    b.   The simple family is usually the most important unit in society.
    c.   The simple family is often not the most important unit in society.
    d.   The simple family is never the most important unit in society.

A more 'general' ('macro' or 'global') question is illustrated below, the correct answer on the basis of the entire passage (whether on the original or adapted text) being item (a), although the other points are all touched on in the text.

6   Most of the information in this passage is about:
   a.   characteristics of the social unit known as 'the extended family',
   b.   contrasts between the extended family and the simple family,
   c.   the advantages (good points) of the extended family system,
   d.   characteristics of extended families in different parts of the world.

An example of a question on pronominal reference is given in (8), with reference to the original text sentence in (7a) and the adapted sentence in (7b).

7 a.   Although the extended family does not take over all the functions of the simple family unit, *it* usually maintains an overall supervision of its members and there are clearly defined rights and duties involved.
   b.   The extended family does not take over all the functions of the simple family unit, but *it* usually supervises its members in an overall way, and it has rights and duties which are clearly defined.

8 The pronoun *it* in line . . . refers to
   a.   the extended family.
   b.   the functions of the simple family unit.
   c.   the simple family.
   d.   any member of the simple family unit.

Results on the test questions showed that of the two groups, those who read the syntactically adapted version did consistently better on all types of questions, thus seeming to substantiate our general hypothesis. Yet relatively more errors were made by readers of the original text on questions of 'specific' information than on 'global' or 'general' content. Thus it appears that intra-sentential syntactic complexity might be more of an impediment to grasping specific details than to overall ideas. Perhaps, then, for purposes of effective skimming, for getting the gist of an entire text, 'syntax' may not be all that crucial. However, if our aim includes students' acquisition of specific information accurately and in detail — which is the case with much scientific or technical material — exact appreciation of syntactic components of each sentence remains an important aim.

Note, moreover, that at least half the questions in this test (those on specific facts and on pronominal reference) focused on *intra*sentential items as such. In other words, our questions failed to tap students' perception of *inter*sentential relations. Consider, for instance, the use of the word *however* in the last sentence of the text, which follows a description of how an American nurse attempting to set up a baby care clinic in China sent out invitations, first to the children's mothers, and subsequently to the paternal grandmother of each child (where (9a) is from the original, (9b) from the adapted version):

9 a. It was, *however*, not the child's mother but the paternal grandmother that decided whether the child should come and by whom it be accompanied.

b. *However*, the child's mother did not decide whether the child should come to the clinic, or who should accompany the child; the paternal grandmother decided these things.

A more comprehensive experimental design would include questions to check comprehension of such relationships, and others.

2.2 A similar type of experiment to the one reported above was conducted by a TEFL student (Cojocaru 1977). Working once again with Hebrew-speakers, Cojocaru had subjects read one of two versions of an excerpt from the article 'The Sea Around Him' by Riley Hughes; she then presented both groups with the same set of 30 questions, constructed along the same lines as those of the test described in 2.1 above. The experimental group's text in this case, however, was adapted by simplifying the vocabulary items, with the syntax being left as far as possible the same in both versions.

Item analysis of the responses of both groups led the researcher to conclude that 'most of the mistakes were a result of poor knowledge of syntax, while the vocabulary, which was not simple, did not cause much difficulty'.

This line of investigation might profitably be pursued, with the element of vocabulary being neutralized so as to focus on the variable of syntax. For instance, one group of students could be given glosses of unfamiliar or difficult vocabulary items, on the assumption that incorrect responses on their part, at the 'micro' level at least, might be attributed directly to factors of syntactic difficulty.

2.3 Evidence of the difficulties caused by syntax has been obtained from classroom observation. The examples relating to (10) and (11) below are based on the author's observation of a class of EFL Israeli college students majoring in biology. The teacher was not informed of the specific purpose of the visit, but she was asked to try to 'get at' students' difficulties with the text as carefully as possible.

10. Chromosomes pair gene to gene.

One student thought that 'pair' was a noun, and so was unable to make any sense of a sentence which seemed to him to lack a verb, and which thus did not meet any kind of svo processing strategies — according to the claims in 1.1 above.

> 11. In many unicellular organisms and in lower plants, nuclei contributing to the zygote are transferred between two cells without the formation of obviously specialized gametes by processes such as partial and temporary fusion of ciliated protozoans.

Most of the students were baffled by this very complex string:
a) several thought that 'nuclei' was singular — failing to find the typical plural marker -s;
b) the plural form of the verb 'are transferring' did not help them, because it is removed from the head noun 'nuclei' by an intervening participial phrase;
c) the participial form 'contributing to the zygote' (where Hebrew would require an overt marker in a phrase like 'that contribute to the zygote', with the verb 'contribute' agreeing with the head noun in number, gender, and person) was interpreted by several of the students as an occurrence of progressive aspect and one student said 'Well, nuclei are contributing to the zygote, so I don't see what are transferred';
d) several students did not understand what the nominal form 'formation' referred to, and when prompted, made clear that they had difficulty in processing the modification of the noun 'gametes' by 'obviously specialized'. (Hebrew would have the equivalent of 'gametes that (are) clearly are specialized', again with number and gender agreement between the noun and its modifier);
e) two students insisted that gametes *were* formed — evidently because they had difficulty in the scope of the negative 'without' across all the rest of the sentence;
f) some students did not realize that 'fusion' was modified by the conjunct 'partial and temporary' — perhaps because Hebrew in such cases requires overt repetition of the head noun, which always precedes its modifiers, to yield the equiva-

lent of 'fusion partial and fusion temporary', again with number and gender agreement between noun and modifier.

These observations thus seemed to substantiate claims made in Section 1 of this paper. They further suggested the important role of special difficulties due to the students' mother tongue — if not for *a priori* purposes of prediction (possibly prevention), then at least for purposes of *a posteriori* explanation of students' difficulties.

Two further examples of EFL classroom information were observed with students working on non-technical texts:

12.   That the note of fear in his parents' voice is uncontrollable is not understood by the child.

Two students thought that 'is uncontrollable' was the main or matrix verb of the sentence, and were thus unable to process it correctly, their perception of constituent structure probably being hampered here by the very 'heavy' sentential subject separated by the very 'light' word *is* from the predicate. When prompted by the instructor, who commented 'Well, there is something that the child does not understand. What doesn't the child understand?' the two students in question got the point right away.

13.   Although Mark predicted inevitable disintegration, history proved his ideas limited.

Several students in the class failed to grasp the relationship between the two clauses, some of them seeming to treat the first clause as independent — despite its heavy semantic import. Again, their dismissal of the role of the subordinating 'although' may be in part due to the fact that Hebrew concessive clauses allow a correlative subordinator in the form '*though* Mark predicted . . ., *yet/but*, history proved'. One student asked the instructor 'What was limited?'; again, the Hebrew equivalent 'history proved *that* his ideas *were* limited' with number and gender agreement between 'ideas' and 'limited' is far more transparent than the English text.

2.4 We conducted an informal study with a class of final year undergraduates majoring in TEFL at Tel Aviv University. They had been assigned to read Chapters 7 and 8 of a book on reading (Smith 1971), and more than half the class reported they had found it difficult. We decided to find out whether 'language' or 'conceptual' difficulty was mainly at issue, and chose an excerpt of two paragraphs (pp. 90–91) which seemed to be syntactically complex, while containing mainly familiar vocabulary. The aim was to elicit introspections or self-reports from a class of some twenty students who were highly proficient though non-native in English. The text was dealt with sentence-by-sentence and students were asked what they had not understood. In some instances they translated the sentence or part of it into Hebrew; in others they were asked to re-word the sentence without changing the meaning or specific vocabulary items and, as these were students with a strong background in linguistics and English grammar, they were also asked to pick out the subject and main verb, the matrix and embedded clauses of each sentence. Students subsequently reported that this had taught them more about the processes and strategies of reading than any of their own prior experience or studies in the area.

Below are some of the kinds of problems which emerged during the 1½ hour session with respect to the first four sentences of the excerpt in question.

14. The fact that the eye is open and exposed to stimulation by light is no indication that visual information is being received and processed by the brain.

Several students did not grasp the relations between the parts of the subject-clause, specifically between 'open' and 'exposed' and between 'exposed' and 'to stimulation by light'; this seemed to be due to the factor of 'truncation' noted in 1.2. The Hebrew equivalent would have overt marking of the subject of 'exposed' in the form 'the fact that the eye is open and *that it* (is) exposed . . .' with *it* agreeing with 'eye' in number and gender. They also tended to gloss over the word '*no*' in the predicate — Hebrew would again require overt pronominalization of the complex subject in the form 'it/this is no indication' and would probably have a simple verb instead of a nominalization here, such as 'it/this does not indicate that'. In general, students reported difficulty in separating out subject from predicate — both 'heavy' strings here — by means of the word *is*. It took several minutes to elicit the propositional 'core' of (14) — that something does not necessarily indicate something — but as soon as this was grasped, students got the point of the sentence as a whole.

15. The eye is exposed to much more information than the brain can possibly use, and the brain selects and processes only as much as it can handle.

Here, two main sources of confusion emerged. One was of the

interrelation of 'information', 'brain', and 'use', owing to the discontinuous *much more X than Y* of this comparative structure, and the Hebrew-speakers' expectation of some kind of resumptive pronoun 'than the brain can use *it*' referring back to 'information'. Again we come across the problem of truncation, or of 'deleted' elements. A few students thought that 'it' in the second part of the sentence had the noun 'eye' rather than 'brain' as its antecedent, so could not understand the writer's point at all. Again, students' difficulty may be attributed to deletion of repeated elements: when asked to translate the latter part of the sentence, they all either repeated or pronominalized the noun, 'information' — e.g. 'and the brain selects and processes only as much *information*/as much *of it* as it can handle'.

16. And while the brain is busy constructing one percept the system appears to be closed to new information that might be arriving from the eyes.

Here, students were asked where they would place a comma to separate off the adverbial clause at the beginning from the main clause. As soon as they became aware of the demarcation line between the two nominals 'one percept' // 'the system', they announced the whole sentence was much clearer. Thus it appeared that constituent structure of the sentence as a whole had been the source of difficulty, particularly in view of the shift in basic SVO+ADVERB to ADVERB+SVO order. Moreover, misinterpretation of the subordinator 'while', as noted in 1.4 above, led some students to expect the main clause to be a contradiction to the adverbial, rather than describing two concurrent events or circumstances.

17. Yet just as we see no spatial discontinuity at the point where the separate visual experiences from the two halves of our field of view are brought together, so we are unaware of the discontinuity over time that occurs with a visual system that is in effect "taking snap-shots" of the world no faster than four times a second.

Students were asked to look at the words starting the two parts of the sentence separated by a comma — *yet just as we . . ., so we are . . .* — and say what kind of relationship they expected. Several students indicated that there would be a contradiction, and when asked why, reported that this was because of the word *yet* at the beginning of the sentence. This could indicate an inefficient reader strategy which might be manifested in the mother tongue as well, where a marker of *inter*sentential rhetorical relations in the form of *yet* is confused with relations between parts of the same sentence.

Two main sources of difficulty were revealed with respect to (17): the discontinuous relation between 'just as . . . so' — and, again, their Hebrew translations favoured *repetition*, for instance: 'exactly as we . . . so exactly we . . .'; they also reported difficulty in processing *negatives*, such as 'we see no spatial discontinuity', 'we are unaware of', and 'no faster than' (compare Hebrew 'at (a) speed that (does) not exceed/is not faster than . . .'). Although the claims noted in Section 1 did not make specific assumptions with regard to the processing of negatives, the kind of elicitation technique used with these students revealed this as an important source of difficulty, perhaps just because English does not allow 'double negatives' which are so clearly marked, but does allow numerous affixal negators, e.g. 'no discontinuity', 'not unpleasant'. Elsewhere, the predictions outlined in Section 1 were largely confirmed: non-apprehension of svo relations and basic constituent structure made it impossible for students to get at the propositional core of these rather complicated sentences; truncation or deletion of grammatical markers rather than overt lexical repetition, subordination or pronominalization made it hard for students to perceive relations between parts of sentences; and discontinuous, logically dependent elements were unravelled only after some prompting.

This detailed reliance on students' reporting on a specific text illuminated many potential sources of difficulty caused by syntactic, rather than lexical or conceptual, factors. Such a technique has certain limitations: there was heavy reliance on translation into the mother tongue and on the investigator's awareness of Hebrew–English contrasts in structure. This is not possible where students are of a mixed-language background. The procedure is also extremely time-consuming. We would suggest that this kind of elicitation be done with smaller groups of students, possibly divided up into different levels of proficiency; that specific problems be isolated in a number of different texts, and students' performance in each case be compared across texts; and that elicitation techniques be more carefully structured than in the informal session reported on here.

Below we review these and other methods of research, in an attempt to arrive at certain recommendations regarding ways of investigating students' processing of FL reading texts at different stages in their course of study.

3. Some methodological conclusions

We started this study by outlining some potential areas of difficulty for the advanced level EFL reader due to factors of syntax, and then reviewed some studies of Israeli students in the area of reading in general. Certain of the assumptions formulated in Section 1 remain *a priori*, though they are derived from extensive experience in the EFL classroom in Israel, and by research into Hebrew–English contrastive structure (for instance, Berman 1978, 1979). However, the evidence emerging from our own experiments as well as those conducted by others with Hebrew-speaking college students does in general substantiate the central claim of this study, namely 'that efficient FL readers must rely in part on syntactic devices to get at text meaning'.

3.1 Several points also seem to emerge with respect to research procedures in this area. Where comprehension questions and item-analysis of responses are used as a research tool, these questions should be carefully controlled to isolate the variables at issue: 'syntax' in general, intersentential connections, vocabulary, pronominal reference, constituent structure, etc. There should, moreover, be a suitable interplay between 'micro' and 'macro' questions, to investigate our suggestion that 'syntax' may be more important at the 'micro' or local, specific sentence level than at the level of overall comprehension of general ideas. Should this be the case, the methodological implications might be as follows: at intermediate-level reading courses, focus should be on syntactic structure, while at a more advanced level focus should be on efficient perception of general ideas, main drift, and overall rhetorical organization of whole texts. This is proposed on the assumption that unravelling of specific syntactic constructions by now might constitute less of a problem, and that advanced students will progress in this area more by exposure and practice in reading than by direct teaching.

3.2 Secondly, very specific elements of discourse structure can and should be isolated for investigation. For instance, a more complex experimental design of the pilot study described in 2.1 above might include questions to check comprehension of logical and rhetorical relations between sentences, and between larger portions of the text, such as paragraphs, relations often marked explicitly by sentence connectors such as *however, furthermore*, or *finally*, and by co-ordinators such as *and* or *but*. Data from Cohen *et al.* (1978)

indicate that some FL student misunderstandings can be traced to ignorance of or inattention to such rhetorical connectors. Perhaps special items need to be constructed to investigate the consequence of ignoring such words, for instance by omitting them from one version of a text for experimental purposes, as well as how they actually are (mis)interpreted by FL readers: by changing the order of occurrence as in example (9) above, by replacing *however* by *but, moreover* by *and also*, and even by replacing them with words in the same category which indicate quite different logical relations.

In general, different variables can be isolated by adaptation of the same text for groups of subjects equated for overall proficiency: by simplification of syntax, of vocabulary, and/or of overall rhetorical structure, to pinpoint specific factors in the reading process. Subjects could also be varied, not only texts; thus, comparison of the performance and responses of native speakers to FL readers of different levels might serve to isolate factors which are peculiarly FL based, and those which require a certain degree of competence on the part of readers in general.

3.3 Another general conclusion is that observation of EFL classroom text work and reading activities may be a good source of information on specific student problems in FL reading. The procedures should be more carefully designed than in the cases reported in Section 2 above, however; the observer–reader should select the texts for classroom work according to his specific hypotheses; he should guide the instructor in the kind of questions to ask; or he might himself construct questions on the text, do an item analysis of the results, and then sit in on the class when the teacher asks why students answered one way rather than another. And the researcher should control carefully for variables such as whether the text is familiar to students from prior reading or general level of proficiency; for instance, the same text may be observed in different classes, in one case with, in the other without prior reading, or in classes at different levels of reading proficiency. Thus, while classroom observation is time-consuming, and tends to be rather diffuse in content, careful design can make it a valuable source of information on how students read what.

3.4 Finally, using students as informants for the purpose of investigating their understanding of EFL texts provides a valuable methodological tool. Procedures for doing this are reported in

Cohen *et al.* (1978) and in Cohen and Fine (1978). In the latter study, a small group of Hebrew-speaking students and some native English-speaking control subjects were asked to read a text in their specialization, history. They were then interviewed (the FL students as a group, the native speakers individually) and asked questions of three types — 'macro', 'micro' and 'vocabulary'. The researchers then did a very detailed analysis of the students' answer to each question, and to each type of question, and despite certain methodological problems noted by the authors (pp. 65–66), they were able to reach pertinent conclusions about the nature of difficulties students encountered with the text, and how the FL readers differed from the native speakers in their responses. A careful item analysis was particularly effective in view of the following: the researchers evolved their procedure on the basis of certain hypotheses about potential sources of text difficulty; they constructed different types of questions geared to these various areas; and they used an interview technique of elicitation rather than the normal type of test, allowing for students to self-correct, reformulate, and in general 'monitor' their answers in a way accessible to researchers when doing their analysis (of tape-recorded transcripts).

3.5 A more direct type of informant elicitation is described in Olshtain and Bejarano (1979). Ten students participating in an 'open university' EFL reading course were asked to keep a diary on their own learning process, and were met with periodically to discuss the contents of these diaries, and to expand on what they had noted down in oral self-reports. Each reading selection in the course followed three steps: an initial rapid reading focusing on main ideas; a more intensive and detailed second reading; and a third integrative reading aimed at promoting student awareness of the reading strategies they had employed. At the end of a six-week period, subjects were met with, their diaries collected, and they were given a questionnaire in the mother tongue to get at their individual working procedures (e.g. by questioning their reaction to the 'first step' rapid reading part of the course). At the end of the four-month (self-teaching) reading course, the subjects were given a comprehension test on an unfamiliar passage, and a questionnaire about the reading strategies they employed with this text (e.g. 'underline the words which you did not understand when you first started reading the passage'). This study was geared mainly to strategies employed by the reader rather than to specific text

difficulties or problems of syntax. Nonetheless, similar procedures
might be adapted to locate specific areas of text difficulty, too.
The use of diaries or of self-reports noted down by the student
while and immediately after his reading of a text should be enlightening, particularly when backed up by more structured questionnaires concerning specific points in the text.

Thus, a variety of techniques for elicitation of information from
the readers themselves emerges, through interviews, diaries, oral
and written self-reports, as well as through appropriately structured questionnaires. Detailed questioning of students in the classroom is time-consuming but illuminating, and it allows for
comparison of students of different language backgrounds. This
can be supplemented by observation of FL reading classes where
the researcher, possibly the instructor, too, is geared to locating
points of difficulty revealed by students' answers, comments,
queries in the classroom situation. And all these procedures can
reveal not only where students do encounter difficulty, but also
'areas of ease' — those areas which many or all students cope with
competently, even though this may not have been predictable on
any *a priori* grounds.

Thus, experimentation in the general area of reading and with
respect to the specific factor of syntax in FL texts can and should
be systematically varied by careful isolation of variables relating
to type of text, type of learner, type of question, and type of elicitation technique — with the aim ultimately of re-integrating the
different variables towards achievement of a more coherent theory
of FL reading.

Note

This is a revised version of a paper presented at the 5th International Congress of Applied Linguistics, Montreal, August 1978.
I am grateful to Elite Olshtain and Roberta Stock for enlightening
discussion of the issues, and to the editors of this volume for
important criticisms of an early version of this paper.

Postscript on Berman

Berman's main thesis, that syntax presents difficulties to the FL reader, would seem to contradict one of Cooper's findings, namely that neither practised nor unpractised readers were strong on syntax, so that presumably the practised group's competence did not owe much to proficiency in syntax. Closer examination, however, suggests that there is no necessary conflict, since the two writers concentrate on markedly different aspects of syntactic processing. Cooper's test examines the ability of subjects to recognize paraphrases or implications of sentences exhibiting particular syntactic structures. Berman's main interest is in factors affecting readers' ability to parse sentences into their main consti-tuents, and thus to derive meaning from these sentences. It is true that, in the case of Berman's first example (p. 139), she seems to insist that readers must recognize that one sentence is a re-ordered paraphrase of another before comprehension can take place. This strong claim, however, whether justified or not, does not seem necessary to her main thesis.

Berman's approach seems to have the following advantages over other approaches to the relationship between syntax and reading:

1. In general, she and her associates have examined syntax as it occurs in actual texts; in other words, the syntax does not form a separate test. In test designs where syntactic test and reading texts are separate, there is always a suspicion that aspects of the test itself may have caused additional difficulties.

2. Berman's approach is aimed at the difficulties of syntax of *utterances*, rather than *sentences* (see Lyons 1968 for an account of the distinction in linguistics). A sentence-based approach often seems to entail a belief that a particular syntactic structure will *always* cause difficulty, e.g. the passive has been held to be simply more difficult than the active. In general, however, the experi-mental findings suggest that, at least for LI readers, syntax only becomes a problem when it interacts with other factors in the utterance (cf. Schlesinger 1968). The features investigated by Berman, such as 'heaviness', are features of utterances. Since the discourse that readers engage with in texts is composed of utter-ances, not of linguistic sentences, Berman's approach seems likely ' to arrive at more valid results.

3. Related to this is the fact that Berman's approach lays emphasis on the processor of the syntax. Many early psycholinguistic studies tended to be very heavily influenced by linguistics, in particular transformational linguistics. The derivation of the passive in English contains more steps than the equivalent active, therefore it 'should' be more difficult. Derivational and processing histories, as it were, were one. Following Bever (1970), Berman lays much greater stress on the interaction of syntax and readers' processing strategies. The theory claims, for example, that, in English, readers tend to look in utterances for agent noun and action verb. Any syntactic feature which hinders this search will be a source of difficulty. This emphasis may be of particular value in the FL field, where the interaction, as Berman makes clear, may be affected by readers' expectations based on syntactic features of the LI.

4. By focusing on readers' attempts to find the main constituents of sentences, a process-oriented approach can succeed in bringing into a unified framework a number of apparently disparate syntactic features affecting such a search, including in Berman's study embedding, ellipsis, deletion and stylistic re-ordering. A more purely syntax-based approach, particularly when not based on any one particular syntactic model, can end up using a number of apparently randomly selected syntactic structures. This matter is not simply one of conceptual tidiness: it would be interesting to discover whether FL readers differed in their ability to parse, particularly when faced with unfamiliar structures, and whether this ability correlated with reading ability. If a positive correlation were discovered, this would be a strong argument in favour of receptive, 'interpretative' syntactic exercises, as Berman suggests, rather than the productive type which are at present the rule.

While it has been remarked above that Berman's and Cooper's findings do not necessarily conflict, there is one curious resemblance which deserves comment. Cooper's practised readers were able to comprehend and extract the gist of texts, yet were apparently weak on the syntactic meanings of sentences. In Berman's text simplification experiment (p. 146), readers of the original 'unsimplified' text made relatively more intrasentential errors than general gist errors. Berman tentatively concludes that syntax is more important at the sentence level. Both findings seem to suggest that it is possible to understand the gist of texts while failing to understand them at sentence level. Partly the problem seems to resolve into a question of what one means by 'gist'. If it is limited to a vague specification such as 'This text is about X', then it would seem that the nature of X could be identified by means of the title, or headings, or frequency of occurrence of certain lexical items, as in early content analysis approaches. If one makes one's requirement for gist more demanding, it is hard to see how a reader could consistently misunderstand the meanings of sentences making up a text, yet achieve a satisfactory comprehension of the overall meaning. One is tempted to suspect the nature of the text used: perhaps the provisional, context-dependent meanings assigned to text sentences are not held with sufficient confidence to stand up to specific, sentence-directed questioning. This area seems likely to repay further research. Certainly we might doubt Berman's methodological suggestion (p. 153) that teaching of 'specifics' should precede teaching of 'general drift'. If her findings are accepted, it is arguable that this order should be reversed!

A process-oriented approach cannot derive its hypotheses directly from a syntactic model. Berman suggests three alternative sources, contrastive studies, observation and student introspection. Contrastive studies have not been very prominent in recent EFL research, for a number of reasons. Berman's paper should remind us that they can be a valuable tool in predicting text difficulty.

Classroom observation is another valuable source of data, particularly when, as Berman points out, the class is linguistically homogeneous. However, as she says, the method does require both a teacher and an observer. Interviews with students are again potentially valuable, though not widely used as yet. The method has links with Harri-Augstein and Thomas's 'conversational' approach. In the FL context, it would seem essential for the researcher to be a fluent speaker of the FL and the LI. Even given this, however, there still remains the problem of finding students who can discuss their difficulties articulately. It is significant that one group successfully studied in this way by Berman had a strong background in linguistics. Perhaps it is necessary for such research to form part of a teaching programme which incorporates the teaching of one or more metalanguages.

Interest in syntax in EFL has recently tended to be eclipsed by interest in a socio-linguistic perspective focusing on discourse, speech acts and linguistic functions. Berman's paper is evidence that a syntax-based approach still has relevance to FL reading and the simplification of texts.

8 The effect of rhetorical ordering on readability

A. H. Urquhart

Is it possible to isolate language factors which affect readability? Readability formulae normally incorporate word difficulty and sentence length as significant factors. However, research suggests that the substitution in a text of 'simpler' words does not lead to genuine simplification (Kueneman 1931). Similarly, it has been shown that sentence length in itself has no measurable effect (Orndorff 1925; Schlesinger 1968). Schlesinger (1968) tested the hypothesis that syntactic complexity caused processing difficulties. Again, however, the results indicated that syntax was not a significant factor, at least as far as L1 speakers are concerned. Syntax relates to organization inside the sentence; a next stage could be to consider text organization beyond the sentence. The experiments below thus tested the hypothesis that rhetorical organization could affect the readability of texts in certain specific ways.

When examining the effects of organization on learning from written texts, it is possible to concentrate on one of two issues. We may ask: can organizational structure be varied so that readers focus on, and remember particular parts of the text? Meyer (1975) embedded the same paragraph in two different texts, in one of which it was the *solution* of a *problem–solution* type of organization, in the other text one of a number of items in a *listing* organization. When appearing as a *solution*, the paragraph was recalled significantly better. On the other hand, we may ask: can we vary the organization of the presentation of a message in such a way as to make the whole message easier to comprehend and remember? In other words, using organization as a variable, can we produce one 'textualization' or version of a text which is easier to learn than another textualization of the 'same' message? The work reported here is concerned with this second issue, as is that of Crothers (1972) and Clark (1975).

Such an approach can be viewed as a part of *readability* studies. That is, just as some have investigated the role of word length, or syntactic complexity in readability, this approach examines another language variable, the organization of the statements, or propositions making up a text. From another point of view, the approach can be seen as an attempt to validate the advice given by pedagogical rhetoricians with regard to organization. Thus, if a rhetorician asserts that in a certain context, a particular type of organization is best, we can often interpret this to mean that if this type of organization is used, the resulting text will in some definable way be more readable. This approach can therefore bring together readability studies and pedagogical rhetoric, and thus have some relevance to both the simplification of reading texts and the teaching of writing.

Readability measures initially derive their validity from being set against measures of text difficulty, e.g. comprehension tests. Such tests provide in a sense a definition of what is meant by 'readable'. The present work focused on the reading of study texts, that is, texts intended to be studied and, to some extent, remembered. For this reason, two criteria for 'readability' were adopted, speed and ease of recall. In other words, all other things being equal, a text was considered more readable if (a) it could be read more quickly, and (b) it could be remembered more easily. This constitutes an operational definition of readability: it is not claimed that it is in any way a complete definition, or the only one.

The two organizational principles investigated here are time order and space order. In time order, a sequence of events is described in the same textual order as they occurred. This is the organization recommended by rhetoricians for narratives (McCrimmon 1963), and descriptions of processes (Hodges and Whitten 1962). In space ordering, objects in a scene, or separate parts of an object, are described in a unilinear fashion, e.g. starting from the left and moving across to the right. This form of organization, naturally, is recommended for physical descriptions. Presumably because most of us consider time and space to be separate from ourselves and from language, these two have been described as 'natural' principles of organization (Lackstrom, Selinker and Trimble 1972).

In order to test the rhetoricians' claims for the effect of, for example, time ordering, it is necessary to have as a basis at least one pair of texts which differ, as far as possible, only in that one employs time ordering and the other does not. The two texts should be as similar as possible not only with respect to content, that is the sequence of events being described, but also in length, vocabulary, syntactic complexity, and indeed in any factors possibly affecting readability. In the experiments described below, pairs of texts were produced by selecting a seemingly suitable original text, and using this as the basis for two texts differing from each other in rhetorical ordering. It would, of course, have been possible to write both versions specially for the experiments: the third alternative, to find suitable pairs of already existing texts, requires perhaps too much searching, not to mention luck, to be practical.

Experiment 1: time order

The first text below is part of a passage from *A Higher Course in English Study* (Mackin and Carver 1968). Sentences 3 to 9 were from one paragraph. The first two sentences are from a previous paragraph, and were included to act as an introduction. The words 'chi' and 'loessial' in the original have been replaced by 'feet' and 'firm' respectively; this was done because both the original terms were likely to be unfamiliar to the experimental subjects. The numbers in the text refer to the units into which the text was analysed:

(1) There are two kinds of cave: earth ones and stone ones. (2) The earth caves are dug into the hillside. (3) Having selected a place where the earth seems to be of the right kind, (4) you smooth the hillside (5) so that you have a vertical face. (6) In doing this, you will see what the soil is like to work with. (7) Next, you make a first hole of two by seven feet (8) and dig in for roughly three feet (9) before you start enlarging. (10) As you dig, the kind of soil will show you how large you can make the cave. (11) The harder and closer the soil is, the larger you can make your cave and vice versa. (12) Having dug out your cave, (13) you polish the earth walls (14) to make them smooth, (15) then you plaster them with mud made of firm earth. (16) All this time, you leave the outer wall untouched, (17) using just the little opening that you made at the beginning, (18) but once the cave is finished (19) you open up this wall (20) so that you have a door and a window.

Two things are immediately obvious about the text. Firstly, it describes an ordered sequence of events. Secondly, at first sight at least, the events seem to be described in the order in which they occur in time. Thus the text was judged suitable to be the basis for the two experimental texts.

Analysis into units:

There are two reasons for analysing the text into a number of units. Firstly, in a study like this involving quantitative recall of a relatively long text, a breakdown into units is necessary simply to provide a scoring scheme for marking recall, which is not likely to be 100%. For this purpose, the precise nature of the units is not, within limits, important, as long as they are of manageable size.

The second reason is more specific to the hypothesis. The rhetoricians' claim is that in time order, events are described in the order in which they occur in time. In order to test this claim, we must be able to relate each event to that part of the text which describes it. It is only when we have identified such parts of the text and labelled them as units that we are able to establish explicitly whether or not a text follows time order, and thus produce the alternative version.

In the text above, the surface structure which refers to single events or stages in the process is generally a clause, whether free or bound. Thus the fifth text sentence contains three clauses, each of which refers to a single event in the process. In general, such structures can easily be transformed into a standard form, YOU + VERB + ETC., e.g. 'You dig in for roughly three feet'. These structures, from now on termed 'narrative units', are the basic analytic units. Details of the analysis are given below:

a.   A text sentence containing more than one narrative unit was decomposed into its constituent units. For clarity, these were written in standard form where necessary and assigned a number. For example, the fifth sentence of the text was decomposed into three narrative units, numbered 7, 8 and 9. Exceptions to this were the structures 'In doing this' (Unit 6) and 'As you dig' (Unit 10). These refer to events which have already been described. It is thus not necessary to include them in a scoring scheme, and consequently they were not decomposed.

b.   Embedded clauses which did not refer to an event or stage were in general not decomposed. Thus the relative clause in the third sentence was included in Unit 3.

c.   Text sentences which did not refer to an event or stage were assigned a unit number for scoring purposes. They are thus non-narrative units. Units 1 and 2, for example, act as a general introduction, and in fact were included in the text to perform this function. Unit 11 appears to be an expansion, or substantiation, of Unit 10.

There are a number of borderline cases. This is perhaps inevitable given the imprecision of such semantic labels as 'event', 'situation', 'stage'. Decisions in such cases, detailed below, were made on semantic grounds; for an attempt to identify narrative clauses in terms of potential displacement, i.e. potential movement in relation to other clauses in the text, see Labov and Waletsky (1968).

The result clause, Unit 5, was treated as a narrative unit, equivalent to 'and (thus) you make a vertical face' or 'and (thus) a vertical face appears'. The other result clause, Unit 20, and the purpose clause, Unit 14, were also considered to be narrative units.

The main clause of Unit 6, together with the very similar main clause of Unit 10, refers to an observation related to an action or event. Formally, both clauses appear to be marked off from the definitely narrative clauses by the modal 'will'. It was therefore decided to treat both Units 6 and 10 as non-narrative units.

Units 16 and 17 look like narrative units, but their common time reference appears to stretch from Unit 9 or 10 to Unit 18. They thus cannot be said to refer to single events or stages in the process, and were consequently classed as non-narrative. They were handled as two units in accordance with the requirement that, for scoring purposes, units should be of manageable size.

According to this analysis, the narrative clauses in this text are:
    3, 4, 5, 7, 8, 9, 12, 13, 14, 15, 18, 19 and 20.

This is the order in which they occur in the text. Reference to the text will confirm that this is also the order in time of the events they refer to. Thus the text follows time ordering. It will from now on be referred to as 1A.

The units were then re-ordered to deviate from time ordering, and used as the basis for an alternative text. The complete sequence of units in Text 1B was as follows:
    1, 2, 4, 5, 3, 6, 7, 8, 17, 16, 18, 20, 19, 9, 12, 10, 11, 15, 13, 14.

On this occasion, most re-ordering of narrative units took place inside sentence boundaries.

Text 1A was 178 words long, consisted of 9 sentences, and had a Fog Index of 10.

Text 1B was 180 words long, contained 11 sentences, and had a Fog Index of 8.

The original of the second pair of texts used in this experiment was taken from a newspaper. Paragraph 11 of the newspaper passage was added to paragraphs 1, 2, and 3 to form the text shown below. Paragraph divisions were eliminated. (Numbers refer to units into which the text was analysed.)

(1) Extreme winds and persistent trouble with their tents forced the British Everest expedition to turn back 2,028 feet short of the 29,028 foot peak yesterday. (2) Climbers from the team of 11 had been struggling to set up Camp Six on the previously unclimbed south-west face of Everest (3) when atrocious weather set in, (4) forcing the climb to be abandoned. (5) The camp is the highest point that any climber has reached on the mountain in the autumn, (6) and it was from there that Hamish MacInnes and Dougal Haston were to have launched their attempt on the summit. (7) But furious winds made it impossible to keep the box-type tents in position, (8) and completely ruled out any possibility of climbing the hazardous 2,000 feet to the top. (9) The expedition arrived in Kathmandu late in August, (10) and set up base camp on the mountain early in September. (11) Progress was quick (12) until the weather delayed the setting up of Camp Five at 26,000 feet for several days. (13) It was finally established on November 4, (14) but from then on the climbers worked in 'incredibly severe weather' with temperatures around −40 deg. Fahrenheit, and wind that made every movement a struggle.

The text was broken down into units in the same way as text 1. On this occasion, there was less need to decompose sentences to isolate narrative units. The narrative units are as follows: 1, 2, 3, 4, 7, 8, 9, 10, 11(?), 12, 13, and 14. (Unit 11 is a doubtful case, since it can be interpreted as meaning either that progress was quick after the setting up of base camp or after the arrival in Kathmandu.)

It is clear that while the text constitutes a narrative in that it describes a number of events occurring in a chronological sequence, it deviates markedly from time ordering. For example, Unit 1, the first textual unit, describes the *last* event in the chronological sequence. The first event in the chronological sequence, the arrival in Kathmandu, is described by Unit 9.

In fact the text can be seen as consisting of 3 episodes, namely,

1. Last event (Unit 1)
2. Events and related observations leading up to 1 (Units 2 to 8)
3. Events from the beginning of the sequence up to, and overlapping, the start of episode 2 (Units 9 to 14).

Inside episodes 2 and 3, the text does, in fact, follow time ordering. In overall organization, however, it deviates sufficiently from this ordering for it to be used as the non-time ordered text.

It was a comparatively simple task to produce the alternative text, which was written to follow time ordering. Basically, this involved moving episode 3 to the beginning, following it with episode 2, and ending with episode 1. The ordering of units for this alternative text was as follows:

9, 10, 11, 12, 13, 14, 2, 3, 4, 5, 6, 7, 8, 1.

As the time ordered version, this is now referred to as 2A, while the other text is termed 2B. Text 2A contained 191 words, and 2B 190 words. Both texts consisted of 7 sentences and had a Fog Index of 16.

It is worth noting that in the case of the 'Cave-building' texts, it was the time ordered textualization, 1A, which was closer in rhetorical structure to the original text. In the case of the 'Everest' texts, the non-time ordered text, 2B, was much closer to the original newspaper article.

The two pairs of textualizations were tested on 44 Scottish secondary school students. The students, aged between 14 and 16, were drawn from 'O' stream classes, that is, classes intending to sit 'O' level examinations.

Subjects were randomly divided into two groups. One group of 21 subjects read texts 1A and 2A, the time ordered textualizations, while the other group of 23 subjects read texts 1B and 2B. They were tested for both speed and recall. Speed was measured by an intrusive word test (Davies 1964). The same 'intrusive' words were inserted into each member of a pair of textualizations, at the same random intervals. Subjects' reading speed was measured by the number of these words they located and underlined inside a fixed time. Thirty-five words were inserted into text 1A and 1B, and 20 into 2A and 2B. Recall was tested by a free recall test. Subjects first completed the intrusive word tests, after discussing an example. They were then given a fixed time to read text 1 without the intrusive words, and wrote down as much as they could remember of it. The procedure was then repeated for texts 2A and 2B.

Recall scripts were marked according to a scoring scheme based on the analysis into units. There were 20 units in text 1A and 1B, and 14 in texts 2A and 2B.

Results: Mean scores are presented in Table 1:

Table 1

	Version A	Version B
IWT		
Cave-building	23·4	20·3
Everest	15·0	12·7
Recall		
Cave-building	6·8	7·2
Everest	5·7	4·2

In the intrusive word test, scores for both 1A and 2A were significantly higher than scores for 1B and 2B, at the 5% level. In the recall test, the mean for 2A was significantly higher than that for 2B. The difference between means for 1A and 1B was not significant.

Thus both time ordered textualizations were faster to read, and one was significantly easier to recall. It is worth noting that, since 2B was much closer to the original article than was 2A, it could be argued that the original had been simplified with respect to quantitative recall by the re-ordering resulting in 2A.

The experiment was replicated with a larger group of 100 Scottish pupils, from a different area. Subjects were drawn from either 3rd or 4th year 'O' streams, and ages ranged from 14 to 17. Again subjects were randomly divided into 2 groups, one of 48 subjects and the other of 52. On this second occasion, however, in order to increase randomization, one group read texts 1A and 2B, while the other read texts 1B and 2A. Mean scores are presented in Table 2.

Table 2

	Version A	Version B
IWT		
Cave-building	23·8	21·1
Everest	17·4	17·4
Recall		
Cave-building	10·9	9·7
Everest	8·7	7·4

With the exception of the intrusive word test for the Everest text, all differences were significant at the 5% level. Thus on this occasion, both time ordered texts proved significantly easier to recall, while one was faster to read.

The recall scripts in the second run of the experiment provided some interesting insights into readers' processing. It will be remembered that in text 2B, the *first* event, the arrival in Nepal, occurred as Unit 9. In the recall, several subjects re-ordered the text so that this event occurred earlier in their recall scripts. It looks as if to some extent they were moving towards a time ordered version. No comparable phenomenon occurred with recall of text 2A. A second phenomenon also related to this part of 2B. In this textualization, the information that 'the party arrived in Kathmandu', i.e. the *first* event, occurred later in order of mention than the information that the expedition had to be abandoned, and that the party turned back. Several subjects clearly interpreted order of mention as paralleling order of occurrence, and interpreted the text as saying that the party turned back *and then* arrived in Kathmandu. Overt signs for this interpretation were the substitution for the original 'arrived in Kathmandu' of 'arrived back', 'arrived . . . on the way down', and 'returned'. This interpretation later proved awkward, since the text went on to detail the initial steps of climbing the mountain. One or two readers were content to leave this unresolved; others attempted to resolve it by interpreting the last third of the text as an account of a *second* attempt to climb the mountain. The fact that several other subjects, with one exception all reading the 'B' textualization, produced this 'second climb' interpretation leads one to suspect that they too had interpreted 'arrived' as 'arrived back', even though they did not make this interpretation overt.

All this is evidence of a tendency, in the absence of clear indications to the contrary, to interpret text order as paralleling time order, or to re-order it in a time order direction for recall purposes. The latter tendency, at least, would go some way towards explaining the results.

These results should not, of course, be taken to mean that the original newspaper article was in some sense badly written. The rhetorical claim investigated in this experiment clearly applies only to situations where it is necessary or desirable for the reader to comprehend and remember each event and its order in the total sequence equally well. If I wish to learn a sequence of actions, then a learning text which facilitates my learning actions 2, 5 and 7 at the expense of 1, 3, 4 and 6 is clearly less than totally helpful.

There is no reason, however, to assume that the writer of the original Everest text had this sort of learning in mind. For a start, we are rarely required to remember all, or even any, of the contents of a newspaper article. Then we may be assumed by the writer to be principally interested in the most current news, which in this case amounts to the last events. Again, the writer may assume that we are already partly familiar with the early stages of the process being described, from having read earlier issues, etc. All this might suggest that in the original text, the last events were considered by the writer as being more important than the other events. It might then be hypothesized that it was this that caused him to front these events, thus giving the text its non-time ordered sequence.

The relationship between different types of organization and the kinds of learning associated with them is a valuable area for empirical investigation (cf. Meyer 1975). This study, however, set out to investigate quantitative differences in speed and recall. The experiment above is evidence that, if speed and ease of recall are being aimed at, the rhetoricians are correct in recommending time order.

An experiment with FL readers

The above experiments were carried out with Scottish L1 readers. A related experiment was conducted with both L1 readers and FL readers by Marenghi and Frydenberg (1980). The original text selected was a newspaper article, which was modified, and then used as the basis for two texts, a time order one, here called 'A', and one which deviated from time order, referred to here as 'B'. As in the case of the 'Everest' text mentioned above, the original article deviated markedly from time ordering, and was much closer in organization to the 'B' text.

All the subjects were students at the University of Michigan. The FL readers were studying English at the English Language Institute there, and were drawn from the three upper levels. The groups were as follows:
1) 22 L1 readers, 12 reading the 'B' text and 10 the 'A' text.
2) 23 Japanese speakers, 12 reading the 'B' text and 11 the 'A' text.
3) 21 speakers of Arabic or Turkish, 11 reading the 'A' text and 10 the 'B' text.

Only a free recall test was used. Mean scores are given in Table 3:

Table 3

	Version A	Version B
L1	16·20	13·75
Japanese	6·45	2·00
Arabic/Turkish	4·09	1·60

In all cases, scores for the 'A' version were significantly higher than scores for the 'B' version. Thus for both L1 and FL readers, a version following time order proved easier to remember.

There are two conclusions to be drawn from this. Firstly, in this case, the validity of an organizational principle appears to have been established regardless of the language background of the readers. Secondly, the large difference between FL readers' mean scores for 'A' and 'B' versions suggests that certain kinds of organizational patterning may present some FL readers with very considerable difficulties.

Experiment 2: space ordering

As mentioned earlier, this principle states that objects or parts of objects in a physical description should be mentioned in a textual sequence determined by some recognizable spatial direction, e.g. left to right, or front to back. A major difference between time and space ordering is that, at least in the orthodox view, time is unidirectional, running from past to present to future. Thus a textual ordering which parallels this direction has, as it were, a unique status; a narrative text either adheres to time ordering or deviates from it. There is, however, no unique space ordering to correspond to this. The rhetoricians recognize this, of course, and tend to substitute for one ordering any order which shows 'some logical or natural progression from one descriptive detail to the next' (McCrimmon 1963 p. 77). In this study, 'logical or natural' was narrowed to mean 'linear'.

The two texts chosen to serve as the basis for alternative textualizations both described roughly spherical objects, and concentrated on the appearance of, and spatial relationships between, their internal parts. Both texts were accompanied in their original form by labelled diagrams, which proved helpful in analysing the ordering employed.

The first text, slightly adapted from Duddington (1966), appears below. Numbers refer to analysed units.

(1) Chlamydomonas consists of only a single cell, but in that cell is contained all the essential attributes of a complete plant. (2) It is usually egg-shaped, (3) one end being somewhat pointed. (4) From the pointed end sprout two (5) very fine protoplasmic 'tails' (6) which by their waving movements enable the tiny organism to swim actively in the water in which it lives. (7) They are called flagella, from the Latin word 'flagellum', meaning a whip. (8) The most conspicuous object in the Chlamydomonas cell is a (9) large (10) green chloroplast. (11) The form of this varies from species to species, (12) but it is usually cup-shaped, (13) and it is situated at the hinder end of the cell, (14) of which it occupies more than half. (15) The remainder of the cell is occupied by the (16) living protoplasm, (17) and this contains a nucleus, (18) which is usually partly hidden in the cup formed by the chloroplast. (19) On one side of the chloroplast there is usually a pyrenoid, (20) similar to those found in Spyrogyra. (21) Some species of Chlamydomonas have more than one pyrenoid, and may even have more than one chloroplast.

Analysis into Units:

In the case of the space experiments, the analysis into units is less essential for establishing what ordering principle is being employed, since this can be done basically by comparing order of mention of the main parts with their spatial position as shown by the diagram. The analysis is essential, however, to the writing of the alternative text, and to the scoring scheme.

The analysis was carried out in the same general manner as in the time experiments. The basic unit in this case was defined as a part of the text which referred to the appearance of the cell, or to the appearance or relative position of any one of the constituent parts. Such units are termed 'descriptive units'. Thus the sixth sentence of the text yielded the following descriptive units:

11. the form of the chloroplast varies from species to species
12. the chloroplast is usually cup-shaped
13. the chloroplast is situated at the hinder end of the cell
14. the chloroplast occupies more than half the cell.

Textual Ordering:

If one omits the opening introductory sentence, an examination of the text revealed the following textual ordering:
1. Exterior cell (Units 2, 3)
2. Flagellae (4, 5, 6, 7)
3. Chloroplast (8, 9, 10, 11, 12, 13, 14)
4. Protoplasm (15, 16, 17)

5.   Nucleus (17, 18)
6.   Pyrenoid (19, 20, 21)

A comparison of the order with Figure 1 below suggests that the writer was guided by the following principles:

a.   In general, the cell and its interior parts were described in an outside-to-inside direction. The exterior shape is described before the chloroplast and protoplasm, which form the interior. The nucleus is inside the protoplasm, and follows it in the textual ordering.

b.   Bigger parts are described before smaller ones. Thus the chloroplast precedes the protoplasm, and the pyrenoid, which according to the diagram is the smallest part of all, comes last.

c.   One might have to add a third principle, that of 'Main body before attachments', to account for the fact that the exterior cell precedes the flagella.

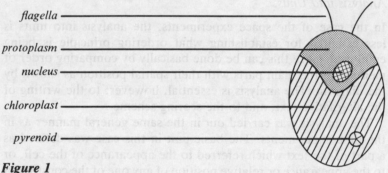

flagella

protoplasm

nucleus

chloroplast

pyrenoid

Figure 1

Thus it appears that in the case of the Chlamydomonas text, the simple unidirectional ordering principle is not sufficient in itself to account for the textual ordering. Nevertheless, the text does appear to exhibit a general outside-to-inside ordering, and was thus used as the linear textualization.

The second pair of texts was based on material from Romer (1954). The first text, shown below, largely retains the ordering of the main parts of Romer's original text passage, but has been supplemented by material from the caption accompanying Figure 2. The text has also been slightly simplified.

(1) The reptilean egg has a complicated structure to which we must devote some attention. (2) As a food supply for the embryo, the egg contains a large amount of (3) nourishing (4) yellow yolk, (5) which is contained in a sac (6) connected with the digestive tract. (7) A membrane called the amnion, (8) which is attached to the skin of the

embryo, encloses a (9) large (10) liquid-filled cavity (11) which develops about the body of the embryo. (12) It provides protection against injury (13) and the danger of becoming too dry. (14) Developing from this, (15) and connected to it (16) is a second membrane, called the chorion, which lies beneath the shell. (17) Out from the back end of the embryo's body there grows a tube and sac, the allantois, (18) in which the waste matter of the body is deposited. (19) The whole egg structure is stiffened and protected by a (20) firm shell (21) on the exterior. (22) The shell, however, is porous. (23) Blood vessels surrounding the allantois (24) carry to the embryo oxygen (25) which has passed in through the porous shell of the egg, (26) so that the allantois acts as a lung.

It can be seen that the order of appearance of main parts is as follows:
1. Yolk (Units 2, 3, 4, 5, 6,)
2. Amnion/amnion cavity (7, 8, 9, 10, 11, 12, 13, 14)
3. Chorion (14, 15, 16)
4. Allantois (17, 18, 23, 26)
5. Shell (19, 20, 21, 22)

Reference to Figure 2 suggests that a unidirectional, outside-to-inside ordering would take the following form:
> 1. Shell 2. Chorion 3. Amnion 4. Embryo 5. Yolk 6. Allantois (It is necessary to invoke the principle 'Main part before an attachment(s)' to justify placing embryo before yolk and allantois).

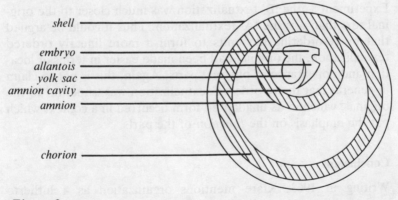

Figure 2

Accordingly, units were rearranged as follows: 1, 19, 20, 16, 14, 15, 10, 7, 8, 9, 11, 12, 13, 2, 3, 4, 5, 6, 17, 18, 21, 22, 23, 24, and a second, linear text, from now on referred to as 2A, was produced. Both texts contained 9 sentences and had a Fog Index of 14.

The two pairs of textualizations were tested on 51 Scottish school children, from 3rd year 'O' stream classes. Subjects were randomly divided, 26 doing the 'A' texts and 25 the 'B' texts. Both intrusive word tests and free recall were used, 35 words being inserted into each textualization. The recall texts were marked using a scheme based on the decomposed units, the Chlamydomonas textualizations out of 20, and the Reptile Egg textualizations out of 19. Mean scores are presented in Table 4:

Table 4

	Version A	Version B
IWT		
Chlamydomonas	25·0	24·7
Reptile egg	19·6	19·9
Recall		
Chlamydomonas	10·3	8·4
Reptile egg	8·0	5·6

There are no significant differences between scores on the intrusive word test. In the case of free recall, the mean scores for the 'A' linear versions are significantly higher than those for the 'B' versions. Thus the linear versions did not prove faster to read, but did prove easier to recall than the non-linear equivalents.

It is worth noting that, as in the case of the Everest text in Experiment 1, the 'B' textualization was much closer to the original text than was the 'A' textualization. Thus it could be argued that by re-ordering the units to form a more linearly ordered textualization, the original had been made easier in terms of location and appearance of physical parts. Again, this is not to claim in general that the re-ordered textualization was 'superior' to the original, which in its unadapted form occurred in a context which put the emphasis on the *function* of the parts.

Conclusions

Writing in 1963, Klare mentions organization as a hitherto neglected factor in readability assessments (Klare 1963, p. 188). The experiments described above seem to confirm that organization can significantly alter readers' recall of text material. It is perhaps worth pointing out that there are degrees of organization. None of the texts used above was really 'badly organized': such a text could have been produced by combining units in a random manner, so that, for example, material referring to the chloroplast of Chlamydomonas was scattered about the text. There is every reason to believe that such a non-organized text would be more difficult than the non-linear text used in Experiment 2.

More particularly, in the cases investigated, the prescriptive advice of the rhetoricians appears to have been validated. The texts written according to their prescriptions facilitated recall of content, and were thus, in situations where such recall was the goal, 'better organized'.

Given the operational definition of 'readability' employed in this study, those texts which were altered to conform to time or space ordering can be considered as 'simplifications'. From a practical point of view, perhaps the most we can conclude from this is that the simplifier should reflect before deviating markedly from, say, time ordering, or, perhaps more likely, before leaving an existing deviation unchanged. Similarly, the reading teacher ought to be wary of exposing low-level learners to narratives which do not conform to time ordering. This is particularly true if some kind of quantitative recall is being aimed at, but we could broaden the scope of the warning if it were accepted that lower recall scores in the above experiments reflected 'lower' comprehension (Carroll 1972).

From the research point of view, there would seem to be two lines of development. In one, we could look for other principles of organization facilitating quantitative recall. Alternatively, we could examine what kind of learning is associated with texts which deviated from, say, time ordering. In other words, we could examine different types of organization and the kinds of learning they tend to induce.

Postscript on Urquhart

Urquhart's paper is of considerable interest to students of reading, for two general reasons: firstly, because within the tradition of readability studies it is one of the few attempts to look at the effects of supra-sentential features that might affect understanding and text processing; and secondly, because it represents an attempt to provide empirical evidence for or against the claims of traditional rhetoricians that have often led to prescriptive advice to writers.

It would seem that other principles of text organization should now be investigated to see what effect they might have on readability — examples of such principles that come to mind are cause-and-effect relations, problem and solution, principles and examples, generalizations and justifications, and classifications from largest or more general to smallest or less general. Doubtless many others could be culled from traditional rhetoric books, or those textbooks, particularly prevalent in the United States, which offer prescriptive advice to would-be writers, especially on college writing courses like Freshman Composition. In the English language teaching world, textbooks like the *Focus* series have taught ESP students how to understand particular rhetorical principles, without much evidence, if any, that the rhetoric causes difficulty to students. Studies like Urquhart's should help illuminate this area.

The results reported in this paper confirm a common sense position on text difficulty which would suggest that texts are made difficult by containing hard words, complicated sentences, complex ideas and a complex ordering of ideas. In this view, an 'illogical' ordering of ideas would be harder to read than a 'logical' ordering. The problem comes when one tries to define 'logical' ordering since there is a danger of tautology: to the layman, 'logical' means 'easy to follow', thus: 'a text that is not easy to follow is hard to read'. Clearly a random ordering of ideas in text would not be 'easy to follow' and this hardly requires empirical support, but what non-random offerings can we predict will cause difficulty? Rhetoricians, of course, have attempted for centuries to define 'logical' more precisely than this, and it is some of these definitions that Urquhart's paper addresses.

In recent years there has been an increase in interest, in foreign language reading, in attempts to establish what causes difficulty for FL readers. Such efforts have partly arisen from a frustration with existing reading courses, which neither appear to help students read in a foreign language, nor appear to be based upon evidence that what they teach actually relates to the causes of reading difficulty that FL readers experience. The need to establish causes of FL reading difficulty comes from the need efficiently to teach students to read in a short space of time. On such special-purpose courses, the pressure is great on materials writers to design maximally effective reading exercises. To teach the whole of English 'grammar' on a reading course might be less than efficient if certain areas of 'grammar' cause no problems for students. Hence the attempt to identify factors causing difficulty in reading with the aim of writing special materials which would only focus on those areas. If we can determine what causes difficulty in text we can either prepare students for those difficulties, or simplify texts (or both). Since students will eventually have to face 'real world' difficult texts we *have* to do the former. But that does not rule out simplifying also, in order to help the student during the process of learning to read a foreign language, whatever the ultimate goal of reading 'authentic texts' might be. Nevertheless, it will remain important to teach students to detect or be sensitive to, the rhetorical organization of texts, and also to detect *deviations* from 'ideal organization'. This latter skill is important because students are unlikely to read only ideal texts: they will need to be prepared to read not only unsimplified, but also unimproved texts — poorly written texts — and to read them adequately for their purposes. Although it has been said that the problem with reading is actually a problem of writing, it is somewhat unrealistic to hope that the provision of well intentioned advice or prescriptions, even backed up by empirical research of the sort Urquhart offers, will have an important effect on writing. Urquhart suggests that writers may deviate from the 'best' order because of what they know or assume about their readers. They may also deviate because they feel, rightly or wrongly, that the content about which they are writing is best presented in some other way. Or they may deviate simply because they are poor writers. The fact is that the reader, be he native or non-native speaker, will likely have to handle texts which are less than ideal.

However, the investigation of causes of difficulty in text is itself fraught with difficulty. There are at least two problems: the first is methodological. How are we to determine such causes of difficulty? What do we take as evidence of understanding, and what textual features do we seek to isolate? The latter issue is taken further by Urquhart, but the former issue remains a problem. Urquhart used reading speed, as defined by the number of intruded words subjects could identify in a given period, and also the number of textual units recalled in a free recall task. Many may quarrel with Urquhart's operational definition of reading success, but like all operational definitions, it has the advantage of being explicit, so that at least we know what he means by 'understanding'. Other researchers have used multiple choice tests of understanding, or cloze or gap-filling tests as a means of getting a measure of reading success. One might even imagine an operational definition relating to the satisfaction of the reader's curiosity or reading purposes, or an agreement between reader and writer (or 'expert' interpreter as in literary criticism), on what the text says.

The second problem, alluded to above, is that the product of reading, the comprehension outcome, will vary according to the reader's purpose (see Royer *et al.*'s and Fransson's papers in this volume, and related postscripts) and according to the reader's experience and background knowledge (see the papers by Bransford *et al.* and Steffensen and Joag-Dev and related postscripts). If purpose and knowledge vary, then so too will understanding. If comprehension varies from reader to reader, it is not clear how the 'causes of difficulty' in the text (rather than in the reader) can be satisfactorily identified or, importantly for the teacher, predicted.

Urquhart himself touches upon this problem when discussing the Everest text, by suggesting that the writer ordered his text in a particular way because of what he assumed or knew about his readers, namely that they would be most interested in particular pieces of information, that other pieces might be known already, and that therefore some propositions needed to be placed before others, regardless of their logical, spatial or temporal place in 'the real world'. The writer, in other words, assumes that a particular set of readers will have a particular purpose and set of knowledge, and he orders his text accordingly. What may be an ideal ordering from the point of view of traditional rhetoric may well be less effective communication within a particular context. Thus if a writer assumes that the reader is already familiar with previous reports of the Everest expedition he will perhaps most *suitably* (and hence most readably for those readers) order the text in terms of new information before old information, especially if his purpose is to attract the reader's attention and the reader's purpose is to gain the latest (new) information about a particular event. By comparison, of course, the subjects in the experiments reported in Urquhart's paper had different knowledge and different purposes in reading the text. The text, in short, has been removed from its context and readership. Readability studies, be they of the traditional formula development type, or the Urquhart rhetorical effect type, perhaps inevitably ignore the reader, and the important variables he brings to the reading event, and they treat readers as in some sense homogeneous (in knowledge, purpose, interest, attention, etc.) in order to examine text variables.

Urquhart's paper and other research within this paradigm do seem to depend upon the belief that it is possible to produce different textualizations of the same ideas and not change the text's meaning. However, whilst there must be some sense, at present highly elusive, in which that is true, it must also be the case that different textualizations may well *mean* different things. To what extent does the re-ordering of ideas in a message distort those ideas and change the message? Of course Urquhart's research is concerned with the effect of different orderings on the recall of information. Varying number of items recalled may not be the same as 'understanding the total message' and was probably not intended to be equated to such a concept. As experimental manipulation may result in a non-text, i.e. a text that would not normally occur, Urquhart's third research alternative — to find suitable pairs of already existing texts — although it may not be practical is an intriguing possibility. Perhaps two draft versions of a written text — novel, poem, academic article — might be found to vary on only one relevant dimension: it might then be possible to ascertain the writer's opinion of the relative readability or suitability of one version. (The notion of suitability appears to be intuitively more satisfactory than readability because of its suggestion of an implicit purpose.) One problem with the research alternative Urquhart adopts — to produce doctored texts — is that it is difficult to change a text on one level without affecting difficulty or readability on other levels. Alteration in rhetorical ordering may well cause syntactic difficulties. One of the possible causes of difficulty, for foreign language readers at least, in text A is clauses like 'Having done this . . .' or 'In doing this . . .', syntactic complexities which are actually caused by writing in a time-ordered fashion. In other words, there may be inevitably contingent linguistic problems when the 'same ideas' are expressed in a different order. Be this as it may, it is notable, and highly relevant for this sort of study, that both pairs of texts in Urquhart's study were equivalent in terms of 'readability' as traditionally defined and operationalized by the Fog Index (sentence and word length). Thus the differences that emerge in Urquhart's study must be due to something that Fog is insensitive to.

The problem of rhetorical ordering for foreign language readers is that their culture may lead them to see a different ordering as more 'logical' — especially in the case of space ordering. But the results with foreign language readers quoted here do not provide any support for that position, unless it can be argued that in Japanese, Arabic and Turkish cultures the 'logical' sequence would be as in English.

We do not wish to understate the importance of readability studies by pointing out the problems associated with trying to capture or identify the elusive sources of difficulty in text, however. We have consistently stressed the importance of both text and reader in an understanding of the reading process, as the organization of this volume indicates. Textual factors must be particularly important when reading in a foreign language. Although there has been a tendency to think that the main problems foreign language readers face are lexical and syntactic, the point Urquhart's paper makes is that there is accumulating evidence that we should be considering rhetorical factors in the text as well as more traditional intrasentential linguistic factors.

9 Simple, simplified and simplification: what is authentic?

Alan Davies

The truth is never pure and rarely simple. (O. Wilde)

Preliminaries

Simplicity is difficult. The explanation of this paradox is that simple and difficult are not always polar opposites: sometimes they are (e.g. a simple and a difficult crossword puzzle) and sometimes they are not (e.g. simple and difficult living, simple and difficult art). I argue in this paper that the simple–difficult contrast in language belongs to the latter rather than the former type, in other words that it is not at all obvious what is simple language and what is difficult language.

It will be useful to distinguish different meanings of simplicity in terms of language and, in particular, to distinguish *simple language, simplified language* and *simplification*. In the first part of the paper I examine the notion of simplicity in relation to language; in the second part I look more closely at the issue of simplification in reading materials and relate this issue to the question of authenticity. Finally, I discuss data from a recent investigation of the comprehension of simplified reading material with non-native speakers of English.

Simple language and simplified language

There is something contradictory about the term *simple language* in view of the equal status accorded to all languages in linguistics. In what sense can a language be simple if it has a structure which is just as complicated as other languages? One example of a simple language is a pidgin. A pidgin is simple because it represents the result over time of speakers' inadequate second language acquisition. A pidgin is simple because it has a very narrow range of functions; its use is restricted to a few activities. Ferguson (1971) extends the pidgin analogy to *simplified language* in which speakers deliberately simplify their normal language in order to make communication possible with certain interlocutors. Ferguson suggests that there are two kinds of simplified language: one in which the functions (what the language is being used for) are restricted by, for example, mothers to children or teachers to second-language learners; the other in which the language forms are reduced as in baby talk and foreigner talk. Notice that it is only in the first of these (the functional restriction) that it makes sense to say that the simplified language is deliberate. Indeed, Corder (1981) argues that to call the second kind, the formal reduction, simplified is illogical since learners, whether babies or foreigners, cannot simplify something they do not already possess.

Pidgins typically develop into creoles as functional demands increase: thus they cease to be simple languages. Similarly the need to simplify for babies disappears and so the one case in which simplified languages acquire permanence is in talk to and by foreigners, most of whom do not achieve full control of the target language in terms of either form or function.

Simplification

Whether or not simple language and simplified language are deliberate products, *simplification* certainly is deliberate. Indeed, simplification belongs to the special class of deliberate production which is labelled pedagogic. And by pedagogic here is meant overt teaching situations when a teacher is teaching, i.e. carrying out his professional task. (The fact that teachers teach at other times and that other people than teachers teach is true but beside the point.) All three, *simple language, simplified language* and *simplification*, are concerned with ease of communication, but this is to say nothing more than that they are all forms of language. What particularly distinguishes simplification is its unique pedagogic purpose.

Now simplification can be seen as a process in which the teacher or his agent consciously adjusts the language presented to the learner (Davies and Widdowson 1974). In the case of the foreign language learner all of the materials, including the spoken, may be simplifications. But it is of reading materials that the term simplification is most often used and in the case of the first-language student it is normally reading materials that are meant, since so much of first-language instruction focuses on the teaching of reading. Simplification, then, of reading materials refers to the selection of a restricted set of features from the full range of language resources for the sake of pedagogic efficiency. 'The code is not affected, the learners are not presented with a simpler language system but with a restricted sample of the full system.' (Tommola 1979).

A useful distinction is made by Widdowson (1978) in discussing simplification between what he calls simplified versions and simple accounts. Simplified versions are, he suggests, 'passages which are derived from genuine instances of discourse by a process of lexical and syntactic substitution'. A simplified version, according to Widdowson, is a simplification of the language code. The original propositions are retained and what is changed is the linguistic connections between them. A simple account, on the other hand, 'represents not an alternative textualization of a given discourse but a different discourse altogether' (ibid). In a simple account it is use of the code, the discourse itself, that is changed, recast to suit a particular kind of reader. Widdowson makes clear that simple accounts are to be preferred to simplified versions in that 'a simple account is a genuine instance of discourse, designed to meet a communicative purpose . . . a simplified version . . . is not genuine discourse, it is a contrivance for teaching language' (ibid pp. 88–9). Widdowson's distinction is a striking one, particularly in extreme cases such as an argument or a description rewritten as a simple account for an encyclopedia, on the one hand, and a simplified reader for foreign language learners on the other, in which the vocabulary and some of the syntax have been changed. However, the distinction is a difficult one to maintain and most rewritings will be partly simple accounts and partly simplified versions. Most helpful is the further distinction Widdowson hints at that simplified versions always have a source script which has been changed, whereas simple accounts have a source but no script.

A more general view of simplification is that it is used to make information available to an audience other than the one originally intended. Making the need of the audience primary helps with the paradox we began with (the simple-difficult relationship). What is meant by simple, therefore, is determined by the needs of the audience even though this may require a longer text or even, on occasion (as in a literary treatment of a folk tale), one with more complex grammatical structure and fewer common words. All discourse, even simplified versions, must be relevant to its audience.

Simplification and authenticity

Realization that even a simplified text can be relevant throws light on the issue of authenticity in language teaching materials. Simplified materials often find acceptance because they prepare the reader for eventual control of authentic texts. Authentic (like simplified) is a term that occurs in the literature of language teaching and applied linguistics but not in theoretical linguistics. In discussions on the authenticity of language data for language teaching purposes, doubts as to what authenticity might mean have already been expressed by Widdowson, who writes (1979) 'I am not sure that it is meaningful to talk about authentic language as such at all. I think it is probably better to consider authenticity not as a quality residing in instances of language but as a quality which is bestowed upon them, created by the response of the receiver. Authenticity in this view is a function of the inter-action between the reader/hearer and the text which incorporates the intentions of the writer/speaker' (p. 165). I would only add that for speech there is no residual authenticity and that for writing, while it is true that the written artefact in the shape of the lines of the page exists, the author may not remember or may not be alive to remember what his intentions were.

In a further discussion of simplification, Widdowson (1979, p. 192) remarks that simplification is the pedagogic analogue of the linguist's idealization of data: 'the teacher simplifies by selecting and ordering the linguistic phenomena he is to deal with so as to ease the task of learning, and the linguist idealizes by selecting and ordering the linguistic phenomena *he* is to deal with to ease the task of analysis'. And, making the connection between authenticity and simplification direct, Lautamatti (1978) argues that 'simplified texts are used in the teaching of foreign language reading comprehension as a ladder towards less simplified and finally authentic texts' (p. 98).

For our purposes the importance of Lautamatti's remark is that she sees simplification and authenticity as ends of the same continuum. In addition we can make use of her further insight (Widdowson's too) that simplification is a pedagogic device and that therefore what is authentic is what is not simplified and what is not pedagogic.

In order to illustrate the relationship between simplified texts and authentic ones four passages were selected:

1. *The Cock, the Mouse and the Little Red Hen*
2. *The Frogs Asking for a King*
3. *English in Focus*
4. *Oliver Twist*, simplified (NMSR)

These are presented in Appendix 1. We are now ready to examine these four passages and place them in the cells of the 2 by 2 table below:

		Authenticity	
		+	−
Simplification or Simplified	+	Passage 1	Passages 3 and 4
	−	Passage 2	

Passage 1 will fit into the top left hand cell. It is authentic in a historical sense, in other words this is how it was originally written. It is also simplified: we note the marked repetition and the co-ordination. Immediately we can see the problem of our earlier definition of simplification only in terms of audience. This passage is (or may be) a story for small children, and yet its language is simpler than in Passage 2. Perhaps then we do need to take account both of audience (i.e. of comprehension) and of language when we consider the simplified status of texts. The implication of accepting Passage 1 as simplified, even though it is not directed at a secondary audience, is that *all* texts can be placed on a more/less simple scale. Texts directed at secondary audiences are likely to be simplified linguistically. Texts directed at primary audiences are intended to be appropriate for their audiences (i.e. within their understanding). What is special about Passage 1, which makes it obviously simple in a way that Passage 2 is not, is that since we have all been children we *all* belong to the primary audience for Passage 1. We can now state that: the wider the audience for a text (primary alone or primary and secondary), the more simplified linguistically it is likely to be. The more limited or specialized the audience, the less need for simplifying.

Passage 2 belongs in the bottom left hand cell. It is not simplified but it is authentic. We may feel it looks simple but its rhetoric is quite different from that of the first passage. As an original Aesop fable it is authentic as a matter of historical fact. Passage 3 fits into the top right hand cell. It is simplified but not authentic. I have here chosen a so-called simple account in which a piece of information (not a story) is made available to an audience which commands a simple register of English. Passage 4 also fits into the top right hand cell; it also is simplified but not authentic. We show it with the original Dickens text. This is the classic simplified version, so that in the top right hand cell we have examples of both simple account and simplified version.

That leaves the bottom right hand cell empty. An original text which has been complexified might fit here. Or a mistake, for example: 'To be and not to be that is the question', since this is not in any sense reduced and yet it is at the same time not quite authentic, giving us both not simplified and not authentic.

In teaching, we select texts on the basis of how simple they are, i.e., whether or not they are comprehensible to the addressee. As we will see again below in our discussion of readability measures we cannot speak of simplified texts without taking into account the understanding of the addressee. It is that understanding that allows us to rank texts on a scale of readability. In other words, while the writer of simplified texts is concerned with the process of simplifying, that process will be effective only if matched by the reader's own involvement. That involvement makes the text authentic for the reader.

As Widdowson says (1979, p. 166) 'Authenticity, then, is achieved when the reader achieves the intention of the writer by reference to a set of shared conventions'. It is here that we look to the creative impulse of the reader who must actively involve himself, cooperate with the writer and come to a comprehension of a text that was a moment before too difficult for him. But true as the statement is it leaves too much to the unresolved formula of the intentions of the writer. Except for the writer's signalling of his intentions in the text itself (Davies and Widdowson 1974) it is unlikely that, as we have seen, we shall ever recover what the writer's full intentions were.

Readability: indices

There is no absolute linguistic index of simplicity. Simplification of texts must be related to audience comprehension. This applies both to text, i.e. simplified versions, and to discourse, i.e. simple accounts. Comparisons between texts on the basis of simplification must always be in terms of comprehension by the reader. That is why measures of text facility/difficulty (or readability) always are based on some evaluation of incremental progression. The numbers attached to texts in terms of readability (by indices or by cloze procedure) are meaningful only in terms of which readers (age for native speakers, years of language exposure for non-native speakers) can cope satisfactorily. To make matters easier for ourselves, we might say that simplicity is a function of the language, readability of the reader. The first tells us what changes are made to the text, the second who can read it easily. But neither characteristic is independent: each one stands by the other. The two concerns reflect different interests, simplification a linguistic interest, readability a psycholinguistic interest. As we have suggested, a comparison between texts in terms of simplification seems always to reflect the audience. There is no clear-cut way of determining linguistically what is simple. It is true, however, that sentences can be constructed in terms of word frequency, number of sentence embeddings, mean length of utterance or simply total length. They can also be contrasted in terms of cohesion markers, marked thematization or quantity of new information. Whether less or more of any of these measures leads to greater simplicity is unclear unless measured in terms of reader's comprehension (Klare 1978). Perhaps a term other than 'simple' would be helpful in labelling this linguistic feature of texts, an index of the amount of linguistic information they contain, a term such as density.

It is equally true that readability becomes measurable only if it makes use of linguistic categories, indeed of the very categories of 'simplified' we have just been discussing. Without the use of these categories there is no way of arranging texts in any graded or sequenced order, save subjectively or after random trials with comprehension questions. Even then the texts would need to be chosen before the questions were applied and the choice of texts made on some principled grounds. It would, no doubt, be possible to make no prior decisions about texts, but to apply a large number gathered in some *ad hoc* way with attached comprehension questions and then to grade the texts on the basis of the results of the comprehension questions. This may seem a bizarre method but, as we shall see, something like this is done with cloze procedure.

A useful discussion on readability measures is given in a report of a Schools Council Project on reading (Lunzer and Gardner

1979). What makes this discussion relevant to our concerns is that the project found it necessary, as Harrison points out in his chapter on *Assessing the Readability of Texts*, to review existing measures in order to decide whether it was necessary to construct new ones. (They decided there was no need for new ones.) Furthermore, they were concerned with differing styles or registers or rhetorics of English, which indicates their awareness of the fact of variation, a notion that links well with the foreign language use of variety in special purpose language teaching.

Harrison, like others before him, points to the multitude of variables that may contribute to text difficulty and then limits his considerations to what is potentially measurable, namely the linguistic variables. 'If a layman is asked what tends to produce readable prose, he might suggest "simple English" or "not too many long words". This common sense view has a good deal to commend it and it has been regularly established that vocabulary and sentence structure are the two most crucial determinants of text difficulty.' (pp. 76–7) Harrison then quotes a typical formula, the Flesch, which has been widely used in the USA since its first appearance in 1948 and was the one used on this project. The Flesch formula is given as a reading ease score (RE):

$$RE = 206 \cdot 835 - (0 \cdot 846 \times NSYLL) - (1 \cdot 015 \times W/S)$$

where NSYLL is the average number of syllables per 100 words and W/S is the average number of words per sentence.

The RE score thus derived is a notional score out of 100 which can be used to determine various reading levels by means of appropriate conversion tables. Given that readability formulae, as Harrison has already observed, typically measure vocabulary and sentence structure, it still remains to be determined precisely what in these areas they focus on. Harrison notes that one of the strengths of the Dale–Chall formula is that it recognized the importance of word frequency as a difficulty factor (in spite of the insight provided in Zipf's Law (1935) that word length is inversely correlated with word frequency). Harrison and his colleagues however did not use measures of word frequency. (The only word variable used in the Flesch formula relates to word length as indicated by the average number of syllables per word.) Again, some formulae take a sophisticated account of sentence structure, providing estimates of grammatical complexity by means of clause structure, number of T units per sentence or percentage of prepositional phrases. Again, Harrison *et al.* do not measure sentence structure other than by sentence length; the Flesch formula's second variable is precisely an estimate of sentence length in terms of average number of words per sentence.

How valid is it to rely on word and sentence length only as estimates of text difficulty? It is partly common sense; our stereotype of simpler reading materials is that they contain short words and short sentences, itself part of our awareness that shorter words are more frequent and therefore normally better known (though not necessarily simpler to understand because more frequent words like 'get' can become loaded with so many denotations that they cease to have any meaning other than a contextual one), and that shorter sentences are less likely to contain complex structures like subordinate clauses. It is partly experimental finding: 'After analysing many linguistic variables, Flesch found' says Harrison (ibid p. 77) 'that two in particular seemed to correlate most highly with difficulty. These were the average number of syllables per word, and sentence length.' And it is partly the saliency of these two variables. They are always present and they dominate other variables such as word frequency and sentence complexity or percentage of word class or type or number of participial phrases. Flesch was going with both science and common sense. As Klare (1978) points out:

> It may seem surprising that counts of the two simple variables of word length and sentence length are sufficient to make relatively good predictions of readability. No argument that they *cause* ease or difficulty is intended; they are merely good *indices* of difficulty. Consequently, altering word or sentence length, of themselves, can provide no assurance of improving readability. How to achieve more readable writing is another and much more complex endeavour. But as long as predictions are all that is needed, the evidence that simple word and sentence counts can provide satisfactory predictions for most purposes is now quite conclusive. (p. 269)

Harrison and his colleagues used the Flesch formula to measure the level of secondary-school texts for native speakers. They found that in the four areas of English, Maths, Social Science and Science the texts given to the 1st year (age 11–12) were not really very different from those given to 4th year children (age 15–16). They argue that the remedy is to lower the 1st year level in all four subjects in that it was for the 1st year that the level seemed most unsatisfactory.

Readability: cloze

The cloze procedure was originally introduced by Taylor (1953) as an attempt to improve on the existing readability measures. Correlations between cloze scores and readability measures in the Harrison study were lower (·5 and ·6) than those found by others. Bormuth (1966) and Miller (1975) noted correlations of ·8 and ·9 between cloze and the same readability formulae. This recent finding is a corrective to the claims made for cloze (for example, Oller 1973). It is useful to have evidence that cloze results are variable and that they are both potentially unreliable and also measures of other things than text difficulty.

Furthermore, cloze is heavily dependent on the actual deletions in any one passage, which is why 5th or 7th word deletions are not necessarily similar in terms of results (Alderson 1978). As Alderson points out, what distinguishes one cloze text from another (even the 'same' text at one deletion rate compared with itself at another) is the deleted words. We need to be cautious therefore (as Harrison *et al.* point out) in making any large claims for cloze. They conclude that readability measures are effective in predicting text difficulty as estimated by pooled teachers' judgements. They are less enthusiastic about the value of cloze procedure. In other words, the best measure of text difficulty is combined expert judgement and, where that is not available, readability formulae. No doubt what the expert judgements take into account over and above the salient variables of the readability formulae are things like potential interest and availability of a text to its intended readers.

Harrison *et al.* raise the interesting question of what makes a teacher a reliable judge of readability and suggest that 'a teacher who is aware of the extensive range of demands made by texts on children at different age levels is likely to be in a much stronger position to make a reliable judgement about potential difficulties' (p. 100).

We assume that texts having different readability levels achieve different comprehension results. Klare (1978) gave two groups of readers two versions of the same text, the original and a specially written simplified one. The group with the simplified passage produced significantly higher comprehension test scores. So there is some evidence that readability levels do make a difference in comprehension. But why do they? The nature of text difficulty is not much discussed in the readability literature. When it is raised one kind of answer concentrates on the comprehension issue; this says that one text is simpler than another if more people understand it. Another kind of answer takes up the linguistic issue: this says that texts become simpler as surface features come to represent meaning more directly, i.e. they lose synonymy, ambiguity, transformations, etc. Essentially this is an argument for idealization, for removing performance phenomena and making sentences as little like utterances as possible, and, as a corollary, it implies that types of words like adjectives, adverbs and prepositional phrases are difficult rather than simple.

Experimental results

We now report an experiment in which a text was simplified and both the original and the simplified version given to the same group of learners (experienced Japanese teachers of English). Passage 1 (the original or authentic text) and Passage 2 (the simplified text) are presented in Appendix 2. The hypothesis was that the linguistically simpler passage would be comprehended significantly better than the original passage.

Passage 1 was selected as being at an appropriate level for this group of subjects. After a one-sentence lead-in, the passage was prepared for cloze testing with every 5th word deleted, making a total of 41 deletions.

Passage 2 was written by the investigator as a deliberate simplification of Passage 1. After a one-sentence lead-in, the passage was prepared for cloze testing, with every 5th word deleted, making a total of 25 deletions.

Subjects were given Passage 2 first and asked to fill in the cloze gaps. Time was unlimited. When all subjects had completed Passage 2 they were given Passage 1 (i.e. the original version was given second so as to obviate somewhat the carry-over effect). Both passages were marked by the verbatim scoring method. Results were as follows:

	Passage 1	Passage 2
Flesch RE Score	49·07	78·25
Mean (N = 29)	8·65	12·86
st. dev.	4·74	4·74
rho of 1 with 2	·7	

By the t test for correlated groups, at 28 df. where the table value of t is 2·048, the obtained value of t is 5·7, which is significant at the 5% level. On the basis of this performance on the cloze tests, there is a significant difference between the comprehension of the two passages.

This is exactly what our hypothesis (simpler means better comprehension) predicted. Of course, there are problems of interpretation due to the research design: no doubt, there was a carry-over effect from Passage 2 to Passage 1 (though that would have worked *against* the predicted direction). Again, the cloze deletions were inevitably quite different from one passage to the other, and we have already noted that this is a serious weakness in the use of cloze as a reliable instrument. (Notice that according to Bormuth a cloze score of at least 38% is required for reading ease. On his reckoning then Passage 2 is well within these readers' capability (mean 51%) but Passage 1 is far too difficult (mean 21%).)

Passage 1 was taken from a fairly popular handbook of psychology (Nicholson 1977), a useful and amusing guide to individual behaviour. The cloze score suggests that the investigator's subjective impression that this was within the reading capability of this group was wrong (as of course the reading ease score also suggests); it also indicates that the reading proficiency of non-native language teachers needs attention and support.

Conclusion

Finally we return to the question of the relation of the learner to simplification. Corder (1981), it will be remembered, rejects the idea that the learner ever simplifies. The learner cannot simplify. This squares well with our view on the relation between simplified and authentic. Just as Corder rejects the learner as simplifier, so we reject the idea of the teacher as authenticator of texts. It is no more the teacher's business to consider authenticity than it is the learner's to simplify. Authenticity as we have seen is a matter of the involvement of the audience. It is not that a text is understood because it is authentic but that it is authentic because it is understood. In teaching our concern is with simplification, not with authenticity. Everything the learner understands is authentic for him. It is the teacher who simplifies, the learner who authenticates. In the teaching of reading as in all language teaching the fundamental task of the teacher is that of selection or of judging relevance.

Appendix 1

Passage 1 Once upon a time there was a hill, and on the hill there was a pretty little house. It had one little green door, and four little windows with green shutters, and in it there lived a Cock, a Mouse and a little Red Hen. On another hill close by there was another little house. It was very ugly. It had a door that wouldn't shut and two broken windows, and all the paint was off the shutters. And in this house there lived a bold bad Fox and four bad little foxes. (*The Cock, the Mouse and the Little Red Hen*, F. Lefevre.)

Passage 2 In the days of old, when the Frogs were all at liberty in the lakes and had grown quite weary of following every one his own devices, they assembled one day together, and with no little clamour petitioned Jupiter to let them have a King to keep them in better order, and make them lead honester lives. (*The Frogs Asking for a King.*)

Passage 3 Although air is invisible it is a substance which fills up space. You know that air rushing along in the form of wind can exert a large force on your body, and if you wave a large sheet of cardboard about you will find that the air resists its movement. ('The Properties of Air', *English in Focus.*)

Passage 4 The evening arrived and the boys took their places. The master stood by the pot; the servants stood near him, and the soup was served. (*Oliver Twist* NMSR, Longman, 1966.)

The evening arrived; the boys took their places. The master in his cook's uniform, stationed himself at the copper, his pauper assistants ranged themselves behind him; the gruel was served out; and a long grace was said over the short commons. (*Oliver Twist*, Charles Dickens.)

Appendix 2

Passage 1 On the basis of their experience as actuaries, the Metropolitan Life Insurance Company of America have published a table which shows the maximum desirable weight for men and women of all heights. Above these levels the 1 <u>rate</u> of mortality rises sharply, 2 <u>and</u> people whose weight is 3 <u>more</u> than 20 per cent 4 <u>above</u> the maximum desirable are 5 <u>classified</u> as obese. The prevalence 6 <u>of</u> obesity is astonishingly high. 7 <u>One</u> survey in London found 8 <u>that</u> over a third of 9 <u>the</u> men and nearly half of 10 <u>the</u> women sampled were clinically 11 <u>obese</u>. It is not therefore 12 <u>surprising</u> that at any given 13 <u>time</u> ten per cent of 14 <u>the</u> British population is actively 15 <u>trying</u> to lose weight, or 16 <u>that</u> each year more than 17 <u>a</u> third of us go 18 <u>on</u> a diet. Obesity is 19 <u>not</u> a peculiarly British disease, 20 <u>being</u> widespread throughout the developed 21 <u>world</u> but it is unequally 22 <u>distributed</u>. It is more common 23 <u>in</u> women than in men, 24 <u>and</u> it is also more 25 <u>frequent</u> among the old than 26 <u>the</u> young. At least in 27 <u>industrialized</u> countries, it is more 28 <u>prevalent</u> among the lower than 29 <u>the</u> higher social classes, presumably 30 <u>because</u> diets rich in carbohydrates 31 <u>which</u> are associated with being 32 <u>overweight</u> are cheaper than those 33 <u>containing</u> proportionally more protein. The 34 <u>immediate</u> cause obesity is 35 <u>clear</u>, you get fat if 36 <u>you</u> eat more than enough 37 <u>to</u> replenish the energy you 38 <u>have</u> used up. What is 39 <u>less</u> clear is why some 40 <u>people</u> get fat while others 41 <u>don't</u>.

Passage 2 An American Insurance Company have given figures to show how heavy men and women should be at different heights. You are more likely 1 <u>to</u> die if you are 2 <u>heavier</u>. If you are more 3 <u>than</u> twenty per cent heavier 4 <u>you</u> are obese. Many people 5 <u>are</u> obese. Over a third 6 <u>of</u> men and nearly a 7 <u>half</u> of women in London 8 <u>are</u> obese. That is why 9 <u>ten</u> per cent of British 10 <u>people</u> try to lose weight, 11 <u>and</u> nearly fifty per cent 12 <u>diet</u> each year. Obesity exists 13 <u>everywhere</u> but not equally so. 14 <u>More</u> women than men are 15 <u>obese</u>, and more old than 16 <u>young</u>. In industrialized countries more 17 <u>poor</u> people than rich people 18 <u>are</u> obese. Perhaps this is 19 <u>because</u> poorer people eat more 20 <u>carbohydrates</u> and less protein. Obesity 21 <u>is</u> caused by eating too 22 <u>much</u> and not using enough 23 <u>energy</u>. It is not clear 24 <u>why</u> some people become obese 25 <u>and</u> some don't.

(Words underlined were deleted in preparing the passages for the cloze test. Numbers were given.)

Postscript on Davies

In this postscript, we limit ourselves to commenting on simplified texts as they are used in the classroom, particularly in the foreign language classroom. Moreover, we limit our use of 'simplified' to refer to texts derived from original texts by means of various deliberate 'simplification' procedures. We take these decisions on grounds of practicality; such texts are what most EFL teachers think of as 'simplified'. The decision is not intended as a criticism of Davies's much wider approach, although one implication of our use of 'simplified' is that Davies's Passages 1, 2, and perhaps 3 (p. 185) are not 'simplified'.

The wider approach adopted by Davies has considerable advantages. One is that simplification in our sense is seen as part of a much broader range of activities. If simplification is defined as making a text appropriate to the audience, then perhaps *any* text may be considered a simplification. A second draft, for example, is a simplification of a first draft. A corollary to this is that there are many kinds of simplification, and, as Davies points out (pp. 183 and 184), the validity of a particular kind of simplification depends upon the needs of the target readership.

In the L1 teaching situation, simplification is often associated with readability formulae. These are intended to measure the readability of existing texts, and as such they seem to work, as Davies points out (p. 189). They are not intended as guides to simplification procedures, and do not work as such; attempts to simplify texts by replacing lexical items with shorter or more frequent synonyms, or by shortening sentences, result, naturally enough, in texts with a 'better' readability index according to the formulae, but which are not, in real terms, easier to comprehend. On the other hand, the evidence discussed by Klare (1963) suggests that when a competent writer produces a 'simplified' version of a text, without explicit reference to the formulae, then the simplified version is not only easier to read, but also rates easier according to the formulae. The interesting question is what writers do in order to produce such texts.

Such findings tend to support Widdowson's distinction between simplifying 'use' as opposed to 'usage' (Widdowson 1979, pp. 185 ff). Altering a text according to invariant, language-directed rules, such as 'Replace polysyllable words with monosyllables' or 'Decompose complex sentences into separate simple sentences' constitutes simplification of usage. On the other hand, a writer who simplifies by using all the linguistic means at his disposal to clarify the referential and propositional meanings of a particular text will, in Widdowson's terms, be simplifying use. The findings reported in Klare suggest that this second is a valid simplificatory procedure for L1 readers, but that the first is not. Widdowson's third category, simple accounts, would probably also be valid simplifications for young L1 readers.

When one turns to the foreign language situation, one of the most noticeable differences concerns the educational range of the learners. Simplified texts for L1 readers tend to be aimed at young beginners, though they may be used with adult illiterates. In the FL context, the range is wider, extending from primary school pupils to post-graduate students. For this latter group Widdowson's simple accounts tend not to be usable: in our experience, educationally sophisticated FL learners tend to be put off by the, for them, inaccuracies and over-generalizations of simple accounts, particularly when these relate to their own subject.

Widdowson argues that it may be necessary to simplify the propositional development of texts. Yet with FL learners familiar with the content of the text, it may be that this will present few or no difficulties; problems may, however, arise at the 'lower' levels of syntax and lexis. In fact, one might argue that the higher the educational sophistication of the FL learner, the 'lower' the text level that needs to be simplified. Berman's students, for example, are not reported as having problems with propositional relationships; their difficulty lay in processing syntactic strings sufficiently to recover the propositions.

Berman's simplification would probably be classed as simplification of use; it was done in order to clarify the meaning of a particular text. In the case of lexis, however, simplification of usage — the code itself — would seem to be valid. If we are aiming at a readership whose L1 is a Romance language, we might attempt to simplify texts by substituting lexis of Latin origin for words with Germanic roots. The French learner might find 'combat' easier than 'fight'. This simplification is not done, of course, in terms of length, or frequency, as is the case with simplifications done for young L1 readers; the code is being restricted with a particular audience in mind.

Thus simplification must be seen to refer to a wide range of procedures, which should be selected and activated with reference to the particular group forming the target audience. The ultimate criterion of validity, as Davies suggests, is that the resulting text should be more appropriate for the audience.

Another crucial factor discussed by Davies is *authenticity*. As she herself points out (p. 145) Berman's simplified texts deviated markedly from what is normally considered 'good' English prose style. In a certain sense, they were not 'authentic'. The same applies to most deliberate simplifications. The question is whether this matters.

We must sympathize to some extent with those who insist that only 'authentic' texts should be used, given the stilted unnaturalness of many made-up 'teacher texts'. The problem is, as Davies's discussion makes clear, that it is impossible to define 'authenticity' in terms of textual features. What is more, any definition in terms of addresser/addressee, e.g. 'by an L1 writer for an L1 audience', is too restrictive.

If it is accepted that the primary function of language is to help communicate meaning, then we could argue that language is only non-authentic when it is intended for a radically different function, e.g. when it is being used by language teachers to illustrate linguistic features. This is not to say that this practice is wrong, simply that it entails using language in an abnormal way.

Even this definition is inadequate, however, since, as Davies points out, the reader's contribution must be taken into account. Suppose a student finds relevant, non-linguistic meaning in a sentence which has been offered to him as an example of some, say, syntactic point: he would thus convey authenticity on the language of that sentence (he might also, of course, frustrate the teacher).

If this is accepted, however, we must reject, or at least modify, Lautamatti's claim that simplification and authenticity are 'ends of the same continuum'. We are committed to believing that simplified texts can be authentic. The claim should read 'texts aimed at an L1 audience', which would fit the common sense view of the function of simplified texts, namely to prepare the learner for dealing with non-simplified ones.

Simplified texts play a prominent part in EFL reading, and will probably continue to do so. The broad approach taken by Davies enables us to discuss them in the wider context of the continuing effort of language users to make their messages more accessible.

10 Aspects of vocabulary in the readability of content area L2 educational textbooks: a case study

Ray Williams and Don Dallas

Readability problems in content area textbooks

For some years, educational publishers have been receiving reports about the readability problems of certain content area titles written for a national or regional market. The problem is particularly acute for pupils entering secondary year 1, when in many countries they are required to make the transition from English as a subject to English as a medium of instruction. Thus the L2 pupil in (for example) Nigeria or Hong Kong simultaneously faces the twin problems of (a) more advanced conceptual difficulties in Science, Social Studies, Mathematics, etc., and (b) studying those subjects through the medium of English. The *reasons* for the reported readability problems differ from country to country and from title to title; but some of the more common are:

1. the spread of universal secondary education, resulting in lower average reading standards;
2. inappropriate reading courses at primary level, in terms of the reading tasks required in the content areas at secondary level;
3. increasing competition between publishers, resulting in pressure to produce new content area titles to over-tight deadlines with (unfortunately) insufficient consideration being given to matters of readability;
4. unrealistic demands of the national syllabus, so that (for example) too much ground has to be covered in a certain year, and/or conceptually complex syllabus content has to be taught at too early a stage in the secondary school;
5. the difficulty of finding authors with a combination of:

— classroom teaching experience at the relevant age level in the country concerned
— command of the content
— an awareness of the reading level in English of the target pupil
— sensitivity to principles of readable writing.

Longman readability pilot study — cloze tests

Longman have been concerned at the reported readability problems of certain of their content area titles in overseas markets. Accordingly, in 1979 they set up a Readability Pilot Study (RPS) to ascertain how readable certain titles were, and to investigate aspects of the readability problems reported. The results of the research — carried out in Northern Nigeria and Hong Kong — are contained in an in-house report to Longman (Williams 1980).

This paper is concerned with one of the titles tested in RPS, viz. *Living Hong Kong Social Studies 1C* (1976). The paper first comments on the title's readability level as indicated by cloze testing. It then outlines one important area investigated in RPS — namely, problems of vocabulary — and summarizes attempts to remedy those problems in the new edition currently being written.

Living Hong Kong Social Studies is a nine book series, with three books (A, B, C) for each of secondary years 1–3. In addition, there is a workbook and a teacher's book to accompany each of the nine books 1A–3C. In RPS, first the mean readability level of 1C was assessed by means of Granowsky and Botel's (1974) syntactic complexity formula (ten extracts, 179 sentences, 2,115 words). Then three passages were chosen, approximating to that mean readability level, and were converted into cloze tests. The tests were printed using the original design, typeface and illustrations; and they were administered in nine Hong Kong secondary schools, one first-year class per school. Results were as follows:

In interpreting the cloze results, we used the most generous criterion level[1] available from cloze research in foreign languages (Cripwell 1976), in comparison with the now generally accepted criterion level of 45% in the L1 context. In other words, the read-

---

1 The criterion level is the minimum score at which a reader can be said to be capable of reading a text unaided by another person.

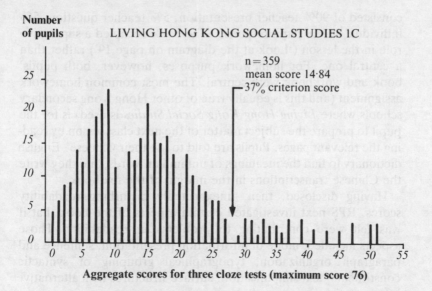

Aggregate scores for three cloze tests (maximum score 76)

ability level of *Living Hong Kong Social Studies 1C* was regarded as too difficult for any pupil who scored 37% or below.

The cloze results are disturbing. They suggest that the old edition of *Social Studies 1C* is too difficult for 91·4% of the pupils tested. Equally disturbing (and highly significant for the textbook writer) is the probability that a sizeable proportion of the pupils tested *simply cannot read English*. If a weaker reader had simply guessed, and had written into the blanks words such as *a, the, and, but*, etc., he would almost certainly have scored a total of 5 over the three tests. If we therefore take 5 or below as indicating an inability to read English (and 5 is a very conservative figure), then we may infer that 52 of the 359 pupils tested (14%) cannot read English.

One might counter these cloze results by saying: 'But surely there is a difference between each pupil completing a cloze test in isolation, and the dynamic classroom reading situation in which the pupil has the help of the teacher, and of other pupils, in the task of reading?' The answer to such a question is two-fold: (a) the 37% criterion score is at the 'frustrational' level, i.e. a level which indicates that the text is too difficult with or without assistance; (b) in practice, it would appear that *Social Studies* is *not* read in class, but is commonly assigned for homework background reading in preparation for the next lesson. For example, a lesson observed in Yuen Long, Hong Kong New Territories, April 1981, consisted of 90% teacher presentation, 5% teacher question, 5% individual/choral pupil response. The book occupied a supportive role in the lesson ('Look at the diagram on page 19') rather than a central one. For homework purposes, however, both pupils' book and workbook were central. The most common homework assignment (and this is equally true of other Hong Kong secondary schools where *Living Hong Kong Social Studies* is used) is for the pupil to prepare the subject matter of the next class lesson by reading the relevant pages. Pupils are told to use their Chinese–English dictionary to find the meanings of unfamiliar words; and they write the Chinese transcriptions in the margin of the textbook.

Having disclosed, then, unexpectedly disturbing readability scores, RPS next investigated certain aspects of the book that it was felt were contributing to problems in readability. Those aspects included: mode of information presentation, sentence and paragraph organization, typographical grouping of syntactic constituents, text simplification, surface structures with alternative interpretations, and vocabulary.

Aspects of vocabulary in *Living Hong Kong Social Studies*

Vocabulary was a particularly important area of analysis in view of the cloze results, since cloze correlates highest with vocabulary and grammar tests, and lowest with reading comprehension (Darnell 1968). Alderson (1978) confirmed Darnell's findings. Furthermore, Alderson's factor analysis showed that cloze — particularly for the non-native speaker — is not associated with areas such as the ability to make inferences and handle text. But it *is* frequently associated with the ability to handle syntax and vocabulary. In other words, cloze appears to test 'core proficiency', and is sentence-bound (Alderson 1978).

In RPS, certain aspects of vocabulary were tested by means of a 40-item multiple choice test. The results of this test contributed towards the revised edition of the *Living Hong Kong Social Studies* series — a revision completed by ourselves, members of the Longman Research and Development Unit, and Hong Kong editorial staff.

The more obvious aspects of vocabulary improvement — simpler synonyms, context support, etc. — are not dealt with in this paper. (Williams (1981) contains a fuller treatment of lexical familiarization in content area educational textbooks.) But the remainder of this paper recounts the RPS testing of certain problematic aspects of the vocabulary in *Living Hong Kong Social Studies 1C*, and indicates how the results of that testing were used in writing the revised edition.

Vocabulary contained in definitions

The most obvious attempt in the old edition to familiarize new vocabulary was a 'Words to Learn' section at the end of each unit. This section contained a list of English words, Chinese translations, and definitions, e.g.:

diarrhoea ⎫
dysentery ⎬ = disorders of the digestive system   (Ic. p. 13)
腹瀉　痢疾

a conflict = a clashing of different ideas   (Ic. p. 34)
衝突

cancer = a malignant disease which is usually fatal   (Ic. p. 41)
癌症

ethyl alcohol = the base of common alcohol found in alcoholic
乙醇　　　　　drinks   (Ic. p. 41)

To test whether the vocabulary itself within such definitions constituted a problem, the following words were tested:

Item no.		Percentage of correct responses	Rank order (/40)
4	disorder	26	35
12	clashing	28	32
13	fatal	53	9
14	recurring	35	25
15	base	42	15
38	lesser	30	29

The results indicate that vocabulary contained within definitions does cause considerable difficulties. This is most unfortunate, as the clear function of a definition is to elucidate, not compound the difficulty. There appear to be a number of problems with the definitions provided in the 'Words to Learn' section:

a The definitions are mostly given in standard dictionary format, e.g.:
   (p. 29) *deformed* = having lost its original shape.

b   They contain too many abstract words, that prevent the formation of a mental image, e.g.:
    (p. 6) *a system* = an organized set of connected parts.
c.   Definitions are given solely in words.
d.   Examples are rarely provided.
e.   Some definitions attempt too broad a coverage, rather than an explanation of the meaning of the word in the context in which it appears in the text.
f.   Some definitions add very little to what has been said in the text itself, e.g.:

text (p. 36)	*definition* (p. 41)
Tobacco smoke contains harmful substances called tars.	tar = a harmful ingredient of tobacco

In addition to definitions in the 'Words to Learn' sections of the pupils' book, each corresponding unit of the accompanying workbook starts with a 'Word Use' exercise, in which given key words have to be added to gapped sentences.

In the revised edition of the pupils' book, the 'Words to Learn' section has been removed. Instead, in-text Chinese translations of unfamiliar words have been given, e.g.:

Industry is very important to Hong Kong. We need a lot of good technicians (技術人員). So the Government is developing higher technical education(工業教育).

(1A, p. 57)

Our reason for adding in-text translations was simply that a study of pupils' books in use showed that this was what the pupils themselves did anyway, and therefore printing the translations of unfamiliar words will reduce their dependence on the dictionary, and so make their reading faster and more pleasurable. In addition, these translations have been collected together, for ease of reference, as an end-of-book English–Chinese dictionary. 'Definitions' themselves have been transferred to the workbook, each unit starting with a 'Learning New Words' section.

In writing the 'definitions', we have borne in mind points (a) to (f) above. In particular, we have chosen a form of familiarization most appropriate to the word itself — example, illustration, formal definition, question, context, etc. Examples from the revised workbook 1C are:

addicted   Many people who take drugs cannot stop. In other words, they are *addicted*.

upright	This man is standing *upright*. This man is not.
nerves	*Nerves* are parts of the body that carry messages to and from the brain.
slogans	NOW WASH YOUR HANDS THINK WHEN YOU CROSS
sympathetic	When the children arrived home from school, they found that their mother had a headache. But the children were very *sympathetic* — they made her some tea, cooked the supper, and were very quiet.

Each unit of the workbook also contains a 'Using New Words' Section, employing a variety of techniques in addition to gap-filling, such as word class change, crossword completion, crossword creation, multiple choice, sentence creation from a table, etc.

Idiomatic expressions

Hong Kong Social Studies contains a number of idiomatic expressions. Items in 1C tested were:

Item no.		Percentage of correct responses	Rank order (/40)
1	a sweet tooth	8	40
8	working off steam	29	31
9	waking up with a start	25	36
10	bury themselves in books	59	6
16	keep a cool and steady head	40	19
31	cut across country	32	27
40	runs the risk	27	33

These test items indicate that idiomatic expressions cause immense difficulty. The probable reason is that unless the pupil already knows the meaning of the expression as a whole, he attacks it word-by-word, e.g. *work* = what my father/mother does every day; *off* = opposite to *on*; *steam* = what comes out of a kettle. But piecing together these individual jigsaw parts does not produce intelligible meaning. Moreover, the problem is not confined to the pupil being unable to make sense of the idiomatic expression alone. This is because such expressions encapsulate the essence of a concept in 'shorthand' form, and thus are central to understanding wider areas of meaning.

In the revised edition, we have taken care to avoid idiomatic expressions. Instead, the meanings they convey have been rewritten in more comprehensible language, e.g.:

(original)	(revised)
Perhaps you can remember waking up with a start from a dream.	Perhaps you can remember waking up suddenly from a dream.
Students who bury themselves in books . . .	Children who spend all their time studying . . .
Don't cut across country . . .	Don't leave the paths . . .

Homonyms

(We stretch the meaning of homonyms to include instances such as the L2 reader interpreting *founded* as the past participle of *to find*.) Items tested in RPS were:

Item no.		Percentage of correct responses	Rank order (/40)
15	base	42	15
30	right	42	15
34	founded	27	33
38	lesser	30	29

The problem with homonyms is that the reader (especially the weaker L2 reader struggling to make sense of a word) is likely to draw on the *primary* meaning of a homonym, which may or may not be the meaning intended by the author. Responses to item 38 give evidence of this:

A concubine = a *lesser* wife or a wife not legally married to her husband.

51% (a) smaller

30% (b) not as important as the others

19% (c) younger

Admittedly, (a) and (c) are not homonyms in the accepted sense of the term, but the pupils who responded (a) presumably were drawing on the more frequent use of *less* in Mathematics, e.g. *Which number is 9 less than 11²?* Pupils who responded (c) were perhaps — quite reasonably — applying this primary meaning in searching for a 'numerical' difference between the wives.

The pupils' confusion with homonyms is ever greater when more than one appear close together, e.g.:

> If there is a fire hazard, e.g. if the staircases are blocked (*? as in a* **block** *of flats, such as Tai Wan Estate,* **Block** 6) with goods (*? opposite of* **bad**), the owners must put the matter right (*? as in* **right**-hand).
>
> (1C, p. 45)

It is clear that authors of content area textbooks should show greater sensitivity to potential problems resulting from homonyms (including the *found*/*founded* type resulting from a faulty knowledge of English). In particular, this requires of the author a knowledge of vocabulary learnt to date by the pupil in his English course. Homonyms likely to cause ambiguity should be replaced. In the revised edition, the example above has been completely reorganized:

> . . . Fire Prevention Bureau . . . Sometimes the staff find that they cannot go up or down a staircase, because it is completely covered with things like boxes . . . the staff of the Fire Prevention Bureau make the owners of the building take the boxes away . . .

Vocabulary contained in 'imported' text

A series such as *Living Hong Kong Social Studies*, covering a wide range of topics, has clearly and necessarily made use of a range of source material. That source material may be either visible (as in the case of extracts from a Hong Kong newspaper, the *South China Morning Post*) or it may be 'buried', as in the case of advice taken from official literature on fire prevention. The vocabulary of newspaper extracts clearly contributes to readability problems, as the following test items indicate:

Item no.		Percentage of correct responses	Rank order (/40)
21	concerned	30	29
22	upsurge	43	14
27	complimented	25	36
28	unique	25	36

In the revised edition, newspaper extracts have for the most part been omitted — since even with simplification of vocabulary, the register and intended audience are inappropriate for a secondary form 1 textbook.

But discussion of vocabulary in obviously imported texts such as a newspaper extract only serves to highlight the visible aspect of a wider, 'buried' matter. This is the fact that all textbooks rely on a wide range of source material — other books, government reports, official documents, newspapers, magazines, etc. The intended readership of these source materials is almost always different from that of the educational textbook being written. An author naturally simplifies the content and overall language to take account of the textbook's target readership. But by constant reference, the author sometimes becomes so familiar with the vocabulary of the original, that that original vocabulary is unthinkingly written into the textbook with insufficient regard to its comprehension by the pupil. An example from *Social Studies 1C* is pp. 43–44, where the source material was presumably a Fire Services Department leaflet covering Dos and Don'ts for various types of fire. Words such as *lighted, inflammable, extinguished, confine, overcome, fumes, alerted* and *smothering* have probably been taken from the original leaflet. We are not suggesting that such words should not be included. (For many of them, there are no synonyms that are more familiar; and in any event, they are part of the language of fire.) But we are suggesting that such vocabulary from 'buried' imported text should be subject to particular scrutiny by the author, and that the reader should be helped by the provision of some form of familiarization (context clue, illustration, translation, definition, etc.) where necessary. Thus in the revised edition of the series, the vocabulary of 'buried' imported text has been given particular attention; it has either been replaced, or suitable familiarization added.

Conclusion

Both RPS and our re-writing of the *Living Hong Kong Social Studies* series have shown us that vocabulary is of crucial importance in the readability of content area educational textbooks. What can be done? A means of control often advocated by editor to author is to write within the vocabulary taught in the EFL/ESL course of the relevant age group of the country concerned. But there are a number of problems:

1.   Vocabulary listed in an English syllabus and taught in English lessons may well be (and frequently is) markedly different from the *actual command of vocabulary* that pupils possess.

2. The L2 secondary level English syllabus is usually very general in nature, i.e. it gives scant regard to the *purpose* for which English is taught. Consequently, vocabulary lists in the English syllabus contain few words that are part and parcel of the language of content area subjects (e.g. Social Studies: *norm, socialize, role, heredity, nuclear family*).

3. Content area textbooks are often written for a *regional* market, within which there may well be national variations in the vocabulary taught in the English course.

4. Our contact with authors of content area textbooks strongly indicates that they would not be happy to accept the strictures of a vocabulary list. They argue that they are physicists, geographers, historians, etc; they will certainly do their best to use appropriate vocabulary, but they draw the line at constantly having to check their writing against a vocabulary list.

At best, then, vocabulary lists found in the English syllabus will assist the author in a very general way, i.e. by providing a broad outline of the *type* of vocabulary that the reader can be expected to cope with. This is particularly useful for the author who lacks teaching experience of the age group and/or the country concerned. But it is doubtful whether vocabulary guidance of this sort will be more than of general value.

Instead, our research and our re-writing experience lead us to believe that a wider, more comprehensive approach is necessary. In addition to the general guidance as to vocabulary levels discussed above:

a. The author needs to consider how the book is used in class and for homework. (For example, in view of the homework use of *Living Hong Kong Social Studies*, the revised edition incorporates in-text Chinese translation of new vocabulary.)

b. The author also needs to develop a repertoire of methods of helping the reader to an understanding of newly-introduced vocabulary (Williams 1981).

c. Further, it is important for the author to acquire sensitivity to the problems encountered by the FL reader, such as the language and form of definitions, idiomatic expressions, homonyms, the thoughtless use of unfamiliar words in imported text, etc.

d. And consideration should be given to 'back-up' devices such as a chapter-initial key words section, an end-chapter or end-book glossary or translation of new words, writing exercises which require the use of vocabulary that has been newly introduced in the book, regularly spaced vocabulary revision checks, etc.

Our experience is that the vocabulary difficulties encountered by FL students in their content area educational textbooks are considerable; that such difficulties are a major stumbling block to the acquisition of knowledge and thereby to the passing of all-important examinations; and that the authors of content area textbooks specifically written for an FL readership need to pay increased attention to the problems posed by unfamiliar vocabulary, and to how those problems can be surmounted. But the author's professional background is unlikely to have equipped him with sufficient awareness of and sensitivity to such problems. Therefore we consider that it is the editor's responsibility to help the author acquire the necessary awareness and sensitivity — by such means as seminars, an authors' manual, demonstration by means of 'before and after' textbook extracts, and dissemination of relevant research findings and of techniques employed by other authors.

Postscript on Williams and Dallas

The situation described by Williams and Dallas is similar to those described by Cooper and by Elley. Whatever one's view of the validity of cloze criterion levels it does seem clear that many of the students in this study were unable to cope competently with their English textbooks.

In such a situation, one might seem to have two broad approaches available, either to work on improving students' reading strategies, as suggested by Cooper and Hosenfeld, or to simplify the reading material in some way, the course taken by Williams and Dallas. The two approaches are not, of course, mutually exclusive.

Within the concept of simplification, we can distinguish two approaches, again capable of being combined. First, one can concentrate on simplifying the text itself. This can be done either in terms of some criterion such as a readability formula, as Davies tried in his experiment, or in terms of eliminating features thought to give particular difficulty to one's target students, the method investigated by Berman. Alternatively, one can concentrate on making the text more accessible by providing what Williams and Dallas refer to as 'back-up devices'. Williams and Dallas combine the approaches to simplification, but seem to attach particular importance to the role of back-up devices.

The incorporation of such devices in a text would seem to have advantages over an exclusive reliance on text simplification. Firstly, it seems to give more acknowledgement to the *learning* aspects of the reading situation, e.g. that students need to increase their vocabulary and must thus be exposed to unfamiliar items. As Williams and Dallas point out, when learning the content subject it is necessary for the student to learn items which may be comparatively specialized. (In Davies's experiment, which relied purely on text simplification, the subjects do not have to *learn* a defined content area.) A second possible advantage is that, since the texts used can be less 'simplified' and more 'authentic', the transition from adapted to non-adapted texts may be made easier.

Of particular interest in their discussion of back-up devices is the reason given for incorporating in-text L1 translations, namely that this represented a formalization of what the students did themselves. Much of the advice offered to students on handling unfamiliar vocabulary, e.g. identifying roots and affixes, guessing using rhetorical clues, etc. seems to depend heavily on input from

applied linguistics: there is seldom any sign of input from observation of students' own behaviour. The danger is that if the gap
between the advice offered and his own practice is too great, the
student will decide to ignore the advice as being unrealistic. Hence
the value of approaches based on observation of students' own
practice.

There is a similar pragmatism about the decision (p. 209) not to
attempt to insist that authors keep to an approved vocabulary
list. The production of texts which are sufficiently accessible in
linguistic terms for a particular target group, yet still capable of
imparting sufficiently accurate information, depends on the skill
of the writer. A realistic editorial aim would then be, as Williams
and Dallas suggest, to help the writer become aware of the likely
difficulties to be encountered by the readership, so that he can
either avoid them or cope with them in some other way.

11 Reading and communication

H. G. Widdowson

It is common these days to refer to reading as a communicative activity. But communication is a more problematic concept than its current popularity might suggest. The paradigm case is usually represented as a situation involving two people in face-to-face interaction: A and B in conversation, with the speaking role shifting backwards and forwards between them like a shuttlecock. But linguistic communication is not always of this reciprocal kind. When listening to a lecture or a speech, for example, communication takes place but there is no overt interaction, no turn-taking shuttlecock exchange. Although the listeners may be actively *engaged* in what is going on, they are not actually *participating* in the activity and so have no say in its organization. One may, of course, choose to challenge convention and seek to convert the monologue into an exchange by interrupting the speaker by questions, or expressions of dissent. There are other communicative occasions, however, when it is not possible to intervene, even if one felt disposed to do so; when the only recourse is to disengage completely by switching off the radio, closing the book.

Reading is clearly an activity of this non-reciprocal kind. The question then arises as to how it is related to the paradigm case of conversation. Is it a derivative version in some sense? If so, in what sense? What is the nature of the derivation? These are the kind of questions that I shall be concerned with in this paper: my purpose is to try to define the communicative character of reading.

We may begin with a consideration of the paradigm case: A and B talking to each other. The one taking the speaker role has some information to impart for some purpose. In general this purpose is to change the state of affairs that obtains in the mind of the addressee at the moment of speaking. Speaker A has reason to suppose that he knows something that B does not know and which he believes it is desirable for B to know. So he alters this state of affairs by passing this knowledge on and the situation then shifts into a new state, itself then subject to further change, and so on. This goes on until one participant resists the change and breaks off the engagement or both participants arrive at a mutual agreement that the situation has reached a satisfactory state of stability, and bring the engagement to a close.

The general purpose of people talking, then, is to bring about some change or other by the transmission of information. The particular purposes associated with particular interactions will, of course, vary greatly. Speaker A might wish to convey information about his desires so that B can satisfy them, he may wish to instruct, to advise, to threaten or command; he may wish to offer a service, or practise a deception, or impose an obligation. He may simply want to impress, or escape from individual isolation. The reasons why people need to communicate with each other are varied and manifold and relate to the whole range of the individual's involvement in social life. Let us then consider what A has to *do* in order successfully to convey what he has in mind.

It might seem as if this is a simple enough matter of A encoding what he wants to say in the language he shares with B. But the assumption here is that a commonly shared code automatically guarantees the common understanding of messages encoded in it and this clearly is not the case. Suppose, for example, that A were to say: 'The man is coming on Monday.' He (or she) is relying on B already knowing who this man is and why it should be a relevant bit of news that he is coming on Monday. So A's utterance does not itself express the information. What it does is to act as a mediator between what A knows and what B knows. The utterance serves to bring two networks of knowledge together and the meaning of what is said is a function of this connection. To adapt McLuhan's well known slogan: the mediation is the message. But very often the production of a single utterance will not be enough to connect up the two networks in this way, in which case the interlocutors have work to do to fix up a circuit. For example, B may not know, or may have forgotten, which man is being referred to and so may not understand what *proposition* is being expressed. We will give our example some human identity. Speakers A and B, wife and husband, Mildred and George. A domestic scene:

MILDRED: The man is coming on Monday.

GEORGE: Man? Which man? (*No connection. The message does not mediate.*)

MILDRED: You know, the builder. (*Circuit repair.*)

GEORGE: The builder? (*Still no connection.*)

MILDRED: Yes, the builder. Don't you remember? He's coming to fix the leak in the boxroom ceiling. (*Still repairing.*)

GEORGE: Oh, yes, that's right. Good. (*Message received and understood. Connection made, meaning achieved.*)

This is a case of propositional repair. But even if George *does* know who the man is, he may not know why Mildred thinks that his coming on Monday is worth mentioning. That is to say, even if he understands what *proposition* is being expressed by the utterance, he may still not grasp its illocutionary force. In this case, one can imagine an exchange of the following sort:

MILDRED: The man is coming on Monday.

GEORGE: So what?

MILDRED: I thought you would want to know.

GEORGE: I do know. You have told me twice already.

MILDRED: Well, I thought you might want to clear out the boxroom before he comes.

GEORGE: Oh, I see. O.K.

Gradually it emerges that what Mildred wants George to know is not only that the man is coming but that she wants him to do something about it. The message is not conveyed until George is led to realize that the utterance 'The man is coming on Monday' is meant to carry the illocutionary force of a request for action.

In both of these cases, the interlocutors are involved in negotiation in order to achieve the propositional and illocutionary value of the message. The last utterance in each exchange marks the successful connection: 'Oh yes, that's right. Good.' (I understand what you are talking about.) 'Oh, I see, O.K.' (I understand what you are getting at.) The two worlds come together and the situation shifts into a new state.

Of course, if the two worlds, the two networks of knowledge, are already in close convergence the need for negotiation is correspondingly diminished. So it is that, given the George and Mildred situation, the following exchange might occur:

MILDRED: The man is coming on Monday.

GEORGE: I'm going out tonight.

This can be understood as a perfectly coherent exchange if we suppose that George knows already that the man is to come to mend the ceiling and that this involves work in the boxroom beforehand. His utterance can then be taken to carry the message: 'I can't work in the boxroom tonight because I'm going out'. So negotiation is not always necessary. When networks are inter-woven by close acquaintance, messages are easy to achieve, some-times without language at all.

But most communication calls for negotiation. It is necessary to establish the meaning of the message, to make it *accessible*. It is also necessary to make it *acceptable*. Why, after all, does Mildred not get to the point straightaway and say bluntly: 'The man is coming on Monday, so clear out the boxroom.' Presumably because she might thereby provoke the response: 'Who do you think you are ordering about?' or 'Do it yourself'.

If you intend to impose an obligation on somebody it is prudent to prepare the ground beforehand, to make him or her receptive to your purpose and the message acceptable. But even when there is no such imposition, the problem of acceptability arises because every occasion of interaction will tend to be an impingement on privacy. It is worth dwelling a moment on why this should be so.

People have need of social contact. It provides them with the means of collaborating in practical action. As Banton puts it:

> Men must organize. In order to obtain food and shelter, to guard against periods of shortage or misfortune, and to propagate their own kind, men are obliged to co-operate with their fellows. (Banton 1965, p. 1)

But contact is also necessary as a means of receiving 'strokes' of recognition and approval which sustain the internal organiza-tion of the individual self. Berne comments on this aspect of cooperation as follows:

> The advantages of social contact revolve around somatic and psychic equilibrium. They are related to the following factors: (1) the relief of tension; (2) the avoidance of noxious situations; (3) the procurement of stroking; and (4) the maintenance of an established equilibrium. (Berne 1967, p. 18)

We may say, then, that people are acted upon by what we might refer to as the cooperative imperative. In language use this is expressed through what Grice calls the cooperative principle: a set of maxims which represent the ground rules we abide by when engaged in communicative behaviour. Thus when a conversation takes place, both interlocutors enter into a socially sanctioned agreement that they will not say more than necessary, that what they say will be relevant to the matter in hand, that they have some warrant in fact for what they say, and so on. (Grice 1975.) To put the matter briskly, social contact calls for a social contract. The management of human affairs depends on the assumption that people will cooperate to achieve understanding. Unless they do so, no negotiation is possible and communication is arrested. But there are risks involved.

Cooperation can only occur if those cooperating allow entry into each other's individual world, and this calls for caution. Human beings, in common with other animals, have a strong sense of private territory, their own circumscribed life space of ideas, values, beliefs within which they find their essential security. In communication, the socially sanctioned cooperative imperative requires the barriers which define this space to be lowered to allow entry. Not surprisingly, therefore, the entry is wary and circumspect. Interlocutors are anxious to avoid offence by seeming to intrude too abruptly, always aware that they are vulnerable to counter attack. So it is that it is in the interests of both parties concerned to be polite, to protect face, and self-esteem, to avoid an abuse of privacy (see Brown and Levinson 1978). Thus on every occasion of language use the cooperative imperative acting in the interests of social contact has to be reconciled with the territorial imperative acting in the interests of individual security. Of course there are occasions when the status or role of the interlocutors is such that customary circumspection can to some degree be dispensed with. One such case is when territory is shared, as it is in families. Familiarity may not always breed contempt, but it will always tend to breed complacency. Another case is when one interlocutor is so privileged in role or so powerful in status that he can invade the other's territory without any fear of reprisal. So it is that officers do not need to be polite to the rank and file, and teachers seldom bother to be polite to pupils. On most occasions of social contact, however, we have to be careful not to infringe rights and offend susceptibilities; we have to be aware of, and wary of, territorial claims.

The points I have made about the territorial and cooperative imperatives can be related to the drives which social psychologists identify as elements in social motivation. Argyle indicates that these drives can be ranged along two dimensions which he represents diagrammatically as follows:

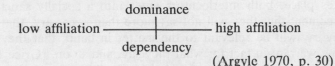

(Argyle 1970, p. 30)

The horizontal dimension here relates to the degree to which people feel they share a life space with those they are in contact with. In the case of low affiliation there will be little or no convergence of individual territory, whereas with high affiliation there will be a good deal. This dimension clearly corresponds to what Brown and Gilman (1960) refer to as solidarity. We may say, then, that a sense of high affiliation and solidarity derives from a recognition of shared experiential territory which reduces the risks of cooperation. Argyle's vertical dimension corresponds to Brown and Gilman's power semantic. This has to do with the extent to which the individual asserts his own territorial claim in cooperative activity. If he is sufficiently confident of his own defences, then he will be assertive and seek to extend his space into that of his interlocutor, thereby exercising dominance. If he lacks confidence, he will invite incursions into his space, and be submissive and dependent. If assertion is frustrated, the result is aggression. If submission is frustrated, the result is anomie, a loss of the sense of social identity.

Linguistic communication has to be understood in relation to these factors affecting social behaviour in general. It can be characterized, I suggest, as a means of bringing individual worlds into convergence by negotiation. These worlds consist of constructs of knowledge and experience, frames of reference for interpreting events (cf. van Dijk 1977). Communication is achieved when the speaker formulates particular propositional content and illocutionary intent in such a way as to make them accessible on the one hand and acceptable on the other. Accessibility is achieved by an alignment of different states of knowledge so that a common frame of reference is created. Acceptability is achieved when the interlocutors locate their interaction on the power and solidarity dimensions and reconcile the conflicting forces of the territorial and cooperative imperatives. So it is that in conversation one is often chary of providing direct access to one's meaning in case it is not acceptable:

Look, you are not going to believe this but . . . .

I don't quite know how to tell you this, and forgive me if I seem to be critical but . . . .

I know that you have been through a hard time recently, but . . . .

and so on.

The greater the threat of disturbance to the ordered scheme of things which represents the internal security of the individual, the more necessary do protective utterances of this kind become. And of course, too much concern for acceptability may lead to obfuscation and a decrease in accessibility. The speaker may be so preoccupied in making sure that what he has to say is not too disturbing an intrusion into the hearer's privacy that the point of his utterance may be lost. The whole business of conversational interaction calls for considerable skill in negotiation.

I shall refer to this process of negotiation as *discourse*. The overt expression of the process takes the form of linguistic signals which can be recorded and studied in detachment after the event. These constitute the *text* of the interaction. A recorded text can be analysed as a product simply as the manifestation of the linguistic code without regard to its character as the realization of discourse; and this, traditionally, is how it has been analysed in descriptive linguistics. The language user, however, does not deal with text as linguistic data in this way but as indications of communicative intent which have to be interpreted in flight, as it were, during the discourse process.

So much, then, for the nature of linguistic communication in general, as represented by the paradigm case of face-to-face interaction involving the overt negotiation of meaning through reciprocal exchange. But now what of written discourse? What of reading and writing? On the face of it these activities are very different from those of spoken interaction. There is typically no shifting of the initiative from one interlocutor to the other, so there can be no monitoring of effect, no adjustment to reaction, no open cooperation in the negotiation of meaning. The reader may give vent to snorts of disagreement, may scribble comments in the margin ('Rubbish!' 'Surely not!') but he cannot alter the development of the discourse as recorded in the text. It is the writer, it would seem, who is entirely in control of events. Indeed one might question whether, in the absence of such interaction, one can legitimately talk about written discourse at all. Is it not, rather, all text? To answer this question, we have to consider the relationship between text and discourse in spoken and written language use.

Written text differs from spoken text in two fundamental ways.

First, it is fashioned by the producer for prospective use and cannot be realized as discourse until it is performed, as it were, as a separate and subsequent activity. Spoken text is the immediate reflex of discourse which disappears without trace unless recorded by third person intervention. The act of writing is the act of recording and if there is no record no written communication has occurred. The act of speaking requires no record but only an immediate textual realization. Second, the written record is onesided. Unlike spoken text it does not usually provide a representation of the entire interaction but only the first person's contribution to it. Written text, then, is a partial record designed to have a delayed action effect, and as such is detached from discourse activity in a way that only analysis can achieve in the case of spoken language use. This detachment has important implications for reading, as I shall suggest presently.

But meanwhile the question remains as to how the writer, being the sole begetter of text, sending his signals out into the void for later reception, can be said to be producing discourse at all. He does so (as I have suggested elsewhere (Widdowson 1979)) by means of a covert interaction whereby he anticipates the likely reactions of an imagined reader and negotiates with him as it were by proxy, by the vicarious assumption of the second person role. In this way he creates his own conditions for communication. He has something to convey and must calculate what additional information he needs to provide to facilitate the conveyance. In the course of his presentation, he shifts perspective to assume and so to assess the second person response and adjusts the development of his discourse accordingly. For example, here is the beginning of a discussion on the relevance of the concept of role in the understanding of social behaviour:

A: The basic psychological function of roles is to provide the individual with a fairly specific model for interaction.
B: Why do you say it's a model?
A: It is a model in the sense that any role is defined in terms of its relation to other roles.
B: I'm still not quite clear. Give me an example.
A: The role of parent is defined in relation to that of children.
B: O.K. I'm with you. Now go on to tell me about roles.

This can be said to be the discourse underlying the following text:

> The basic psychological function of roles is to provide the individual
> with a fairly specific model for interaction. It is a model in the sense
> that any role is defined in terms of its relation to other roles, as the role

of 'parent', for example, is defined in relation to that of children. Each role is associated with what, for the moment, is best called norms of 'behaviour'. (Kelvin 1971, p. 139)

So it is that the writer can be said to conduct a covert interchange to establish a convergence of frames of reference so that the information he wishes to convey is made accessible to his supposed reader. To do this he has recourse to the kind of tactical procedures illustrated here whereby he anticipates the immediate reactions of the imagined second person addressee and so provides for the linear development of the discourse. But he also makes use of procedures of a more strategic kind to foreground or bring into focus the main points of his presentation and to distinguish them from information which is only intended to serve an enabling function. Such strategic procedures occur commonly in conversation when they are generally used retrospectively to summarize or recapitulate the gist or upshot of what has preceded:

'What has emerged from our discussions, then, is . . .'
'So we are agreed that . . .'
'In short, the indications are that . . .'

Such procedures have been referred to by the ethnomethodologists as 'formulations' (Garfinkel and Sacks 1970; Heritage and Watson 1979). Apart from these retrospective procedures for formulating, however, the writer also makes use of prospective procedures to give *pre*formulations of what he intends to say:

'There are three points I wish to make: first . . . second . . . third . . .'.
'The purpose of this paper is . . .'

Such devices make explicit in advance the hierarchical structure of the discourse and compensate for the absence of immediate feedback which in conversation allows for the structure to be monitored into shape through reciprocal interaction.

The discourse procedures mentioned so far are directed at providing for what I have referred to as accessibility. The writer may also need to take acceptability into account so that he does not project an image of dogmatic rectitude or insult the intelligence of his reader. Hence expressions like 'of course', 'perhaps' and the mitigating use of modality. However, the writer is not in a situation of actual physical confrontation and is under no immediate threat of reprisal should he cause offence by unwarranted trespass. Furthermore, whereas spoken interaction, no matter how formal, must inevitably involve individuals and expose them to the dangers of attack, written discourse is, with the exception of personal correspondence, not typically directed at individuals at all but at groups. Writers are therefore less concerned with the protection of persons. Indeed, the problem of the writer is not so much to avoid conflict as to create conditions for an engagement, and to this end he will sometimes provoke reaction by flouting acceptability. Consider this example: 'To see, we need light'. Such a statement invites the riposte: 'You don't say. Now tell us something new!' But as the discourse develops it becomes clear that this is a deliberate ruse to engage our attention:

> To see, we need light. This may seem too obvious to mention but it has not always been so obvious — Plato thought of vision as being due not to light entering, but rather to particles shot out of the eyes, spraying surrounding objects. (Gregory 1966, p. 13)

I have characterized written text as the partial record of a discourse enacted by the writer on behalf of a supposed reader. This enactment involves the use of tactical and strategic procedures to convey a scheme or pattern of information which is a projection of the writer's world. His purpose is to induce the reader to recognize his territorial claim. If the actual reader is prepared to play the role that the writer has cast him in, then he will seek to recover the underlying discourse from the textual clues provided. In this case, in respect to the point made earlier about dominance and dependence in social behaviour, reading will be an act of submission. The reader, recognizing the authority of the writer and wanting to allow access to the information given, will adjust his own frames of reference to accommodate it. He will then allow himself to be directed by the writer and be content to keep to the course that has been plotted for him. He will follow the text like a script.

But the reader may not wish to submit to writer control in this way; he may not be willing, or may not be able to accommodate the writer's conceptual scheme into the patterns of his own life space. Nor is he obliged to do so. In spoken interaction the co-operative imperative imposes constraints on freedom of action and will direct interlocutors towards accommodation and convergence (cf Giles and Smith 1979). But the reader is not under such constraint. The text is there before him, dissociated from the discourse which created it, and so he can use it in whichever way best suits his purposes, free to disregard the discourse that the writer has enacted on his behalf. Instead of adjusting his scheme of things to accommodate that of the writer, he can project his own scheme on what he reads and change the direction of accommodation so that the text is adjusted to fit the patterns of his own significance. In this case reading is an act not of submission but of assertion.

Communication involves the transmission of information from one individual world to another, from one schematic setting to another. Negotiation is necessary to bring about the required adjustment so that there is an alignment of frames of reference. But in spoken interaction the very social nature of the activity, and in particular the acceptability requirement, calls for circumspection and compromise. The interlocutors, caught up in a social event, have to act in accordance with the requirements of social behaviour, and the discourse that results represents not only the negotiation of meaning but also the management of interpersonal relations. The written text, on the other hand, is produced as the report of a discourse enacted in detachment from the immediacy of a social encounter; and the reader, in like detachment, can choose to relate it to his own scheme of things in whichever way serves his purpose best. He may choose to be dependent and to adjust in submissive fashion to the writer's scheme, following the discourse development plotted for him. Alternatively, he may choose to be dominant and to assert the primacy of his own conceptual pattern, fitting textual information into it directly and short-circuiting the discourse process.

I am suggesting, then, that since the reader is not under social pressure to key his reactions into the structure of an actually occurring interaction, he is free to take up whatever position suits his purpose on the dominance/dependence scale, asserting his own scheme at one point, submitting to that of the writer at another, alternately using the text as a source of information and as the script of a discourse. But the positions the reader takes up will not be determined by the *interpersonal* factors that are so crucial in conversation, but by *ideational* factors (to use Halliday's terminology). That is to say, the reader's concern is to derive as much information as he needs from his reading so as to consolidate or change the frames of reference which define his particular conceptual territory. If he seeks to consolidate he will tend to be assertive, and if he seeks to change he will tend towards submission.

Whether the reader adopts an interpersonal attitude of submission or assertion, to achieve his ideational purpose he has to make a connection between the writer's frames of reference and his own.

There has to be some coincidence of what Sanford and Garrod refer to as 'scenarios', which, as they point out, provide the basis for prediction:

> The scenario is an information network called from long-term memory by a particular linguistic input . . . in all cases the basic principle is one of enabling the knowledge of the reader to be used in such a way as to allow for direct interpretation of entities or events predicted by his knowledge. To the extent that any text conforms to the predictions it is readily interpreted, to the extent that it does not, it will be more difficult to understand. (Sanford and Garrod 1981, p. 127)

The first circumstance mentioned here, where the text keys in closely with reader predictions, will encourage assertion. The second, where the text is relatively unpredictable, will require submission to the writer's discourse. But in both cases the aim is to relate what the writer says to a pre-existing scheme.

A consideration of reading as the ideational matching of frames of reference or scenarios requires us to shift our attention from the psychology of interpersonal relations to the psychology of perception. For the process of prediction which Sanford and Garrod refer to is engaged as much for the interpretation of visual images as for the interpretation of linguistically coded information. Thus Neisser makes reference to 'anticipatory schemata' which correspond to the scenarios of Sanford and Garrod:

> In my view, the cognitive structures crucial for vision are the antici-patory schemata that prepare the perceiver to accept certain kinds of information rather than others and thus control the activity of looking. Because we can see only what we know how to look for, it is these schemata (together with the information actually available) that deter-mine what will be perceived . . . . At each moment the perceiver is constructing anticipations of certain kinds of information, that enable him to accept it as it becomes available. (Neisser 1976, p. 20)

The schema, then, like the scenario, is projected on to events which are then interpreted with reference to it. But clearly if actuality always fitted neatly into anticipation and predictions were always confirmed, then schemata would fossilize into fixed stereotypes and nothing would be learned from reading or visual experience. Allowance, therefore, must be made for information to modify existing schemata. In view of this Neisser proposes a perceptual cycle whereby a schema directs the perceiver to explore reality by sampling the available information and modifying the original schema where necessary. Diagrammatically, the cycle is presented like this:

Object
(available information)

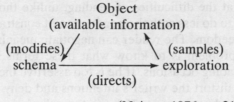

(modifies)   (samples)
schema ⟶ exploration
(directs)

(Neisser 1976, p. 21)

It seems clear that the reading process can be characterized in terms of this perceptual cycle. The reader applies a schematic frame or scenario to the textual object, samples the information it represents, and makes whatever modification is necessary to incorporate information not previously accounted for into the structure of his knowledge. There are, however, complications. To begin with, the object to be sampled is itself schematically organized and so represents a structural order which the reader has to reconcile with his own. Where the two orders are similar little sampling and modification will be required to make them congruent. Where they are different, the reader may choose to sample the text to make minimal modifications, thereby asserting the primacy of his schema, or may feel the need for major schematic modification and in this case the sampling will take the form of a submission to the writer's discourse, of which the textual object is a realization.

I have tried in this paper to indicate what seem to me to be the salient characteristics of reading as a communicative activity. Essentially they derive from the detachment of first person addresser and second person addressee and the consequent dissociation of text from discourse in written language use. This enables the writer to concentrate on accessibility and the reader to use the text for ideational purposes, sampling the information it offers without being involved in the management of interpersonal relations, and without having to process it as it emerges in real time. The reader is free to deal with it as a perceptible object. On the other hand, the text is the report of a discourse and so the interaction which originally informed it can be recovered as required by the reader assuming the second person role presupposed by the writer. Thus the reader is able to adopt the social attitudes of dominance and dependence to suit his own personal purposes in acquiring information without being troubled by their implications in social interaction.

So it is that the difficulties of reading, unlike those of conversation, have to do less with the negotiation of constraints than with the use of freedom. The reader can negotiate meaning on his own terms. His problem is to know what these terms should be on particular reading occasions. If he is too assertive there is a danger that he may distort the writer's intentions and deny access to new knowledge and experience. If he is too submissive, he runs the risk of accumulating information without subjecting it to the critical discrimination necessary to incorporate it into the schematic structure of existing knowledge. In both cases, reading is deprived of its essential purpose since it does not result in the change of state which, as I suggested earlier, is a defining feature of the communicative process.

Postscript on Widdowson

One of the most original aspects of Widdowson's paper is its attempt to explore the *differences* between reading and listening, or perhaps better, between reading interaction and conversational interaction, and it is this aspect we concentrate on in this postscript.

As we suggest in the postscript to Elley's paper, there is a respectable, and to some extent commonsensical argument that, beyond the phonemic/graphemic level, the written and spoken languages are, in major respects, the same. This applies only to the code; certain writers, however, notably Sticht (1972) extend this similarity to language *performance*, and claim that reading and listening are fundamentally the same activity. According to Sticht there are not two separate skills, i.e. reading and listening, but one, holistic ability to comprehend by language (p. 293).

The standard view of the relationship between spoken and written language abilities is summarized in the table below:

	Productive	Receptive
spoken	speech	listening
written	writing	reading

This simple classification at least has the virtue of pointing out a similarity between listening and reading; however, it is seriously defective in that it fails to make due allowance for what Widdowson refers to as the paradigm case, that of face-to-face interaction. Such a classification can thus lead to the teaching situation in which the syllabus includes a speaking class, where presumably students speak but do not listen, and a listening class, where, more believably, students listen but do not speak. The dual skills nature of the paradigm situation, with its associated abilities such as turn-taking, makes it so different from other situations, such as eavesdropping, listening to radios, reading novels, etc. as to justify use of the following categorization:

	Dialogue	Monologue	
		PRODUCTIVE	RECEPTIVE
spoken	Conversation	Lecturing, etc.	Listening
written	Letter exchange Telexes	Writing	Reading

Thus lectures, sermons, etc., and writing have in common the factor of pre-planning, which marks these activities off from other activities such as taking part in conversations, unscripted interviews, etc. When Sticht argues that listening and reading fundamentally involve the 'same' abilities, he seems to be thinking largely of reading and listening to monologues.

Widdowson sees one of the main differences between conversational and reading interaction in the fact that the latter permits the reader–participant much more scope in deciding what to take from the discourse (pp. 222–3). That is, in conversation, there are strong social conventions pressuring us to cooperate. In reading, the face-to-face aspect is absent, and there are fewer pressures on us; we can skip chapters or put the book down. Clearly also, the permanent nature of written text makes it much easier for the reader to select what he wants than it is for the listener to a spoken text. We will refer later to other factors that could be taken into account when examining this little known area. First, however, we shall attempt to describe briefly what we think are significant positions along what Widdowson refers to as the dominance/dependence scale (p. 223).

It should be made clear that the dominance/dependence distinction is *not* equivalent to an active/passive one. In Widdowson's, and other writers' view of discourse, even the most dependent reader must create or recover the discourse from the text. Having said that, however, for the sake of completeness, we shall begin with the passive approach, referred to by Fransson as the 'reproduction oriented' approach.

A. *Passive* 'I don't know what you're talking about, but I'll do my best to learn it.'

Active approaches focused on by Widdowson can be categorized as follows:

B. *Active* 1.   'I'm doing my best to understand what you're saying.'
                 (This is the *submissive* approach.)

2.   'I understand what you're saying, though I disagree with a lot of it.'
     (This is the *assertive*, or *dominant* approach.)

3.   'I don't care what you have to say: there's a piece of information in your text somewhere that I want.'
     (This activity is sometimes referred to as 'scanning'.)

Now, it seems clear that, in Widdowson's terms, B2 and B3 would be located towards the 'dominance' end of the scale. However, it also seems clear that B1 and B2 have significant features which mark them off from the other two types. One could argue that B2 is simply B1 with the addition of an evaluative component (cf. Bloom *et al.* 1956). More fundamentally, however, B1 and B2 have in common the fact that in both cases, writer and reader share the same goals. Suppose, for example, that someone wants to learn about the unification of Germany. He selects a suitable history book. The writer's goal is presumably to explain to the reader the salient facts leading up to unification. The reader is looking to have such facts explained. Thus their goals converge, even if the reader disagrees with what the writer says. If, however, the reader uses the same book with the aim of discovering the name of Bismarck's country estate, then his goal is quite different from that of the writer. Thus, in approaches B1 and B2, the reader tries to recover the writer's message; in A, he tries to learn the text; and in B3, he makes use of an isolated piece of the message. This suggests that the situation is more complicated than can be handled on a single dominance/dependence scale.

It is not clear whether reading can be divided off sharply from conversational interaction according to a cooperation/self-assertion dichotomy, as Widdowson seems to suggest. One can always, after all, break up the narration of someone's pet story by waiting till a point just before the punchline, then asking the teller whether he always pronounces such and such a word in such and such a way. This is clearly an example of divergent goals in a speech situation. In general terms, however, Widdowson is clearly right: the permanent nature of written language makes readers' self-assertion far more possible. It is, for example, impractical in most cases to scan a lecture for a particular bit of information.

Is it, however, true (p. 223) that the reader is not affected by interpersonal factors? One of the editors, for several years, felt uncomfortable about abandoning any book he had started reading, and thus took some eight years, on and off, to finish *Kangaroo* by D. H. Lawrence. It cannot be said that this behaviour was dictated by 'ideational' factors; one suspects he was, deep down, unwilling to be rude to an author conventionally considered 'major'. Similarly, many students may be affected by respect for the author as an authority in their field, or perhaps, for the received wisdom of the whole subject area.

Finally, there would seem to be other factors relevant to a discussion of how people approach written and spoken language. Individuals within the same culture may vary; some people can read for hours, yet become uncomfortable after listening to a lecture for 20 minutes; the reverse may be true of other individuals. Different cultures may vary in the respect they accord the different media. In Europe, written texts have often been granted more respect. In India, for example, the reverse seems to have been true (McNeill 1963). Finally, differences may exist between different subject areas; we have little empirical data about the possibly complex relationships between written and spoken sources of information in different academic disciplines. The analysis of the needs of language learners may answer this question, although the research is likely to be complex and protracted.

12 Case studies of ninth grade readers

Carol Hosenfeld

Introduction

The rhetoric of the '80s in maths education and science education is a call for research on problem solving. For example, the National Council of Teachers of Mathematics places problem solving first on its agenda for action in the '80s (*An Agenda for Action*, 1980).

It is natural that problem solving would be an important category for thinking about mathematics. In fact, there has been a long tradition of research in the area of problem solving in the field of maths education.

Perhaps less obvious is that problem solving is also an important category of analysis in research in second-language acquisition. H. H. Stern and J. Cummins (1981) come close to this realization — though they never use the language — when they place research on learning processes first on their agenda for research in the 1980s in foreign language education. But perhaps it would be very helpful to view their call for research on learning from a problem solving perspective. This would open up lines of research in other areas (e.g. psychology, artificial intelligence, mathematics education, science education, and English education) which would contextualize our own endeavour.

In my own research I have been focusing upon problem solving. Specifically, an effort is made to uncover the kind of strategies students use in performing foreign language tasks. The focus has been on trying to understand those strategies that are used when youngsters confront problems.

The specific techniques I have used for that purpose have been the thinking aloud and introspective/retrospective research techniques. Briefly, a thinking aloud approach consists of asking students to perform tasks and to verbalize their thought processes;

an introspective/retrospective approach consists of asking students to reflect upon their operations as they perform a task or after they have completed it. (For an extensive discussion of these techniques, see Cohen and Hosenfeld 1981)

When these techniques are used with reading tasks, every attempt is made to implement the following principles. (For further information, the reader may wish to consult Hosenfeld 1977a and 1977b.):

1   Begin each interview with a practice session. The length of the session will depend chiefly upon the student's ability to self-report and the interviewer's skill. For practice tasks, select tasks that are similar to the actual tasks you intend to use to elicit students' reading strategies. As an introduction, you might say, 'I'd like you to read this passage and to tell me what you are doing as you read it. Do what you would ordinarily do if you were reading the passage in class or at home. You are not expected to know the meaning of all of the words in the passage. Let me know what you do when you come to unfamiliar words.'

2   Obtain as complete a description of a student's reading strategy as possible. A reading strategy can be viewed as consisting of two categories of operations: what students do when they read in a relatively uninterrupted manner (their 'non-stop' reading behaviour) and what they do when they come to unknown words (their 'interrupted' reading behaviour). A complete description would include both categories of operations.

3   Use the think aloud approach with students who translate and the introspective/retrospective approach with students who do not translate. Because students who translate usually sub-vocalize as they read, it seems appropriate to ask them to report their sub-vocalizations. As they 'mutter' in English, they provide information needed to describe their 'non-stop' reading behaviour. Because they must stop 'muttering' at unknown words and use specific strategies to decode them before continuing to 'mutter', they provide information needed to describe their 'word-solving' strategies. By contrast, students who do not translate appear to sub-vocalize less; it seems appropriate, therefore, to ask them to report their thoughts.

4   Ask indirect rather than direct questions. At times it is necessary to ask students questions in order to clarify certain

features of their problem solving processes. Questions should be so worded that they do not impose directions upon students' thought-processes or self-report. For example, to a direct question, such as 'Do you translate?' students might answer 'yes' because it is easier than trying to perceive what they actually do with the tasks or they might answer 'no' because the question is intimidating to them: they might feel that they *should* read without translating. An interviewer should obtain the information by a more indirect approach. Often, during a practice session, the following exchange occurs:

s: Do you want me to translate?
i: Do you usually translate?
s: No.
i: Do what you usually do.

When information is obtained in this manner, the interviewer can have greater assurance that it reflects what the student actually does with the task.

I have used these techniques in three studies to discover strategies students use to solve problems of understanding foreign language texts. In the first study (Hosenfeld 1977a), high and low scorers on a test of reading proficiency were asked to self-report as they read the next unassigned reading in their text. High scorers (called successful readers) tended to: keep the meaning of the passage in mind, read in broad phrases, skip inessential words, guess from context the meaning of unknown words and have a good self-concept as a reader. By contrast, low scorers (called unsuccessful readers) tended to: lose the meaning of sentences as soon as they decoded them, read word-by-word or in short phrases, rarely skip words, turn to the glossary for the meaning of new words, and have a poor self-concept as a reader.

Further analysis of the protocols obtained in the first study and analysis of additional protocols indicated that as well as using the strategies mentioned above, successful readers tended to: (1) identify the grammatical category of words; (2) demonstrate sensitivity to a different word order in the foreign language; (3) examine illustrations; (4) read the title and make inferences from it; (5) use orthographic information (e.g. capitalization); (6) refer to the side gloss; (7) use the glossary as a last resort; (8) look up words correctly; (9) continue if unsuccessful at decoding a word or phrase; (10) recognize cognates; (11) use their knowledge of the world; (12) follow through with a proposed solution to a problem; (13) evaluate their guesses (Hosenfeld 1979).

Once I had identified some strategies of successful readers, I asked the following research question: can unsuccessful readers acquire the strategies of successful readers? Two case studies were designed to answer this question. The purpose of this chapter is to present: (1) a summary of the report of the first case study (Hosenfeld 1979) and (2) a report of the second case study.

The first case study

The subject of the first case study was a fourteen-year-old girl enrolled in a level two French class in a large suburban high school in western New York. The daughter of two university professors, 'Cindy' lived in an upper middle class neighbourhood. She had maintained an A average in the French course and was considered a good student by her teacher. The diagnostic sessions, however, revealed that she was having difficulty in reading.

Analysis of her reading strategies indicated that she guessed the meaning of words without regard to context, i.e. as though they existed in isolation; failed to evaluate her guesses (which were often 'bad' guesses); translated word-by-word; and forgot the meaning of sentences as soon as she decoded them. She seemed to use only one of the strategies of successful readers listed above (No. 10): she recognized some cognates. But she certainly did not always use this strategy appropriately.

During the teaching phase of the diagnostic teaching study, Cindy was asked to compare her reading strategies to those of a successful reader (protocols obtained during the first study) and to list the differences between them. Her list included the following comparisons: 'He keeps the story in mind as he goes along; I just think about the word I'm translating. After he guesses a word, he checks to see if it fits into the sentence; I don't stop to see if it makes sense. He brings in outside information to figure out some words. I just never thought of doing that.' (Hosenfeld 1979). She then practised the strategies with new reading tasks.

The results showed marked improvement. After instruction, she read (translated) in broad phrases, kept familiar phrases in the foreign language, remembered the meaning of sentences, guessed contextually the meaning of new words, and used many information sources in decoding, e.g. illustration, side gloss, glossary (as a last resort), cognates, and her knowledge of the world.

There were, however, some strategies she did not learn. Even after instruction, she did not: (1) identify the grammatical function of words; (2) skip inessential words; or (3) change the form of words, e.g. verbs, before looking them up in a glossary. Further research is necessary before we can understand why she did not learn these strategies.

The second case study

The second case study, designed to answer the same research question (Can unsuccessful readers acquire the strategies of successful readers?), differs from the first in several important ways: the socio-economic backgrounds of the subjects are different; they read in different ways; and the instructional approaches are different. Specifically, this section intends to show: (1) how the second subject, Ricky, obtained meaning from printed text; (2) how he was taught new techniques of obtaining meaning; and (3) how he obtained meaning after remediation.

Context

Ricky is a student at a Buffalo, New York State, high school. The school is located in South Side, the industrial section of the city. Of the 1,800 students in grades 9–12, two thirds are white and one third black. Black students are bussed from the East Side. Once a high-priority issue, segregation has been replaced by other issues: high absenteeism, drinking, drugs, and low achievement. (Students obtain the lowest stanines in the city in reading and mathematics.)

The neighbourhood in which Ricky lives would be termed working class.

His father is a clerk in a steel mill; his mother a secretary for the school department. He has an older sister who dropped out of school and works as a waitress, and two brothers, one and two years younger.

Ricky, a fourteen-year-old freshman, is considered a quiet, cooperative student by his teachers. His performance in school is best described as uneven: he is about average in most subjects, excels in English and mathematics, and struggles with Spanish. He is a very articulate, winsome boy. At times, he seems wise beyond his years; at other times boyish, almost childlike. This combination is reflected in his explanation of how he selected a career:

I was thinking about all these different types of jobs and I was trying to figure out which would be the one where I could open my own office and where I wouldn't have to worry about someone else paying me. I started thinking about law and then last year my English teacher said to me 'Ricky, you'd make a beautiful lawyer' — because I'm always reading — and I thought a lot about it and I decided she was right and that would be the best thing to do and I'm sticking with it.

When asked if he thought Spanish would be useful in his chosen career, he replied:

Yes. At the beginning I might just get jobs at night court and probably there will be people there who can't speak English and who only speak Spanish and I could converse with them and I could help them by translating what they are saying to other people. And so as a lawyer, there would be this whole group of people I could help if I knew Spanish.

Despite Ricky's apparent eagerness to learn Spanish, his actual language classroom experience has not been a happy one. His difficulties began in the sixth grade during his first year of language study when he was told at mid-term to switch from Spanish to French for one semester. Although he switched back to Spanish (his preferred language) the following year, his grades dropped sharply; there was little improvement in eighth and now in ninth he is struggling to keep up with his classmates. He gave several reasons for his poor performance: a personality conflict with a teacher, crowded classes, and uninteresting learning activities.

The pedagogical method used in Ricky's Spanish class is chiefly an audio-lingual approach including memorization of dialogues and manipulation of pattern drills. On days devoted to reading, students read aloud one after another; they write out answers to questions accompanying the text passage and turn them in to be corrected and graded. When I asked Ricky what he had been told about reading, he replied that the only thing he could remember was something his seventh grade teacher had said: 'Take your time. Pronounce the words correctly. If you don't know a word, look it up and remember it.'

Ricky's problem solving behaviour

To discover Ricky's strategies, I planned to meet with him twice, first for a practice and then a diagnostic session. Ricky, however, could think aloud so easily as he read that one session was sufficient. As a reading task, I selected the next unassigned reading in his text, *Nueva Vista 2* (p. 55). Following are a portion of the task, a translation, and a transcription of the decoding segment. (H = Hosenfeld; R = Ricky)

Excerpt from: Los pueblos hispanoamericanos
La vida diaria (daily) de un pueblo es tranquila, casi monótona.Nadie tiene prisa (Nobody is in a hurry). Los hombres se levantan temprano y van al trabajo. Muchos cultivan la tierra (land); algunos trabajan en las minas o en las pequeñas industrias del pueblo.

Mientras los hombres están trabajando, las mujeres se quedan en casa cuidando de los niños y preparando las comidas.

Los domingos por la mañana se oyen las campanas de la iglesia llamando a la gente a la misa.

A Translation of the Text: Spanish American Towns
The daily life of a town is tranquil, almost monotonous. No one is in a hurry. The men get up early and go to work. Many cultivate the land; some work in the mines or small industries of the town.

While the men are working, the women remain at home caring for the children and preparing the meals.

On Sunday mornings the church bells can be heard calling the people to mass.

R: (He reads aloud one sentence) The daily life . . . of the town is tranquil . . . tranquil . . . *casi montana* . . . *casi* (He turns to the glossary.) almost . . . *montana* (He repeats the word, spells it out, and then returns to the text.) The daily life of the town is tranquil . . . always . . . *manotano* . . . (He turns to the glossary.) monotonous (He turns back to the text.) The daily life of the town is tranquil . . . and always monotonous. *Nadie tiene* . . . Nobody is in a hurry. The men . . . *se levanta* (He turns to the glossary, repeats *levanta*, and spells out the first letters as he scans the columns.) to get up (He turns back to the text.) The men . . . get up . . . early and go . . . *el trabajo* (He turns to the glossary, repeats *trabajo*, and spells out the first letters.) to work (He turns back to the text.) The men get up early and go to work. Many cultivate . . . the land . . . *algunos trabajan* (He turns to the glossary, repeating the word *algunos*.) I think it means many . . . any (He turns back to the text.) Any . . . Many work in the mines . . . or in . . . the little industries of the town. *Mientras los hombres* . . . *mientras* (He turns to the glossary and scans the columns, spelling out *mien* many times.) While. (He turns back to the text.) While many men . . . have to get up . . . the women . . . *quandan* (He turns to the glossary, repeating the letter q; turns back to the text, spelling out many times the first three letters of the word; turns back to the glossary, spelling out the beginning of the word.) remain (He turns back to the text.) While many men . . . have to get up . . . have to leave . . . the women . . . remain . . . in the home taking care of the children . . . and preparing . . . the meals. *Los domingos* . . . *domingos* (He turns to the glossary, repeating the word.) Sunday (He returns to the text.) The Sundays . . . *por la mana* (He turns to the glossary, and then back to the text.) Sundays in the morning . . . *se oyen* (He turns to the glossary.) hear (He turns back to the text.) you hear . . . the *campanas* (He turns to the glossary.) bells (He turns back to the text.) You hear the bells of the church . . . *llamando* (He turns to the glossary.) They don't have this word in the book.

H: What word?

R: *Llamando*.

H: What would you do?

R: Well it seems to me that . . . it sounds like . . . somebody's calling something . . . *ando* . . . it ends with i/n/g . . . let's see . . . the bells *llamando* . . . are ringing . . . *a la gente* (He turns to the glossary.) people (He turns back to the text.) They are calling the people . . . *a la mesa* . . . It sounds like they're calling them to mass (He turns to the glossary, scans the columns, repeating the word *mesa*, and turns back to the text.) *Misa* (He spells out the word and turns to the glossary.) (Sigh) mass . . . yes (He turns back to the text.) The bells are calling the people to mass.

To obtain meaning from printed text, Ricky engages in a careful, word-by-word decoding of sentences, providing (either from memory or from the glossary) English 'equivalents' of the Spanish words. Because so many words are unfamiliar to him; because his only response to these words is to turn to the glossary for their meaning; and because he often forgets the word he is seeking in the glossary, reading for Ricky consists chiefly of shuttling back and forth between the glossary and the text. (It is interesting to note that one of the few words whose meaning he guesses contextually, *llamando* — and he does so quite skilfully — is a word he cannot find in the glossary.)

There is no way to know for certain why Ricky reads in this plodding fashion, but several explanations are plausible. One explanation pertains to Ricky's first response to new words. Ricky might have started to read before he had a large enough vocabulary to guess the meaning of new words (Jarvis 1979; Saville-Troike 1979). At that time, turning to the glossary was necessary since the glossary was the only available source of new meanings. At some point, however, turning to the glossary may have become a habitual response: he may have continued to use the glossary when it was no longer necessary, that is, when he knew the meaning of enough words to guess contextually the meaning of new words.

A second explanation pertains to the type of reading instruction Ricky has received. As mentioned above, when I asked him what he had been told about reading, one of the few things he could remember was that his seventh grade teacher had told him to look up unknown words and try to remember them. This directive might be responsible for Ricky's reading style.

A third explanation pertains to the relationship that exists between the readings in Ricky's text and subsequent tasks. Each chapter begins with a story which is followed by exercises including comprehension and personal questions, vocabulary and grammar tasks. The exercises all relate in some way to the story. It is little wonder, therefore, that Ricky tries to obtain as accurate, detailed, and complete an understanding of the story as possible. In other words, his constant reference to the glossary and his word-by-word approach may result from a general goal to obtain 'perfect' comprehension of reading passages (Coady 1979).

It is also possible that all three explanations presented above account for Ricky's approach to reading, i.e. lack of prerequisite information (vocabulary) when he first began to read, reading instruction, and the textbook format of reading tasks may all contribute to Ricky's approach to reading.

Remedial Work with Ricky

Ricky was willing to explore a different approach to reading with me, and I was eager to get started, so several days after diagnosis we began remedial work. Over the next two weeks, I made four half-hour visits to the school. We met three times in the school cafeteria during his regularly scheduled Spanish class and once in his Spanish classroom after school.

The general purpose of the remedial sessions was to teach Ricky some of the strategies successful readers reported using. A portion of the time was spent teaching him how to guess the meaning of new words. Specific techniques included: (1) substituting the filler word 'something' for new words and guessing their meaning from remaining words in the sentence; (2) using information in preceding and succeeding sentences and from the broader meaning of the entire reading passage to decode new words; and (3) asking a series of questions about new words including: (a) what kind of word is it (e.g. verb, noun)? (b) Does it look like an English word? (c) Given my knowledge of the world, what word would I expect to find in the sentence?

The following excerpts from two remedial segments illustrate the instructional technique and Ricky's response to it. The reading tasks are taken from *Nueva Vista 2* (pp. 55 and 61); transcripts of the interview are provided:

Los pueblos hispanoamericanos
   . . . En la plaza hay árboles y flores, una fuente en el centro y varios
bancos. En la plaza se encuentran tiendas, cafés, restaurantes y otros
edificios. El edificio más alto, más bello y más importante es siempre
la iglesia del pueblo.

R: In the plaza there are something and flowers, *una* something in
     the center and various benches.
H: Let's look at the first word, *árboles*. What kind of word is it?
R: A noun.
H: Does it look like an English word that would be appropriate in the
     sentence?
R: No.
H: What do we often find with flowers in a plaza?
R: (Silence)
H: Something in the same category.
R: Trees.
H: Does the word 'trees' fit into the sentence?
R: Yes.
H: Let's look at the next word, *fuente*. What kind of word is it?
R: A noun.
H: Does it look like an English word that would be appropriate in
     the sentence?
R: No.
H: They're talking about a plaza where there are trees and flowers.
     There is something in the center of the plaza. What might we find
     in the centre of a plaza?
R: A fountain.
H: Okay. Let's go on to the next sentence.
R: In the plaza something, something, cafés, restaurants and other
     something.
H: What is *se encuentran*?
R: A verb.
H: Does it look like an English word?
R: Yes. Encounters.
H: Let's figure out *tiendas*. In the plaza are found something, cafés,
     restaurants and other something. In the plaza are found cafés and
     restaurants. What else do we find in a plaza?
R: (Silence)
H: In the plazas we have around here?
R: Stores.
H: Let's look at the last word in the sentence. What kind of word is
     edificios?
R: A noun. It doesn't seem to look like a word in English.
H: Think of the whole sentence. In the plaza are found stores, cafés,
     restaurants and other what?
R: (Silence)
H: Look at the word again.
R: If you put the words all together . . . if there are restaurants and
     cafés, there would have to be other buildings along with them.
H: Okay. Let's go on to the next sentence.

R: The building something something, something something and something *importe* and is always the church of the village. If it was like a backward country where they have great pride in their religion they'd make the churches the best, the biggest, the tallest, so that it would signify their great respect for their religion. So this sentence must be the building, most tall, most beautiful and most important . . . the tallest, most tall, most beautiful and most important . . . the tallest, the most beautiful and most important building is the church of the village.

Preparativos para el viaje

SEÑOR BROWN: ¿Necesitan Uds. pasaporte?

SEÑOR ROBERTS: No, solamente tarjeta de turista y ya la tenemos.

SEÑOR BROWN: ¿Lleva Ud. cheques de viajero?

SEÑOR ROBERTS: Si, siempre llevo cheques de viajero, pero todavía no los tengo.

SEÑOR BROWN: ¿Llevan Uds. mucho equipaje?

SEÑOR ROBERTS: No podemos llevar mucho en avión. Llevamos solamente cuatro maletas.

Preparations for the trip

MR BROWN: Do you need passports?

MR ROBERTS: No, only a tourist card and we already have it.

MR BROWN: Do you carry traveler's checks?

MR ROBERTS: Yes I always carry traveler's checks, but I do not have them yet.

MR BROWN: Are you carrying much luggage?

MR ROBERTS: We cannot carry much on the plane. We are only carrying four suitcases.

R: Do you need a passport? No, something something and I already have it. (Pause)

H: Look at the question and answer again.

R: He says he doesn't need a passport . . . he needs a *tarjeta de turista* . . . it's a thing . . . *tarjeta* is a noun . . . *turista* looks like tourist . . . maybe it's a tourist ticket or a tourist card.

H: Would that be appropriate here?

R: Yes. Do you carry checks of something? (Pause)

H: What does Mr Roberts reply?

R: Yes, I carry checks of something, but we don't have any (Pause)

H: In the dialogue what is Mr Brown asking Mr Roberts about?

R: In this question?

H: No. In the whole dialogue.

R: He's asking him about a trip he's taking to Mexico.

H: What kind of checks do people often carry on a trip?

R: Oh. Traveler's checks. Are you carrying much something? I think it means team.

H: What does Mr Roberts reply?

R: We can't carry much on the plane. We can carry only four . . . *maletas* must be suitcases.

H: Is 'team' appropriate in the question?

R: No. It must be luggage.

Ricky's problem solving behaviour improved considerably during the remedial sessions. Before remediation, Ricky's habitual response to new words was to look for their meaning in the glossary. He did not know that there were many other strategies he could use to decode new words and that using these strategies was preferable to turning to the glossary.

As a result of the remedial sessions, he now guesses the meaning of new words by using: (1) known words in sentences, (2) his knowledge of cognates, (3) his knowledge of the world, (4) context (either to predict meaning or as an information source to which he can circle back for pertinent information), and (5) his knowledge of grammar. He also came to appreciate that guessing the meaning of words is preferable to obtaining their meaning in a glossary.

The remedial sessions had other positive effects. Ricky now reads the title and draws inferences from it; examines the illustration and uses information contained in it in decoding; decodes in broad phrases; skips inessential words, and uses the glossary as a last resort.

After considerable encouragement and prodding, Ricky began to keep easy phrases in Spanish. The remedial sessions ended, however, before it was possible to determine if he would continue to keep more and more of the text in Spanish. In other words, he is still basically a translator.

The deductive instructional approach used with Ricky involved teaching him the strategies of successful readers as he continued to translate (since he insisted on doing so) and encouraging him gradually to keep easy phrases and then more and more of the text in the foreign language. An alternative approach would be first to encourage him to process meaning directly in Spanish (perhaps with easier reading tasks) and then gradually to teach him 'successful' strategies.

So little information is available about teaching reading strategies that case studies like this one should be viewed as exploratory in nature. Although Ricky did acquire some strategies of successful readers, to conclude that the instructional approach used in this study is the best approach for him would be premature.

Implications for research

We need more small-scale studies like these based on systematic observation of foreign language readers engaged in the processes of reading and acquiring new reading strategies. These studies would elucidate the reading process and identify useful remedial techniques. In these studies we should include students of a wide range of verbal abilities, vary the remedial techniques, and try to obtain answers to the following questions: (1) Under what conditions do students process meaning in the foreign language without translation? (2) How lasting are newly acquired strategies? (3) Do students transfer their L1 reading skills to FL? Does their low language proficiency in FL 'short circuit' this transfer (Clarke 1980)? Or do other factors (e.g. lack of schemata) account for the lack of transfer (Hudson, in press)?

In addition to small-scale diagnostic teaching studies, foreign language reading should be approached descriptively as it occurs in the language classroom (Bloom 1980). Longitudinal case studies of students starting from the time they begin to read and continuing through intermediate and advanced levels of language study would shed light upon: (1) developmental dimensions of the foreign language reading process both for individual students and groups of students; (2) interactions of teaching procedures, materials, etc. and students' reading processes; and (3) learning environments that are optimal for and those that are detrimental to learning how to read in a foreign language.

The research method used to identify students' strategies seems to provide useful descriptions of how students obtain meaning from printed text. This method should be subjected to constant, careful scrutiny. The following questions remain unanswered: Do the thinking aloud and introspective methods cause some students to translate more than they normally do? Does self-reporting *in English* have a similar effect? Does the method change students' strategies in other ways? What are these ways? If we had another method of identifying reading strategies, one method could provide a crosscheck upon the other and help us to answer these questions. One such method could be to use miscue analysis in combination with self-report techniques to provide a more complete description of students' reading processes (Chen 1982).

Implications for the classroom

Students clearly need help in learning to read in a foreign language. Unassisted, many students learn strategies that impede their obtaining meaning efficiently from printed texts. The instructional methods used in the two case studies can be adapted to classroom use. The method (inductive) used with Cindy would be appropriate for individualized classrooms. The method (deductive) used with Ricky, however, is essentially a dialogue between teacher and student and consequently lends itself to many classroom arrangements. For example, a teacher can engage students in a tutorial exchange when they come to the teacher's desk; while moving from desk to desk as students work on a homework assignment; in small or large group settings. With different arrangements, the size of the 'audience' changes — an important consideration when students' inefficient learning behaviours are disclosed. In one-to-one settings, a teacher can be more direct than in small and large group settings where a teacher should usually ask for volunteers to perform the task or use protocols of unidentified students.

Classroom reading instruction is usually limited to activities that precede or follow the reading of texts (e.g. introduction of new vocabulary and discussion of a story). Teachers rarely help students while they are in the process of constructing meaning. As an example of such help, a teacher might: (1) assign the first paragraph of a story for silent reading; (2) ask several student volunteers to identify words which were new to them and to describe their strategies with these words; (3) discuss identified strategies with the entire class. This sequence — silent reading, disclosure and discussion — can be used with several paragraphs. (For additional activities teachers can use to help students *during* the reading process, see Hosenfeld, Arnold, Kirchofer, Laciura and Wilson 1981.)

The definition of reading underlying the teaching and materials used in Cindy's and Ricky's classrooms is essentially that reading consists of careful, phrase-by-phrase decoding of reading passages. Foreign language teachers need to investigate other definitions of reading, e.g., a psycholinguistic definition of reading (Goodman 1967, Smith 1971; Weaver 1980) and to observe reading classes where the definition is implemented with foreign language readers (Hosenfeld, Brinton and Allwright 1982) and native language readers who need remedial help (Hosenfeld, Frankel and Brinton 1982).

Postscript on Hosenfeld

Hosenfeld's work is part of a growing emphasis on *process* rather than *product*, which has been commented on at various points in this book. Traditional teaching and research practices emphasized product — the right answer, the desired terminal behaviour. Students' or research subjects' reasons for arriving at an answer could at best only be inferred. The new approach, on the other hand, is more interested in ways in which readers approach the problem.

Hosenfeld's paper represents an attempt to gain insights into the process of reading through a relatively novel set of techniques, and has resulted in the beginnings of an identification and categorization of the sorts of strategies that readers use when grappling with foreign language texts.

The sorts of strategies that are revealed by Hosenfeld's work relate particularly to problem solving strategies, when unknown words are encountered. They may be classified into several types: narrowly linguistic, as in identifying the form class of words, recognizing cognates, or chunking strings into phrases. Others are broadly semantic, in that they relate to a reader's attempt to make sense of a text, to keep the meaning of the text in mind whilst solving a particular lexical problem, checking to see if his guess fits into the context, evaluating the sense of his hypotheses.

Other strategies might be termed paralinguistic, in that they involve relating the verbal information to accompanying visuals, tables, etc., using punctuation and orthographic clues as cues for meaning, and typographic devices like titling and sub-headings.

Hosenfeld's work carries the implication that it may be possible to make a categorization of different types of reader, whose differing needs could then be catered for perhaps by self-access material. On the other hand, perhaps what we should be looking for is repertoires of different kinds of reading behaviour, different 'reads', to use Harri-Augstein and Thomas's term. It seems likely, after all, that learners, as well as mature readers, will vary their behaviour to take account of different tasks.

A categorization of strategies might be useful not only because it creates a sense of order in the somewhat *ad hoc* appearance of the strategies which emerge from protocols, but also because it might then inform a focused search for types of strategies in readers' protocols. In other words, what might emerge from case studies conducted on the lines Hosenfeld follows and proposes might be less exploratory research, and more confirmatory and experimental investigations of the process of reading.

Importantly, however, the paper goes beyond the gaining of fresh insights into the reading process by using these insights pedagogically, to help relatively unsuccessful readers to improve their reading in a foreign language. Hosenfeld's approach to the teaching of reading may be characterized as psycholinguistic, since she does not appear to teach her students language, but to provide them with *ways* of getting at meaning. The strategies that students develop as a result of her lessons do not directly involve the acquisition of linguistic knowledge — new words, or new grammatical or rhetorical structures — but are rather *ways of processing* linguistic information. The results of the two case studies convincingly demonstrate the usefulness of developing students' awareness of the strategies they currently use, and of consciously trying to get them to use new strategies. One problem that bedevils the teaching of reading, in our experience, is that students are highly resistant to having their 'habits' changed, especially if they already consider themselves to be perfectly adequate readers in their own language (as is the case with many ESP students at tertiary level, for instance). Moreover, Hosenfeld's work provides evidence for one's feeling that many learners' difficulties are caused more by an inadequate or counterproductive view of the task than by the inherent difficulty of the task itself.

In particular, the Ricky case study seems to show that Ricky's foreign language reading behaviour could be induced by the sort of instruction he has received. The explanations offered by Hosenfeld of Ricky's reading all relate to instructional effects: either he began reading too early in his language course, or at least he began by reading texts that were far too difficult for him linguistically, because they contained too many unknown words. Alternatively, he may have simply followed his teacher's advice to look up unknown words. Or the nature of what passes for reading exercises has itself led to his behaviour: the exercises, through comprehension questioning, emphasize the importance of understanding texts in detail, and they are linguistically biased, in the sense that they focus on the language — vocabulary and grammar — of the texts. Such a pedagogic practice — of focusing on the language of a text — may be justified as a language lesson, but it may very well be counterproductive as a *reading* lesson. Often what is known as 'intensive reading' (as traditionally opposed to 'extensive reading') is actually not reading at all: the lesson consists of a series of language points, using texts as points of departure. Reading texts, in other words, are sources of language exercises, rather than reading exercises. Yet students are likely to be influenced in their *reading* behaviour by this language focus in 'reading' classes. The Ricky study is a good example of how attention to reading strategies, rather than to language, can result in reading behaviour which is at least arguably better in that it resembles the behaviour of successful readers. Hosenfeld's pedagogic techniques offer some hope that students' 'habits' can indeed be changed, and with the willing consent of the student. In this respect, the Hosenfeld paper has a clear connection with the work of Harri-Augstein and Thomas, who concentrate on at times highly sophisticated techniques for consciousness-raising in native speaker readers.

There are, in fact, important resemblances between the work of Hosenfeld reported here and that of Harri-Augstein and Thomas. In particular, they share (i) a partial reliance on the readers' reports of their own behaviour, and (ii) the practice of encouraging readers, after such introspection, to compare their behaviour with that reported by or exhibited by more efficient readers. An important difference between them, on the other hand, is Hosenfeld's concentration on readers' handling of unfamiliar vocabulary.

Hosenfeld's paper is also connected with the first paper in this volume by Alderson, on the relationship between native language reading and foreign language reading.

The questions she raises towards the end of her paper on the possible transfer of reading strategies from one's first language to a foreign language are also examined in Alderson's paper. Interestingly, Ricky himself appears to be a good reader of English — we are told that he does very well in English at school, and that he is 'always reading'. Yet his foreign language reading is very slow and inefficient. One might conclude from Alderson's paper that the solution for Ricky's problems would be to teach him more language. Yet this is precisely what Hosenfeld does not do: to good effect. In this case, at least, it appears that reading strategies have not transferred, yet such transfer can be encouraged by instruction and consciousness-raising, without language instruction. (This is of course speculative since we are not told *how* Ricky reads in English.)

Hosenfeld's work is also interesting because it employs a research technique which has fallen out of favour in recent years, at least within applied linguistics, and that is the use of the reporting of thought processes as empirical evidence for analysis. Research into the process of reading is notoriously difficult because the process is invisible. Hosenfeld's think-aloud technique, and the use of introspective and retrospective reports, are limited but welcome additions to the range of research tools. And they have the advantage of being relatively simple to use, so that they are actually capable of use in classrooms, in genuine action research. There are obvious limitations to the techniques. These include the possibility that thinking aloud or consciously reflecting on the process may itself distort the process. This, however, is true of any technique known to us for research into reading processes.

Having established a protocol of the reader's thoughts, the analysis of such protocols presents formidable problems of identification and categorization of strategies, but we have suggested that this may not be unsurmountable.

Since the best reports are presumably, with most foreign language readers, gathered in the mother tongue, the researcher or teacher must either be proficient in that language or have a reliable informant who can help with the research. Yet although this practical problem is admitted, it is arguable that a language teacher should in any case ideally be proficient in his students' own language.

Although there are limitations in the methodologies that Hosenfeld employs, the methodologies are useful, and further experimentation both with the techniques and into the techniques, along the lines that Hosenfeld suggests, are to be welcomed.

Many questions are, of course, unanswered by this paper, and this sort of research. Seeing reading as problem solving ignores what happens when no problems are present. How do readers read when they are not encountering difficulties? The 'nonstop' behaviour that Hosenfeld mentions is even more difficult to investigate than the problem solving, or the 'interrupted' behaviours that Hosenfeld's paper largely refers to.

Hosenfeld describes a reading strategy as consisting of two categories of behaviour, namely what the reader does when faced with unfamiliar words, and everything else. But it should be possible to describe this latter category in more detail. What, for example, does the learner do when confronted by an unfamiliar syntactic construction, by an unfamiliar fact, by an unfamiliar juxtaposition of statements? What happens if different sorts of texts are used? Does the reading of literary texts, rather than the language-teaching texts used in this study, result in different strategies? How does the introduction of purposeful reading — as dealt with by Fransson, Royer *et al.* in this volume — affect the sorts of strategies that readers might use? If readers — typically ESP readers — are reading for factual information, do they engage different sets of strategies? Are adults more likely to use their background knowledge, and 'pragmatic strategies', than these schoolchildren? Would readers from different language backgrounds, especially those with radically different scripts, like Chinese or Japanese, reveal the same sorts of strategies? Do the strategies of successful readers vary from text to text, and purpose to purpose? And so on.

It would be unfair, of course, to expect all these questions to be tackled by a single piece of research. Nevertheless, the tasks performed by Hosenfeld's readers, while familiar enough in the language class, appear rather remote from reading behaviours in the real world and we may ask ourselves whether the tasks themselves could have produced the observed behaviour.

Despite this reservation, the area of reading strategies and the nature of the reading process is clearly a fruitful one for future research, and we believe that Hosenfeld's paper offers some guidance both in terms of research methodology, and of likely outcomes, as well as in terms of the undoubted pedagogic usefulness of such results.

13 Conversational investigations of reading: the self-organized learner and the text

Sheila Harri-Augstein and Laurie F. Thomas

Print provides a major resource for tapping vicariously a vast store of human experience. The quality and range of purposes which a person can generate together with an effective control of processing the resource will influence the richness of response to print. Our studies indicate that different purposes lead to different kinds of processing of the linear strings of the words, sentences, and paragraphs on a page. These are sampled, selected and related in order to attribute a 'structure of meaning' (Harri-Augstein 1978). Although purpose partially determines strategy and this influences outcome, these must be seen as co-existing; the process is dynamic and interactive. The self-organized learner interacts with a text by entering into a series of cycles in which purpose, strategy and outcome become progressively more precise and clearly articulated, i.e. refined, elaborated, modified, differentiated or even completely changed. Conversational investigations of reading demonstrate that an awareness of a wide range of needs and purposes that can be met through reading, together with the competence to organize and achieve these purposes, enables a reader to interact with the printed resource in ways which lead to self-development.

Early research by the authors on how students read (Augstein 1971) revealed, almost inadvertently, that increased awareness enabled learners to break free from long established habits and begin to experiment with a wider range of strategies. This resulted in greater flexibility in their use of reading as a learning skill. In the next phase of research, originally crude techniques for recording reading behaviour and for describing the structure of meaning in a text were improved and additional techniques were developed. Conversational exchanges between the experimenter (henceforth referred to as tutor) and the subjects (henceforth referred to as reader/learners) were systematically studied and subsequently developed into 'talkback' procedures. These gradually developed into a conversational methodology which recruits conversational tools and a process model of reading for investigating how people of various age groups and linguistic backgrounds learn by reading. A programme of action research spanning a ten year period carried out in schools, colleges and with adults in training departments in industry has enabled the authors to investigate how conversational methods can enable learners to explore, review and develop their reading competence.

This paper contains three related themes. It outlines a conversational approach to the study of reading as a learning skill. It then attempts to illustrate this by reference to specific talk-back procedures: in raising awareness of personal reading processes these procedures serve not only to give insights into the complex processes of reading but also function as learning opportunities for the participants. Lastly a process model of reading is briefly sketched out. This model provides the basis for negotiating the conversational exchanges described.

The conversational approach

Until recently, the widely accepted tenets of experimental methods have largely restricted the psychological investigation of reading to the short-term recall of letters, words or sentences; yet a complex text offers a rich resource for investigating more sophisticated cognitive processes. The text serves as a common reference point, but the meaning attributed to it varies from person to person. Subjects bring a uniquely personal experience to reading and this must be incorporated into the investigation process if 'reading' is to be properly understood.

The orthodox cognitive experiment uses stimuli which are 'completely known' to the experimenter. The pursuit of objectivity demands repeatability of events, prior specification of experimental conditions and the pre-selection of measures. But studies aimed at developing self-organization demand that learners have freedom to explore opportunities in their own terms. As the learner begins to exercise greater choice, so the tutor loses the capacity to insist on a pre-planned design. If the tutor does so insist, the highly structured events yield data which may trivialize the experiences of the learner. Concern with experimental control may also lead the tutor to lose personal contact with learners. This reduces the reality and relevance of the research findings. Thus an orthodox view of objectivity within the physical science paradigm and the pursuit of self-organization would appear to be incompatible. This is a brief statement of the dilemma in educational research which led the authors away from the more traditional 'before–after', statistically based experimental method towards a conversational research design.

In a conversational approach experimenter and subject share the responsibility for the observation and measurement of a continuously changing process within a 'context sensitive' framework (Thomas and Harri-Augstein 1978a). Thus, the empirical investigation becomes a cooperative effort. The conversational approach adopted in our investigations accepts the reader/learner as full participant in the descriptive and interpretative enterprise. It uses the reader/learner's unique position as observer of those internal events whereby meaning is attributed to a text, and admits the personal validity of the reader's attempts to explain such personal processes. The tutor with the technology at his or her disposal can observe and record external aspects of the reader's behaviour. Such records can then be used to help the reader to introspect and describe personal reading events. The advantage of the conversational approach lies in involving the reader in the observation and explanation. He or she is unlikely to tolerate oversimplified or highly abstract descriptions, which the tutor might otherwise formulate in his role as interpreter of experimental results within the traditional paradigm.

Systematic tools have been developed by the authors (Thomas and Harri-Augstein 1978a) to assist in such a conversational enterprise. These mediate to give validity and rigour to the unique descriptions offered by the reader. The tools enable the reader/learner to be talked back through a reading event giving evidence from the reader's own *behaviour* and *experience*. Together, the tutor and reader/learner interpret the findings revealed by the use of these tools and relate these to the original text. Part of the skill in the conversational method is to be able to talk a reader back into his or her earlier process with some evaluative commentary so that he or she is encouraged to review the meaning attributed to a text. Whilst there is obviously no objective check on the validity of the re-creation of the experiential process, there are a number of corroborative indications. Spontaneous remarks which relate to the read record, to the content of a text, the structure of the flow diagram, the description of a text and to the monitoring and decision making processes, together with the reader/learner's recognition of the earlier experience, all add up. The validity lies within the reader/learner and tutor's personal experiences of 'how it is' within the conversational process itself and not in terms of standardized pre- and post-test procedures.

In a conversational investigation of reading, any preconceptions which the tutor harbours about the 'meaning' in a text are rapidly dispersed. The reader/learner's explanations may be different. Mismatch of meaning is recognized and explored in the experimental conversation. Goodman (1974), Augstein (1971) and Marton and Säljö (1976) have demonstrated the complexity and enormous individual variation in students' response to print (reading outcomes). Any method, therefore, which evaluates meaning only by reference to a pre-established experimenter-defined version inevitably discards most of the information relevant to a more complete and significant understanding of the cognitive processes involved in its attribution. Although conversational in one sense, Piaget's studies assume that the experimenter's view is comprehensive (Piaget 1961). Pask's approach is more truly conversational but the formalism of his cybernetic method often hides the explanations from both subject and experimenter (Pask 1969). The approach advocated by the authors, based on verbal language rather than formal mathematics, is capable of infinite expansion and variety; readers are free to harness their own experiences of the process of attributing meaning into a personal model and description. The experimenter's role is to assist them to achieve this.

In essence, the conversational paradigm advocated is aimed at enabling readers to arrive at personal descriptions of their reading process, so that they can reflect upon and develop their competence.

Such descriptions include:

(1) Comments on *how* learners map meaning onto the words on a page;
(2) Terms expressing personally relevant criteria for assessing comprehension;
(3) Personally acceptable explanations of how learners invent, review and change meaning until a satisfactory outcome is achieved.

This description of the process takes place at several levels of text organization (word, phrase, sentence, paragraph, chapter). Thus mapping meaning, monitoring, reviewing, coupled with a hierarchical view of the process present a basis for the conversational approach to the study of learning by reading.

The conversational tools

Given this conversational approach to reading, a number of tools have been developed for enabling readers to explore, review and develop the ways in which they attribute meaning to texts. For instance, tools for the diagnosis of one's own reading problems and for articulating purpose hierarchies and personal taxonomies of reading purposes are often recruited early on in any conversational exchange. The whole range of tools is described elsewhere (Thomas and Harri-Augstein, 1977, 1978a, 1978b, 1978c, 1979b). This paper focuses on two tools, the *Brunel Reading Recorder* for exploring reading behaviour and the *flow diagram technique* for describing the structure of meaning in texts. These tools can be used singly or together to explore the interaction between the organization of texts and the behaviour of readers in ways which result in heightened insight into the active, conversational, meaning-attributing process of reading. Each tool is used to record and organize a specific experience and to offer personally relevant feedback arising out of the reading process. Understanding out of direct experience enables the reader/learner to experiment and change.

This is a very different approach from that where the tutor encourages the reader/learner to study research findings on reading, as reported in the literature. Such reports provoke only vicarious understanding and in our experience fail to achieve the heightened awareness of process which enables a reader/learner to achieve enhanced levels of competence.

Briefly, the basic requirements of a conversational tool are:

(1) some observational record of that aspect of reading (e.g. purpose–strategy–outcome) being investigated;

(2) a display which facilitates 'talk-back' so that a precise language for thinking about the process can be acquired;

(3) this display should include the facility to move up and down between levels in the hierarchical organization of that aspect of process being investigated (e.g. hierarchies of purposes, strategies, and outcomes);

(4) a facility for the negotiation of a description of reading behaviour and experience;

(5) a procedure for gradually weaning the learner away from depending on the tool, with an enhanced perception of the reading process.

Conversational tools have been used singly or together for 'mirroring' the reader's experience and behaviour back to him or her. This leads to heightened awareness and enables the reader/learner to reflect upon and so develop personal reading processes.

The Brunel Reading Recorder

One way of expressing what goes on during reading is that the structure of the words on the page provokes the reader into a search for stable meaning. This view of the process is commented on later in the paper. The thoughts and feelings associated with this search take *time*. Therefore the patterns of time revealed in detailed records of reading behaviour can be used conversationally to infer the sequence of feelings and thoughts that accompanied

Figure 1: The Reading Recorder

it. But how can such detailed records be obtained? A series of prototypes led to the development of the Reading Recorder.

This is a robust, easy-to-use machine which is commercially available on a limited basis. Developments in techniques for recording reading behaviour include a prototype mini-recorder which works directly on to the pages of a book, and various simple paper and pencil methods (Thomas and Harri-Augstein 1973). In its variant forms the Reading Recorder is a tool specially designed to make the behavioural process of reading explicit.

> The text is printed on continuous stationery and is viewed through a window (represented by this rectangle). The size of the window can be varied to expose one, three or five lines of text.

The movement of the continuous stationery is under the direct control of the reader. He or she turns a handle on the side of the recorder to move the text past the window. The movement of this handle is transmitted directly to the pen of a chart recorder incorporated in the machine. This produces a graphical record. Figure 2 shows a very simplified version of a record obtained on the Reading Recorder.

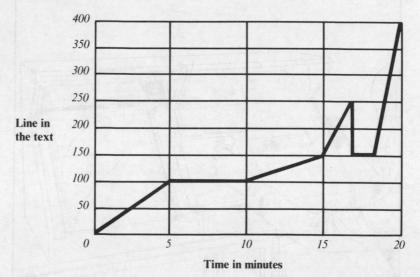

Figure 2: A Simplified Version of a Record Obtained on the Reading Recorder

This record shows the reading of a four-hundred line article in twenty minutes. We can see that the lines were *not* read at an even rate of $\frac{400}{20}$, i.e. twenty lines per minute. The first 100 lines were read in five minutes, i.e. at an average of twenty lines per minute, but then the reader spent five minutes not reading at all. Observations show that he sat thinking for three minutes and then made some notes. From the tenth minute to the fifteenth, he read more slowly from line 100 to line 150, i.e. $\frac{150 - 100}{5} = \frac{50}{5} =$ ten lines per minute. Then he speeded up and read from lines 150 to 250 in two minutes, i.e. 100 lines in two minutes at fifty lines per minute. At line 250, he stopped and then turned quickly back to line 150 and spent one minute making notes, not reading. He then scanned evenly and very quickly through from line 150 to line 400 in two minutes, i.e. at $\frac{250}{2} = 125$ lines per minute.

Reflection upon this read record is the starting point of a conversational exchange between the reader and the tutor, aimed at discovering:

1   What was in the first 100 lines that made the reader pause and think after reading them?
2   Why were lines 100 to 150 so difficult to read?
3   Why did he or she go back from line 250 to line 150?
4   Why was it then so easy to read through from line 150 to the end?

Conversational investigations may reveal that the first 100 lines were a simple introduction; the next fifty explained in detail the author's intentions; line 250 referred to an idea dealt with first in line 150; and the last 150 lines repeated the author's aims more elaborately. The tutor and reader can begin to infer quite a lot from the reader's behaviour i.e. the read record.

The read record shows how time was spent. It shows changes in pace, hesitations, skipping, backtracking, searching, and note-making. Conversational interpretations of read records have led the authors to identify five types of 'read'. These are described in detail elsewhere. (Thomas and Harri-Augstein 1972, 1974, 1976, 1978b).

These 'reads' are seldom observed in pure form, but usually any read can be classified as one of five idealized types. Actual records often contain a mix of these, but nevertheless the types serve to provide a common terminology for conversational exchange.

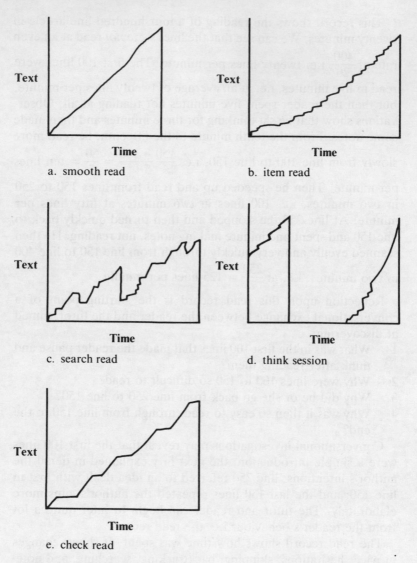

a. smooth read

b. item read

c. search read

d. think session

e. check read

Figure 3: Five Types of Read

Read (a) a fairly rapid, more or less smooth continuous read from beginning to end;

Read (b) a slow read from beginning to end with detailed hesitations and possibly notes;

Read (c) a read that shows considerable search backwards and forwards within the text;

Read (d) an activity associated with 'thinking', note consultation, drafting sessions and so on during which specific parts of the text may be consulted briefly;

Read (e) a fairly rapid read with a few hesitations at selected parts of the text.

These basic read patterns combine in various ways to produce a *reading strategy* of greater or lesser effectiveness. Conversational investigations have shown that this depends on the purpose, on the previous knowledge and skills of the reader, on the structure of the text, and on the personal criteria used by the reader for evaluating the outcome.

Read (a), the smooth read, appears to serve three functions within a given strategy.

(1) It is the only type of record produced by people whose outcomes are ineffective on a variety of tests, e.g. summarizing or multiple choice tests. One or more repeated smooth reads, which become the strategy, are in most cases ineffective on a wide range of reading purposes (see Table 1).

(2) It can be the only type of record produced by someone who is quite familiar with the content of the text and with the topic in general. Such readers score highly on a wide range of tests related to a number of different purposes. Obviously very little learning has taken place.

(3) It can form part of a more complex strategy, either as the first read, last or both. At the beginning it appears to perform an orientating or preparing function (survey). At the end it serves a checking function (review), possibly analogous to (2) above. Sometimes a few hesitations or back-trackings characterize this last read, indicating that particular attention is being given to some parts of the text. In this instance it approximates to read (e).

Read (b), the item read, shows a linear processing of the text. The 'items' may be small units of meaning such as phrases or sentences, or they may represent larger units of meaning such as groups of sentences or paragraphs. Item reads are always associated with good scores in multiple choice tests and any test demanding factual knowledge or recall at the *literal level* of a purpose taxonomy (Barrett 1968). Again, a purpose involving the *selection* of relevant data in the text can be successfully achieved with the implementation of this type of read. The more selective the purpose in terms of the content of the text, the fewer the hesitations in the read, and a really efficient reader shows hesitations only in those parts of the text relevant for his or her chosen purpose.

Read (*c*), *the search read*, can represent highly sophisticated cognitive processing of the text. It shows the kinds of relationships which the reader is constructing from various items in the text, which may be located quite far away from each other. In other words he or she reorganizes the text. 'Signposts' by the author may influence the reader to search backwards and forwards in an attempt to trace out the author's meaning. Again, 'text cues' referred to may influence the reader to search in the text as he or she attempts to attribute meaning to it. The reader's own purpose for reading is yet another factor which will influence the sampling and searching activities. Readers attempting to prepare flow diagrams for describing the structure of a text always produce search reads as part of their strategy. Sometimes the searches are unsuccessful and show that the reader has failed to draw useful relationships from the text. People who are successful in the higher order purposes in the taxonomy almost inevitably recruit this type of read as part of their strategy.

Read (*d*) is not really a 'read'. Yet conversational investigations show that people are actually 'reading in their heads', searching and checking relationships and recalling details, main ideas and so on, using some visual cue sequence of the text as an aid. Occasionally, specific items in the text are referred to.

Read (*e*), *the selective check read*, approximates to the highly selective item read described in Read (b), when the reader's purpose is that of locating specific 'bits of information' from the text. Again, the pursuit of an evaluative or summarizing purpose may result in this type of read only, if the reader is quite familiar with the content area dealt with in the text. Hesitations relate to those aspects of the text which may be new. A last read in a strategy as described in the smooth read (a) may be of this type when readers explain that they are 'checking bits of the text' against their defined purposes. A very brief résumé of three kinds of strategy, which combine these reads in different ways, serves to illustrate that different reading strategies lead to different kinds of learning outcomes. These findings have been repeated by the authors in several studies and reported in detail elsewhere (Thomas and Harri-Augstein 1972, 1976). Recently they have been replicated by another researcher in a study using our conversational techniques (Beard 1978). Strategy A is usually effective for recall at the literal level, Strategy B can be effective for summarizing purposes as well as literal recall, and strategy C is effective for summarizing, abstracting and evaluative purposes. Figure 4 illustrates these.

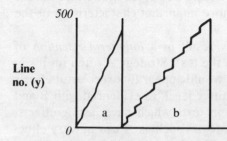

Strategy A: effective in literal recall (objective tests)

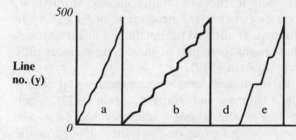

Strategy B: effective for summaries and literal recall

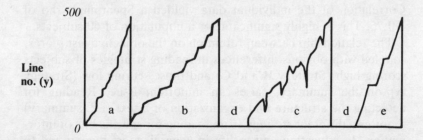

Strategy C: effective for summaries, abstracts and evaluations

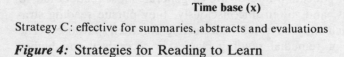

Figure 4: Strategies for Reading to Learn

Table 1 summarizes the results of one study in which 60 subjects took part. They were given an article from *Scientific American* and were asked to summarize this and to answer objective tests.

These results indicate that the longer a subject spent reading the more likely he or she was to be successful in the summary. However, inspection of the reading strategies shows that time is simply a crude indicator of more important characteristics of the reading process.

Strategies B and C usually result in a *long-term retention* of items of information found in the text. Strategy A often results in a *short-term retention* only. It would appear that successful efforts to comprehend at a high cognitive level, as evidenced with B and C, initiate acts of operation on texts which have lasting effects. Low level comprehension strategies such as A can be very effective in the short term for literal level recall but the reader fails to organize these and the information is forgotten quite quickly. This agrees with the findings of Ausubel (1967) who has shown that 'advance organizers' help learners to retain complex information. The reader has to create an organized structure to order and relate the items of information. If allowed to remain in a linear unstructured sequence, these items form part of short-term memory only (Thomas and Harri-Augstein 1972).

Table 2 shows in simplified form some experimental results which support this (Thomas and Harri-Augstein 1972). Each figure on the top line is the average summary score for 5–6 subjects. The corresponding figures on the bottom line show the *average loss* for the same subjects between objective tests given at the same time as the summary task and again one week later. These tests were designed to measure literal recall in a text. Correlation of the individual data yielded a Spearman's rho of -0.76. This is highly significant for a population of 60 subjects.

The relationship between retention on the objective test scores, coupled with obvious differences in reading strategies of subjects scoring high (Strategy B and C) and those scoring low (Strategy A) on the summary, raises an important issue. Reading for detecting the structure and organization of a text (i.e. summary) requires a different strategy from reading for specific bits of information. In education and in life in general, most readers fail to realize this, and, often unconsciously, they pursue reading strategies which may be totally ineffective for their purposes. The explosion of remedial reading classes in secondary and higher

Table 1 Distribution of Subjects into Short, Medium and Long 'Reading and Note-Making' Times for Different Levels of Effectiveness

	Reading Time			Read Types	Strategy
	Short (up to 70 mins.)	Medium (71–95 mins.)	Long (96 mins. and over)		
Effective on summary and objective tests	3	1	22	a, b, c, d, e	B, C
Effective on objective test only	10	7	3	a, b	A
Effective on neither	14	0	0	a	—

chi² = 57.4 p < 0.001.

Table 2 Amount of Information Lost After One Week Compared to Score on Summary

Score on summary	50	47	41	35	31	23	17	13	11	9	6
Loss on objective test	1·8	2·6	3·4	4·0	3·6	7·6	9·5	9·0	10·0	8·2	8·4

education substantiate the inferences we have drawn from our own research findings.

Talk-back through records of reading behaviour and flow diagrams of texts.

How much a reader can learn from going back over personal records of reading behaviour depends on an ability to interpret these. The reader is encouraged to go through each record and think himself or herself back into the frame of mind that he or she was in when the record was first produced. This is done by identifying on the record all significant events, e.g. hesitations, backtrackings, changes in pace, skipping forwards and searches. These events are related back to the particular parts of a text where they occurred. The reader is then encouraged to recall the original experience of reading and think carefully why at these points in the text a certain word, phrase, sentence, or idea led him or her to behave in a particular way.

We have found that behavioural records of reading can be effectively recruited to enable students to explore, review and develop their self-organized capacity to learn from print. When students embark on conversational investigations of their own reading they are seldom aware of the cognitive and affective processes which underlie their reading behaviour. To the extent that they remain unaware, reading remains a marionette-like mechanical activity which they have little control over. By guiding learners into contact with their own processes, they become more aware of the existing state of their skills and attitudes towards reading and so bring these under review. An awareness of a wider range of skills and attitudes opens up alternatives which hitherto were non-existent. How is this achieved?

A read record used haphazardly in a 'talk-back' conversation does not allow a participant to achieve significant states of awareness. The uninitiated learner is unable to make accurate inferences. This is always a dilemma for the tutor, who has to manage the conversational exchange. The tutor takes on a directive, guiding or facilitatory role depending on the learner's ability to generate personal feedback. As this ability develops, the tutor offers greater freedom for the reader/learner to explore the consequences of relying on personal feedback. Gradually the learner acquires the perceptual skill to interpret his or her own records. The quality of the talk-back conversation depends on this sensitivity of the tutor to the information that the learner constructs from the read record.

In interpreting the read records the learner attempts to reconstruct the original reading experience. Briefly, this is achieved as follows. The learner is talked through the read record by the tutor: ' . . . you started at line (X) and read evenly through to line (Y) where you began to slow down and read at half your original speed until line (Z). Here you stopped for 10 (30, 50) seconds. Was this of any significance? Now on line (P) you stopped and skipped back to line (E) and made a note. Why was this? How did this relate to your purpose? What kind of notes did you make? Is this your usual way of making notes? Did you get bogged down in the text here? Why was this?' and so on. An evaluative assessment leads to a review of the reader/learner's purpose, strategy and outcome.

Systematic talk-back through the read record enables the reader to identify key habits and to challenge these, so that new strategies can be tried out. We have found that learners experience anxiety as they become aware of the limits of their skill. In attempting to improve they may often start by getting worse! Old habits must disintegrate before new skills can be developed. Part of the conversational skill is to be sensitive to this and to empathize with the reader/learner. Is he re-living the reading experience, or is he simply going through the motions of reproducing the behaviour? Talking a person back into the reading-for-learning experience and encouraging reflection and review in a supportive way is an important component of the awareness-raising technique.

When a record of the reader's behaviour is combined with a procedure for recording comprehension a more rigorous reconstruction and evaluation of the process of reading becomes possible. Having created an awareness of the personal process of reading by talkback through the read record, the flow diagram technique is introduced into the conversation.

The reader/learner is shown how to prepare flow diagrams. The text is divided into 'items of meaning'. The sequence of items is preserved in the flow diagrams and each item is allocated a number according to its position in the text. The size of each item depends upon the text being analysed. If a *paragraph* is the unit for analysis, then each *sentence* (or small groups of sentences) may represent the appropriate item. In larger texts paragraphs may be the most appropriate items. Each item is classified into one of the designated categories and then assigned a relationship to other items by means of arrows. Figure 5 illustrates this. The original

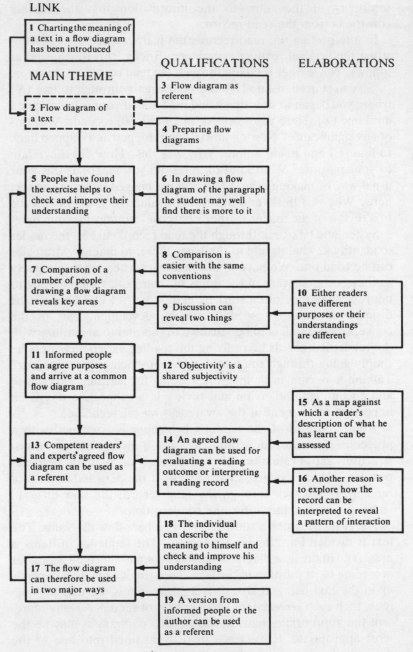

Figure 5: Flow Diagram of a Paragraph

text from which this flow diagram was prepared is presented below.

Paragraph for Analysis

1	The idea of charting the meaning of a text in the form of a flow diagram	1
2	has been introduced in a number of Reading-for-Learning Activities.	2
3	In Unit 2 you were encouraged to use the flow diagram as a referent	3
3	against which to assess your reading outcome. In Units 3 and 4 you were	4
4	asked to prepare flow diagrams of two texts. People working with the	5
5	flow diagram technique have found that the exercise of clearly describing	6
5	their own understanding of a text helps them to check and improve it.	7
6	By the time you have drawn a flow diagram of this paragraph, you may	8
6	well find there is more to it than your first cursory reading led you to	9
7	surmise. When a number of people each draw a flow diagram of the same	10
7	text, comparison reveals key areas of agreement or disagreement. Com-	11
8	parison of flow diagrams is made much easier if everybody uses the same	12
8	conventions. Discussion about areas of disagreement can reveal one of	13
9	two things: either the readers have approached the text with different	14
10	purposes or if their purposes are similar their understandings are different.	15
11	When discussion is focused in this way it is possible for informed people	16
11	to agree on purposes and arrive at a common flow diagram. The 'objec-	17
12	tivity' of such a description is no more than a shared subjectivity among	18
12	the participants. When the participants can reasonably be judged to be	19
13	both competent readers and experts in the subject matter, their agreed	20
13	flow diagram can be used as a referent against which the reading of other	21
14	people can be evaluated. An agreed flow diagram can be used as a basis	22
14	for evaluating either a reading outcome or interpreting a reading record.	23
15	As we have seen in the earlier Reading-for-Learning Activities, the agreed	24
15	flow diagram can be used as a map against which the reader's description	25
16	of what he has learnt can be assessed. Another reason for describing the	26
16	meaning structure of a text in the form of a flow diagram is to explore	27
16	how the record obtained by the observer can be interpreted in the light of	28
16	the purpose of the reader to reveal a pattern of interaction with the text	29
16	which may or may not result in the reading outcomes which he is seeking.	30
17	The flow diagram can therefore be used in two major ways. The individ-	31
18	ual reader can describe the meaning of the text to himself and by exter-	32
18	nalizing this structure of meaning, he can check and improve his	33
19	understanding. When informed people or even the author can provide	34
19	their version, it can be used as a referent against which other readers'	35
19	understandings can be reviewed.	36

1–19: Items of meaning   1–36: Lines in text

The flow diagram technique was developed to exhibit in structural form the non-linearity of the meanings which readers attribute to a text (Thomas and Harri-Augstein 1973). The technique can be used to analyse a sentence, a whole book or any size unit of meaning in between. Whilst words, phrases and sentences in a text are organized in a *linear sequence*, a reader seeks cues in a text and creates relationships which form part of a complex pattern of meaning. This pattern of meaning can be displayed as a flow of related items in a text. The example illustrated in Figure 5 shows how one student divided a paragraph into 19 items. These were then classified into one of the four categories shown and related to each other within a pattern of meaning. The statements in each box are abbreviations of the sentences in the text.

In its basic form the technique contains four categories for describing the structure of a text:

(1) text links, i.e. connections to other sections of text;
(2) main theme, i.e. the major ideas expounded by the author;
(3) qualifications, i.e. statements which add to the main ideas but are of a lower order of importance such as definitions, justifications, explanations and so on;
(4) elaborations, i.e. reference to details such as dates, numbers, quantities, examples and so on.

These display a structure of meaning particularly suited to a *general description* of a text. A *summary* of the text is described in the meaning flow within the *main theme* column. Other sets of categories more appropriate for a particular range of texts and for more specific reading purposes have also been developed. For instance, *symbolism, metaphor, alliteration, imagery*, and *rhythm* for a critical analysis of poetry, and *character descriptions, plot, style, dramatic episodes* and *physical context* for describing sequences of text in novels.

Having mastered the technique, the reader is encouraged by the tutor to prepare a flow diagram either during or immediately after reading a chosen text. If the text has been read on the Reading Recorder, and the reader has constructed a flow diagram, the tutor can map the flow diagram on to the read record as shown in Figure 6.

This combination of the read record and the reader's own personally relevant flow diagram of a text can be recruited by the tutor into the conversation. The reader thus becomes explicitly aware of the ways in which meaning is attributed as he or she hesitates, slows down, or skips forward or backwards through a text. The tutor and reader can use this 'mirror' of process to reflect upon how the read record and flow diagram relate to each other, to the original linear text and to the purpose(s) for reading. The tutor can also prepare a flow diagram of the same text and as the

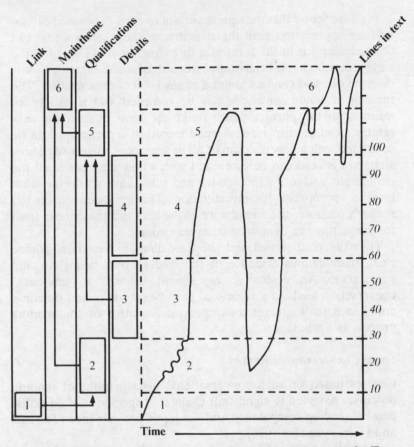

Figure 6: Mapping a Read Record onto a Flow Diagram of a Text

conversation develops this can be introduced for comparison with the reader's own. Almost inevitably, the tutor's flow diagram will be different. Part of the conversational exchange deals with any significant differences, so that some sharing of the meaning attributing process is achieved. However, the onus must remain with the reader/learner to decide which of the two most usefully describes the meaning in the text. The process of comprehending the meaning in a text is essentially subjective. To extend an individual's understanding we have found it extremely useful not only to offer a tutor's flow diagram as one external referent in the conversation but also to encourage students working in small groups to exchange each other's flow diagrams.

We have found that the significance of reading behaviour cannot be fully appreciated until the structure of meaning in a text can be made explicit in the form of a flow diagram and shared in the ways described. A behavioural record of reading and a flow diagram of a text can be obtained at any level of organization. The reading of single sentences can be recorded and a pattern of meaning of the phrases which make up items of meaning in a sentence can be displayed. A read record of a paragraph can be combined with a flow diagram of all its sentences. A record of how a chapter is read can be combined with a flow diagram of all the paragraphs within it. The reader and tutor have to decide what level is appropriate for investigation. This may depend on the reader's purpose, the complexity of the text and the criteria used for evaluating the quality of comprehension.

Thus the read record and the flow diagram together provide clear unambiguous evidence of the reader's own behaviour and experience. An evaluative assessment through a 'talk-back' conversation leads to a review of purpose, strategy and outcome and hence to a greater awareness and control of the reading process as a whole.

Some Conversational Results

Courses based on such conversational investigations of reading processes have led to significant changes in specific reading skills, general reading competence and academic performance (Thomas and Harri-Augstein 1976).

A questionnaire of 59 items designed to diagnose the habits and attitudes towards reading was administered immediately before and shortly after the reading courses. Students were asked to respond to each question on a five-point scale. A computer program for McQuitty hierarchical cluster analysis (Thomas 1969) was used to analyse the questionnaire results. Nine distinct clusters emerged. Significant trends were noted as shown in Table 3. For example, six questions clustered along a dimension of:

| I plan my reading | ←————————→ | I seldom plan my reading |

Comparison of responses *before* and *after* the course shows a highly significant change *towards planning* ($p < \cdot001$). After the course students question more what they read, plan their reading more rigorously, search for organization in texts, make fewer notes, and find reading for learning more enjoyable.

Table 3 Change in Student Responses to a Questionnaire

No. of Q's	Sub-scale +	Direction of change and significance level	Sub-scale −
7	I find words and sentences easy to read	NS 0	I often stumble over unusual words and long sentences
9	I read for main ideas	NS ←	I read to remember facts
5	I question what I read	·01 ←	I accept what I read
6	I read fast	NS 0	I read too slowly
9	I am flexible in using various methods of reading for learning	NS 0·1 ←	I always read in the same way
6	I plan my reading	·001 ←	I seldom plan my reading
5	I search for organization in a text	·01 ←	I take a text as it comes
6	I like reading for learning	·001 ←	I dislike reading for learning
6	I take few notes	·01 ←	I take many notes

KEY: NS = Not significant
·01 = Significance level

An inventory of records of reading behaviour shows that students have become more flexible and use a broader range of 'reads'. Again there is a clear positive correlation between reading performance and academic performance. Figure 7 illustrates that after one course there is a significant improvement in reading performance which correlates with improved academic grades.

Students' subjective reports emphasized that they valued the talk-back procedures, and that a greater awareness of purpose and strategy, coupled with mastery of the flow diagram technique to aid comprehension, had contributed to the success of the course. Comments from teaching staff almost invariably included the following: students who participated in reading-to-learn courses

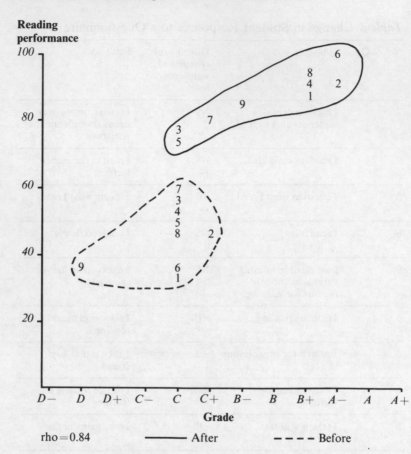

Figure 7: The Relationship Between Improvement in Reading Performance on the Course and Academic Grade

were more active in seminars and tutorials and the quality of their *written* work had improved. They seemed to be better able to work on their own, to plan schedules of work and implement these fully. Some members of staff in colleges where such courses had been run, themselves enrolled on subsequent courses.

A capacity for process model of reading

Conversational research into personal reading processes using the tools and procedures briefly described in this paper as well as several others not here described, have enabled us to clarify certain issues about a model of the reading process. To be useful the model needs to describe:

1. The complexity and variety of structure in the reader's purposes, strategies and outcomes;
2. The hierarchical nature of purpose, strategy and outcome;
3. The uniquely personal relationship which can exist between these within an individual's system of attributing meaning to a text;
4. The mechanism by which the system is (or is not) brought under review;
5. The active and interactive aspects of the ongoing relationship between the reader and the text.

Reading is an active generative process whereby meaning is attributed to the words on the page (Goodman 1967 and 1974). This process represents the core of the eyeball-to-print interaction. The sophisticated reader samples, searches, selects and relates the items of meaning in a text, in ways which make sense to him or her depending on self-defined purposes. This process continues more or less intuitively depending on the degree of conscious control exercised. Our studies show that the more the reader can bring the process under review the greater the probability that he or she can recruit an optimal strategy for effective interaction.

Figure 8 illustrates that as a person reads, he or she is predicting meanings that will be symbolized by the words on the page. The reader's eyes scan the words to discover whether they are compatible with the meaning he or she expects. When they are, closure is achieved and the meaning generating, comparing, scanning process proceeds. When comparison reveals mismatch between expected meaning and what is being read, the process of attributing meaning to the text falters. If the reader has a strategy, the hesitations or searching lead to revised meaning. If not, meaning is no longer attributed to the text.

The difficulty may be caused by failure to attribute meaning to a particular word, phrase or sentence. The reader has to search within the text to locate 'cues' which will aid comprehension. Again mismatch may be caused by an inappropriate purpose or ill-defined criteria for checking reading outcome. It is when such difficulties arise that an awareness of the process becomes essential for diagnosing failure to comprehend.

The process is essentially similar at all levels of organization. Figure 8 illustrates how the process is conceived as a series of meaning-achieving cycles. The content of a cycle can be words, phrases, sentences or paragraphs. At each level the expected meaning is generated out of the series of revised meanings achieved on the level below, i.e. the sequence of meanings attributed to words may generate a 'sentence-sized' expected meaning. The sequence of meanings attributed to sentences may generate a 'paragraph-sized' expected meaning, and the sequence of meaning attributed to paragraphs may combine into meaning attributed to the whole article, chapter or book. Search and comparison at a lower level may lead to match at a higher level. Match leads to closure, so that the meaning generated becomes incorporated into the long term store to form part of the individual's 'personal knowing'. The alternative 'structures of meaning' which a reader can generate from a finite set of words is practically infinite. This is perhaps best illustrated by reference to reading poetry. In the short term, meaning depends on the immediate specific purpose and that part of the text being processed. In the longer term it relates to a complex set of purposes and to the text as a whole. Thus purpose forms the basis against which comparisons are made and match is achieved.

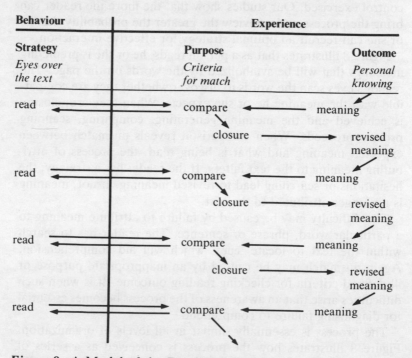

Figure 8: A Model of the Reading Process

This process model of reading, here briefly described, offers a starting point for each 'conversation'. The 'tools' are gradually introduced as tutor and students decide to experiment with particular aspects of the model. Each tool enables the participants to exhibit their reading experience. The tools we have concentrated on in this paper (the read record and the flow diagram technique) exhibit reading behaviour and how this relates to the reader's own comprehension. As mentioned in the introduction, other tools have been developed to exhibit reading purposes, reading outcomes and reading problems.

These tools are recruited into the conversation to elaborate a personal model and to negotiate a personal system of operational metalanguage. This is what an awareness of process through conversational exchange actually accomplishes. Thus, the conversation becomes a vehicle for constructive development of a new language in which to think about the learning process and this enables the learner to experiment with change.

The focus of the conversation is reflection and review of process. The tutor's function can be described as 'mirroring' the process to the learner. Mirroring leads to heightened awareness and this enables the learner to explore a personal language in which to think about and experiment with reading so that he or she moves towards greater competence. The authors have systematically analysed conversational transactions and developed 'a science of learning conversations'. Different levels of discourse can be identified and within each level it has been found useful to identify a number of interwoven dialogues. It is beyond the scope of this paper to discuss this in greater detail but the concept of 'learning conversations' is described in a number of publications (Thomas and Harri-Augstein 1976, 1977, 1978d, 1979b).

The self-organized learner

During a 'learning conversation' the tutor acts as articulator and manager of the conversation as the learner explores the resource. Gradually, the learner internalizes the conversation and develops a capacity to articulate this. In reading, the self-organized learner is able to identify and define personal needs; translate these into purposes; develop these into a wide-ranging repertoire of ever expanding purposes; recruit effective strategies; interact with the text by generating alternative purposes and strategies depending on its structure and organization; treat texts that challenge and frustrate differently to those that fit easily into existing understanding; and assess the quality of learning outcomes within the context of the whole process. The self-organized learner acquires the ability to be flexibly aware of the process of learning. He or she can relax into the non-conscious or intuitive use of reading skills without losing the ability to bring these back into conscious review. Finally, he or she can identify the dimensions of personal problems, intellectual, attitudinal or skill, so that appropriate assistance can be sought. In so doing, a learning network made up of books, tutors, peers, experts and a whole range of other resources is created (Thomas and Harri-Augstein 1978d and 1979a).

Implications for education

Conversational methodology offers a productive alternative to more content-specific programmes for promoting the development of reading as a learning skill. The tools used to raise awareness of process, already effective, are being refined, developed and supplemented as more operational experience is gathered. Complex models of language usage such as information theory, phrase structure, deep structure, or even cybernetic/logic systems, have not in our experience proved useful to help people to reflect upon and develop their reading. Pragmatic approaches, typical of various study skill courses, are too prescriptive to serve as vehicles for developing personally meaningful experience (Robinson 1961 and Merritt 1969). A process model such as that offered in this paper, being capable of infinite expansion and variety, appears to us best to serve the conversational method. Students are free to harness their own mythologies of the process of reading into expanding personal models and metalanguages. These provide them with sufficient insight to achieve individually valued changes in learning capacity. Models and their metalanguages are thus valued within a conversational theory as conceptual tools for effecting change and maintaining flexibility.

In offering 'language experience' and 'experience exchange' in our educational institutions, three basic questions need to be faced: what variety of language, type of experience, and form of exchange? In the authors' view, meeting this challenge depends on elevating the quality of tutoring transactions so that learners of any age group are enabled to attain a *metaview* of what learning is about.

Postscript on Harri-Augstein and Thomas

This paper brings together into a coherent research programme a number of themes dealt with individually by other writers in the book. Because of this, the following discussion is limited to comments on what are considered to be the major of these themes.

1. *Text Description*

This is handled in the Harri-Augstein and Thomas scheme by the flow diagram technique, which is in essence a method of analysing texts into main units, and various kinds of subordinate units, marking the relationships between them, and to some extent relating the units to the linear ordering of the text. Considered as a form of discourse analysis, the apparatus is very simple; compare it with, for example, the complexities of Meyer's analysis (Meyer 1975). The technique is more fairly viewed, however, as an attempt to provide *readers* with a metalanguage with which to discuss their separate interpretations of texts. As such, its simplicity is obviously a major advantage. Moreover, the simplicity means that the technique is very flexible in that, as Harri-Augstein and Thomas point out (p. 268), new categories can easily be substituted to cope with new situations. The validity of the analysis must be measured in terms of the success it achieves in enabling useful conversations about a text to take place. A simple, commonly accepted set of terms, i.e. a metalanguage, is clearly needed in the reading class in general in order to allow discussion of text structure (cf. Widdowson and Urquhart 1976).

2. *Reading Behaviour and Outcomes*

External aspects of reading behaviour are measured by the Reading Recorder. Investigations of this sort are reminiscent of early studies of eye movements, but the results of the method are much more strategic, giving information on the time spent on large sections of text. When classified, and correlated with reader's performance on different kinds of test (pp. 259–263), the reading records provide very interesting empirical data on efficient and inefficient reading behaviour. The data lend support to existing pedagogical advice; for example, they show that repeated re-reading of a text in the same way does not ensure success at every comprehension task. Types (c) and (d) seem to be similar to the pattern recommended in the so-called sqr3 technique (skim, question, read, review, revise). In addition, the reading patterns and their outcomes seem to be relatable in an interesting way to some of Fransson's findings. One might hypothesize, for example, that reads (c) and (d) would be likely to result in conclusion-content recall, and it would be interesting to have confirmation of this.

3. *Reader/Text Interaction*
    When the record of an individual read is put together with the reader's analysis of the text in terms of a flow chart, we get a description of reader/text interaction of a particularly explicit form. A focus on such interaction, in both theoretical and practical studies, is often accompanied by an acceptance of the view that different readers will interpret the same text differently. Harri-Augstein and Thomas were among the first researchers to attack the possibility of what might be called the 'received total meaning' view of text, that is, that a text has an overall meaning which will be arrived at by all right-thinking readers (cf. Thomas 1968). In other work, Harri-Augstein and Thomas have made use of the valuable concept of 'shared common meaning', to refer to the consensus of meaning attributed to a text by a group with similar knowledge of the content area. This common meaning can then be compared with the interpretation of readers with a different level of knowledge, e.g. experts in the content area. The implications of this for teaching and especially the testing of reading comprehension in a foreign language are self-evident and enormous.

4. *Conversational Techniques*
    Investigation of interaction is deepened and made more precise by the use of conversational techniques of investigating readers' interpretations of texts, i.e. of systematically examining readers' introspections into the reading process. A completed flow diagram is a *product* analysis; a comparison of the diagram, the reading record, and readers' introspections is an attempt at a *process* analysis.
    The conversational approach is also used by Hosenfeld, and, to a lesser extent, by Fransson and by Berman. Harri-Augstein and Thomas go further than the others in attempting explicitly to substitute conversational approaches for orthodox experiments (p. 252). It is true that the orthodox

experiment, by sticking to examination of experimenter-defined variables, can miss much valuable information which, so to speak, is there for the asking. Moreover, as Fransson's experiment illustrates, prior assumptions made by the experimenter, and then built into the design of the experiment, can seriously distort the results. Nevertheless, we still believe that experiments can play a useful part in reading research, providing a measure of objectivity and generality to results, which it seems likely the conversational method cannot match. There is nothing to prevent one from combining the methods, e.g. by using conversational investigation to arrive at a hypothesis, which can then be tested by an experiment.

5. *Control*

As we suggest in our postscript to the paper by Royer *et al.*, it seems possible to draw a rough distinction between those who believe in experimenter/teacher control, both of directing activities and defining success, and those who see the experimental subject, or the student, as being ultimately self-directed, with the experimenter as observer, or the teacher as guide and advisor. Clearly, Harri-Augstein and Thomas belong to the second category, considering the tutor's task as being one of helping the reader become more aware of his own processes, and by means of this increased awareness, develop his abilities. In part, at least, this view is the cause of their rejection of the orthodox experiment. It should be noted that their criticism of the experimental technique, using as it does 'pre-established experimenter-defined' versions of meaning (p. 253), is at least partially applicable also to the situation in the conventional reading class, in which not only questions, i.e. what information is judged worth extracting from a text, but also answers are equally 'pre-established' and defined by either teacher or materials writer. If we accept Harri-Augstein and Thomas's contention that, in reading, the learning process consists of the learner becoming more conscious of his own activities, and with guidance, developing his own strategies and defining his own purposes, then the implication is that we need radical changes in classroom approaches.

6. *Final Outcome*

That the aim of developing readers' self-awareness is not just idealistic is shown by the table on p. 271 and Figure 7. After the course, students reported themselves more aware of main ideas and organization, and felt themselves to be more flexible and more critical than before. The results reported in Figure 7, if generalizable, are even more impressive. After all, in the teaching of reading for learning, improved academic performance by students is the ultimate criterion of success.

14 Exploring the reading difficulties of second-language learners in Fiji

Warwick B. Elley

Fiji is an independent multilingual country within the British Commonwealth. It is made up of 600,000 people, nearly 50% of whom are Hindi-speaking Indians. Another 44% are indigenous Fijians who speak Fijian as their native tongue. In addition there are small communities of Chinese, Rotuman, Europeans, and other Pacific Island groups, each with their own vernacular and cultural traditions.

The children of this diverse community, however, are all exposed to a common education system which has English as the medium of instruction after the first 3 or 4 years of elementary school. Fiji thus provides the applied linguist with an interesting cross-cultural laboratory for studying acquisition and development phenomena in second-language learning. Regrettably, this opportunity has not been exploited to date, and few educational policies in language learning or language planning are informed or supported with empirical data (see Moag and Moag 1977). There is, however, considerable concern expressed in the community about the quality of English teaching in the schools, and the evidence cited below suggests the need for a rethinking of current approaches.

At present the universal method of teaching English throughout the South Pacific is an audio-lingual programme, based on principles popularized by Fries and Bloomfield in the 1950s. Known as the Tate Oral English Program, it was prepared almost single-handed by an experienced teacher, Gloria Tate, in the early 1960s and has been followed religiously by education departments and teachers throughout all South Pacific island nations for over a decade, without investigation or evaluation. One of the distinguishing features of the Tate Program, relevant to this article, is the extraordinarily minor role assigned to reading in language learning. It is argued below that this neglect could well be a dominant factor in explaining the language problems of children in Fiji.

In this article I propose to outline some of the ways in which the reading difficulties of children in Fiji have been studied and to reveal some disconcerting findings about the extent of these difficulties.

I will examine the validity of the techniques used in exploring the children's language problems and conclude by pointing briefly to the likely causes and possible remedies for the state of affairs described.

Surveys of reading in Fiji

In recent years there have been several large-scale surveys of the English reading competence of Fijian pupils. The procedures and main findings of these investigations are summarized below.

1. *Nationwide Reading Survey in Grade 6*

   In 1977 a research committee of the Suva Institute for Educational Research undertook a nationwide survey of reading in Grade 6 in order to determine levels of performance in various sub-sections of the population. The committee developed a standardized reading comprehension test of 36 multiple choice items, based on simple prose passages written around local themes. After suitable trials and revisions, the test was administered to a sample of 1,234 Grade 6 pupils in 54 randomly selected schools during November 1977 (Elley and Mangubhai 1979). While the performance of many Suva city pupils was found to be most creditable, it was found that more than 25% of pupils, mostly in rural areas, scored sufficiently low to indicate that they were virtually non-readers of simple English prose. This finding was a disturbing one, as the test passages were rated for readability at a level lower than that of the textbooks used by the same pupils in Grade 6. Moreover, this result was obtained after the pupils had had six years of exposure to English, and at least three years of instruction in English as the medium.

2. *Cloze Test Survey in Grade 7*

   In order to clarify the disturbing findings of the Grade 6 survey, the writer selected four typical passages from the early pages of currently used Grade 7 textbooks in English and Social Science, and administered them as cloze tests to an above-average group of 98 pupils (from 4 schools) who had been tested in the 1977 survey in Grade 6, and who were then in Grade 7. The method used was similar to the conventional cloze procedure. Four typical passages of 150 words were chosen and every seventh word was deleted after the first line. Each pupil completed two passages. Two methods of scoring were used, the 'exact replacement' and the 'contextually acceptable' method, but the results were virtually identical in rank order (rho = 0·99). As predicted the correlation with the results of the multiple choice test used in the Grade 6 survey was high (rho = 0·79). However, the mean score of this group of pupils was very low. The 'exact replacement' scoring scheme produced a mean score for this above-average group of 13·81 out of 40 or 34·5%. The estimated mean cloze score for a more representative sample would therefore be less than 30%. This percentage is well below the levels recommended by American researchers for comprehension at the instructional level (see Bormuth 1968).

From this small survey it becomes clear that if these textbooks are intended to be a resource for learning, they will be quite unsuitable for large numbers of Grade 7 pupils. As more than one quarter of Fijian pupils are unable to read simple English with understanding at the end of Grade 6, this result should not be surprising. Nevertheless it is cause for concern.

3. *National Grade 6 Norming Project, 1979*

Another survey which threw further light on the scope of the reading problem was the national test norming project conducted in 1979 by the Fijian Ministry of Education. A new set of twelve locally produced standardized tests in English reading comprehension, listening comprehension, and vocabulary, was administered along with tests in other subjects to 1,400 Grade 6 children in 50 representative schools. The tests were prepared by local teachers, and all used multiple choice format. This norming exercise formed part of a Grade 6 test development project in which the writer was involved as consultant.

Once again the reading scores were lower than expected outside the main urban area of Suva, and the national distribution of reading scores revealed a large bulge around the tail. By contrast, all other tests showed the expected normal curve distribution, with very few pupils concentrated at the 'chance score' mark. The reading results of this project confirmed the disturbing findings obtained in 1977 on a different test. At Grade 6 level more than one child in four was unable to read simple English prose with comprehension.

4. *High School Cloze Study*
High school investigations show that the problem continues well beyond elementary schools. A study by Stamp (1979), using cloze tests drawn from students' textbooks in Grade 8 and 9 Science, Social Science and Industrial Arts, produced results even more disconcerting than those quoted above. The mean cloze scores obtained from large groups of typical Fijian students were all between 20% and 26%, well below the 'frustration level', as defined by Betts (1946).

5. *Cross-Cultural Comparison*
Finally, to introduce a cross-cultural comparison into the picture, another survey was conducted by the writer on a smaller sample of 75 pupils in Grade 7. These children were also part of the same sample tested in the first Grade 6 survey reported in (1) above, and were slightly above the national average in reading test scores. They were given the Progressive Achievement Test of Reading Comprehension, which was developed and normed in New Zealand (Elley and Reid 1969). Judging by the New Zealand norms, it was concluded that the Fijian sample was reading at a level approximately two and half years below their New Zealand counterparts.

Some would claim that such results should give no cause for alarm. The Fijian pupils are learning in their second language, and comparisons with New Zealand pupils are unhelpful.

However, it should be noted that Fijian pupils are regularly exposed to textbooks which are comparable in reading difficulty to those used in New Zealand. Moreover, all Fijian pupils are expected to study New Zealand curricula and to take New Zealand external examinations in the high school. No systematic allowance is made for their language difficulties in these contexts. In relation to their initial baseline, the pupils' reading growth may seem creditable; in relation to what is expected, it is disturbingly inadequate.

6. *Surveys of University Students*
Further studies have been made of Fijian students at the

Foundation Level (first year) at the University of the South Pacific. All such students were tested in two successive years with the Progressive Achievement Tests (PAT) of reading, vocabulary and listening comprehension. Whereas 97% of New Zealand first-year university students scored in the top two levels (9 or 10) on the criterion-referenced PAT Reading Comprehension Test (Cleveland 1970), only 53% of the South Pacific students reached this level in 1978 (Elley and Thompson 1978), and 42% in 1979. Yet most of the texts and reading materials for Foundation courses require a comprehension ability of at least Level 9.

The results of the other two English tests were regrettably no better. According to the PAT vocabulary test, the average Foundation Year student at the University of the South Pacific knows the meanings of about 7,500 common English words. Amongst those words known by less than two-thirds of students were 'frequent', 'anxiously', 'explanation', 'diligent', 'radical'. These Pacific Islands students have an English reading vocabulary comparable to that of New Zealand thirteen year-olds on the same tests. The results for the listening comprehension tests were even lower.

Subsequent studies of first and third year students by the writer revealed cloze test scores, based on typical selections from their prescribed textbooks, well below the levels of apparent intelligibility. Furthermore, a survey of student opinion showed that 45% of Foundation students regarded their English reading skills as below adequate (O'Sullivan 1978). 80% admitted they 'often' have difficulty understanding their textbooks. Before 1977, virtually no evidence existed on the English reading skills of Fijian students. On the basis of the eight different surveys summarized above, we are surely justified in concluding that the present policy is seriously inadequate. After six years of primary school instruction, large numbers of pupils are reading with insufficient competence to cope with the expected reading tasks of the classroom. Throughout high school the problem becomes more serious, despite a severe dropout rate and a series of selective examinations. By the time they reach university, the surviving students are still struggling with what must be largely meaningless English prose in their texts and reading assignments. By their own admission, many students are out of their depth in coping with English as a second language. In this writer's view it takes indomitable persistence on the part of these L2 students to succeed against such daunting odds.

How valid are these measures with second-language learners?

While other evidence could be cited to support these disquieting findings, it is important to examine more closely the kinds of procedures used to produce them. The tests used were predominantly multiple choice and cloze tests of English prose. Are they appropriate for the L2 users of Fiji?

Multiple choice tests are in fact used widely in elementary school tests and national examinations in Fiji. Because pupils have to face four or five of these examinations in English, between Grade 6 (12–13 years) and Form 6 (18–19 years), teachers in Fiji frequently encourage their pupils to take multiple choice tests for practice. In the Grade 6 national norming survey conducted in February 1979, by the Ministry of Education, pupils had little difficulty in responding to multiple choice questions in the twelve tests which were standardized at that time. Indeed, the high results gained on some items in Mathematics and Social Studies (over 80% correct) indicates that they are able to handle such questions satisfactorily. Furthermore, the writer has recently used multiple choice tests without problem in tests of Fijian and Hindi language at Grade 4 level in Fijian schools.

The particular multiple choice tests used in most of these surveys were designed and trial tested on representative samples of Fijian children before national figures were obtained. Content validity was high, as the tests were deliberately designed to fit local circumstances. In the case of the Progressive Achievement Tests, which were trialled and normed in New Zealand, an inspection of their contents shows very little evidence of cultural bias. For instance, the words of the vocabulary test are sampled from the most common 10,000 words in English (Wright 1961). In the reading comprehension test only three of the eighteen passages have a New Zealand context, and in these the setting is only incidental to the main theme. The remainder of the passages would be appropriate in most English-speaking countries.

The question of the validity of cloze tests with second-language learners is more debatable. Numerous studies reported by Oller (1973) have shown high correlations with conventional reading tests. The cloze method does appear to be a valid measure of reading comprehension with FL students. However, it is another matter to use the procedure as an indicator of readability, using the criterion cut-off points established by American researchers. Indeed, the high rate of meaningless responses found in the Grade

7 study in four schools, as reported in 2 above, raised the question of whether the cloze technique might operate in a different way for L2 learners. It is conceivable, for instance, that the discrepancy between their receptive and expressive skills in English is greater than for L1 users, making it possible for L2 users to comprehend more than the evidence of their expressed responses would suggest. If this were the case, and some of the writer's colleagues claimed that it was, it would be important to clarify the position before curriculum revisions and policy decisions were made in Fiji and elsewhere, on the basis of cloze test findings on textbooks and other reading materials for L2 learners.

Comparison of cloze and multiple choice tests in ESL

In order to explore this problem of the validity of the cloze criterion scores, when estimating the readability level of English prose with L2 learners, a cross-cultural study was made of the reading ability of L1 and L2 learners in Fijian schools.

The basic research on suitable criterion levels for first-language learners was undertaken by Bormuth (1968) in the USA. He found that a score of 75% on typical multiple choice and completion style reading comprehension tests was equivalent to a score of 44% on a cloze test of the same reading passages. He found further that a multiple choice test score of 90% was equivalent to a cloze score of 57%. Follow-up studies of these figures by others have shown remarkable consistency with L1 learners (Rankin and Culhane 1969; Peterson *et al.* 1973). As a result of these and other studies, Bormuth concludes that criterion levels between 45% and 55% on a cloze test are close to the optimum for L1 students in an instructional context (Bormuth 1971).

Regardless of the finality of these figures, it is of considerable importance to determine whether these criterion levels, now widely accepted in several English-speaking contexts, are equally applicable for L2 users in Fiji. A Papua New Guinea study by Anderson and Hunt (1972) gave promising results with upper primary schools pupils. However, contrary findings by Baldauf and Propst (1978) in American Samoa suggested that cloze tests were unsuitable because many of the Samoan students 'lacked the English production skills, as contrasted with the recognition skills, necessary to complete the conventional cloze tests'.

To throw more light on the relationship between cloze and multiple choice performance levels in L2 users, samples of 74

Fijian and Indian pupils in Grades 5 and 6 in two typical Suva schools were administered cloze and multiple choice forms of the same passages in the Fiji Reading Comprehension test. The tests were given one week apart, and the cloze test was administered first. The results were compared with those obtained from 98 English-speaking Europeans of similar reading ability, but younger age. The European children were mostly New Zealand, Australian and British, and were drawn from two schools of predominantly European pupils in Suva and one on the island of Niue. The Fijian and Indian children learned English as their second language, through the audio-lingual Tate syllabus. They were in their second or third year of reading in English. All of the European pupils had English as their first language, and all were in Grades 3, 4 or 5 at the time of the investigation.

As expected, the correlations between the two reading tests were high; 0·81 for the Fijians, 0·83 for the Indians and 0·84 for the Europeans. In this respect the two tests were performing in almost identical ways in all three language groups. Furthermore the slope and intercepts of the regression lines for this relationship were very similar in each group. Such statistics were calculated in order to estimate more precisely the equivalent cloze test scores of 75% and 90% correct on the multiple choice tests. Table 1 shows the means, standard deviations and correlations for all three groups.

Table 1 Summary statistics of cloze and multiple choice tests for three language groups

	Cloze			Multiple choice		
	N	Mean	S.D.	Mean	S.D.	Correlation (Cloze and Multiple choice)
Fijians	38	21·24	7·98	20·29	5·81	0·81
Indians	30	18·50	8·47	18·67	6·81	0·83
Europeans	95	32·20	9·79	24·78	5·92	0·84

It is apparent that the European group, although younger, still performed at a higher level on both tests. However, the overlap was considerable, and the distributions sufficiently similar in all three ethnic groups to make possible an estimate of comparable regression lines and consequently of the equivalent cloze test scores for the conventional criteria of 90% and 75% correct on the multiple choice test. These figures were calculated using the appropriate regression equation for each ethnic group, and the results presented in Table 2, along with those of earlier researchers, in the USA and Papua New Guinea.

Table 2 Comparison of cloze and multiple choice criterion levels

	75% on Multiple choice	90% on Multiple choice
Fijians	44%	56%
Fiji Indians	42%	53%
Fiji Europeans	48%	63%
Bormuth (1968) USA	44%	57%
Rankin and Culhane (1969) USA	41%	61%
Peterson *et al.* (1973) USA	42%	–
Anderson and Hunt (1972) PNG	44%	53%

The table indicates a remarkable consistency from one investigation to the next, particularly for the 75% multiple choice criterion, the operative one for the judgements made in this article. This consistency was found, regardless of grade level (which varied from Grade 4 to Grade 12), or country of testing, and regardless of whether the students had English as their first or second language. If we can generalize from these findings, it is apparent that the cloze criterion scores for estimating appropriate readability levels in first-language situations are equally helpful in the second language. The hypothesis that prompted this investigation was that cloze test scores are unsuitable in assessing readability for L2 learners because of a discrepancy between students' active and passive vocabularies. (See Baldauf and Propst 1978). Such a hypothesis finds little support in this study.

Analysis of cloze errors

The somewhat unexpected findings presented in Table 2 prompted further analysis of the kinds of cloze errors made by the three language groups. It is conceivable that the consistency in the total scores concealed a fortuitous combination of compensating errors in the tests. Therefore a breakdown was made of the errors made by each ethnic group, firstly to check on this hypothesis, and secondly to determine how useful the cloze procedure might be as a diagnostic tool in error analysis in multi-lingual classrooms.

As a first step a frequency count was made of all errors on each of the 35 deletions in the first three passages for each language group. The highest-scoring European pupils were omitted in order to make them comparable to the other groups in the total number of errors occurring.

Table 3 lists the first ten deleted words and the number of errors made by the three groups on each word.

Examination of the table shows a remarkable similarity amongst the three columns, a similarity which continued throughout the passages tested. Clearly the same words presented difficulties for first and second-language users alike.

Table 3 Cloze error frequencies by language group

Deleted word	Fijian	Indian	European
the	0	1	1
at	11	10	11
water	2	4	3
ground	10	6	12
enough	4	5	4
stones	9	9	9
them	11	9	12
and	9	14	10
when	13	12	18
the	8	3	10

A follow-up study was undertaken subsequently in order to determine whether the observed similarity amongst the three groups extended to the actual insertions made by the pupils in each case of error. Thus each error in the first three passages was recorded for the complete sample of Fijian and Indian pupils, and for a matched group of Europeans. This analysis showed that many of the same incorrect words were in fact chosen in similar proportions by all three language groups. For instance, in one passage the pupils were required to insert the word 'not' in the blank — 'but he was *not* afraid'. Of the 36 errors made, 'very' was chosen by 3 pupils from each language group, 'so' by 7, 5 and 3 pupils, and 'too' by 2, 3 and 5 pupils. In the phrase 'Every *Saturday* for weeks now . . .' the word 'Saturday' was replaced with 'day' by 10, 7 and 5 pupils; with 'one' by 2, 1 and 2 pupils.

A few of the discrepancies which did occur were best accounted for by cultural background, e.g. in one sentence a bird 'tried to knock over a jug, so that he could *at* least have a little of the *water* when it spilt on the *ground*'. In this case, 7 European pupils wrote 'floor' for 'ground', but no Fijian or Indian chose this response presumably because this would not be seen as an indoor activity in their experience. 'Bucket' was replaced with 'tap' by 6 Europeans, but only 1 Indian. The latter group preferred 'village' or 'river', a more likely response in their culture. It was difficult to see any consistent patterns in the remainder of the discrepancies between the errors of the three groups. Once again the similarities between them are more impressive and more easily explained than the differences.

A study of the literature on interference in language learning would have predicted many systematic differences in the errors made by these language groups. Cloze test responses, however, showed no clear differences at all in the categories of errors made nor in the specific words chosen. The inherent difficulties in the language, which are affected by the variations in redundancy throughout the texts, appear to play a much greater role in this kind of exercise than interference advocates might have predicted. Either these interference phenomena are not significant in written language exercises, or else the cloze test is not a sensitive enough tool to identify them. Certainly this evidence does not support the use of the cloze procedure as a diagnostic tool for identifying specific weaknesses which might be attributable to the learner's first language.

What the results do confirm, however, is that the cloze procedure operates in a similar way for second-language users as for first. For each language group, the correlations between cloze and multiple choice tests were consistently high; the points of ease and difficulty were almost identical; and the nature of the specific mistakes made was very similar. It is clear that the cloze procedure can be used to assess reading comprehension of pupils and the readability of texts in much the same way for L1 and L2 language users. It is worth noting, too, that the non-European pupils in this study had acquired their English through a highly structured audio-lingual programme, whereas the Europeans had learned their English in the informal unstructured context of the home. Apparently the method of acquisition of the language has no influence on the kinds of cloze errors made.

Reasons for pupils' difficulties

The eight surveys outlined earlier in this article revealed that Fijian pupils are frequently unable to cope with the language expectations of teachers, textbooks and examinations. There is no doubt that it is a matter of concern. Community surveys in Fiji and other Pacific Islands (Williams 1977; Thaman 1977; Thomas and Titiali'i 1973) have shown that the teaching of English is by far the biggest 'unmet need' of the school system in the eyes of parents, teachers, employers and pastors. University students in Fiji have likewise listed it as their major concern (O'Sullivan 1978). And an analysis of external examination results shows that English is consistently the weak subject for most students. Why has this problem become so serious?

It is too easy to explain it merely in terms of the fact that pupils are learning in their second language. This is clearly one significant explanatory factor. However, we should remember that Fijian children are exposed to English from Grade 1, and have it as the medium of instruction from Grades 3 or 4 onwards. The predominant language of government, of commerce, of the media in Fiji is English, and the motivation to learn English is high. It is true that many rural pupils do suffer from a lack of good models in the classroom and the community. Since the proclamation of independence in 1970 there has been a steady withdrawal of expatriate native English teachers from the primary and secondary schools in Fiji, and the standard of oral English amongst the local teachers is often cause for concern. These kinds of explanations are facts of life, and little can be done to alleviate their effects in the short run.

More significant, in the eyes of the author, are two factors which are subject to policy change. First is the lack of suitable literature for children in the schools; second is the nature of the English language teaching programmes in the elementary schools.

Dearth of children's books

In the national survey of children's reading cited above (Elley and Mangubhai 1979) a multiple regression analysis was undertaken to identify the major correlates of pupil reading ability in English. As predicted, home background factors accounted for over a third of the variance. Children from homes where English was regularly used, where the parents were well educated, where socioeconomic levels were high, where there were many books in the home, and where parents took an interest in their children's school work, such children read English with greater comprehension. The multiple correlation found between the best combination of these home background factors and pupil reading ability was 0·58, a relatively high value for this kind of study.

When the influence of home background was removed, however, several school factors also showed correlations with reading scores. Amongst these, the most important was size of the school library. Those schools with libraries of more than 400 books produced consistently higher mean scores than those with smaller libraries or none at all. The correlation was 0·31 across 54 schools, but reduced to 0·23 after the influence of home background was partialled out. No school had high scores without a large library.

It would be premature to conclude from such a correlation that the solution to better reading lies in larger libraries. Other factors may explain the correlation. However, the hypothesis that the availability of a plentiful supply of books is a prerequisite to reading growth is a promising one. It is now being pursued with an experimental 'book flood' in 20 Fijian elementary schools, in order to determine the effects of a large supply of books on children's reading skills. There is good reason to be optimistic about such an experiment. A small but comparable study undertaken in two New Zealand schools with large numbers of Pacific Island children did show marked improvements in reading habits, reading skills and listening skills, after only six months (Elley *et al.* 1975).

Unfortunately, the current situation in Fiji, as in most Pacific countries, is that most schools have very few books for children's leisure reading. The typical Fijian elementary school has just over 200 books, many of which are instructional readers (Ragni 1979). In some of the countries of the South Pacific there is not a single library in any primary school. Part of the reason for this paucity of books is economic; part is professional — the teachers do not value reading as a way of learning language. Just as serious is the fact that there is no indigenous children's literature. The number of fictional books written in any language for Pacific Islands children can be counted on the fingers of one hand. Most of the books that Fijian children read are imported from and set in foreign cultures. While these will hold the interest of some children, the vast majority need to start with the kinds of fictional characters they can identify with, set in the kinds of contexts they are familiar with.

Recent approaches to language learning place high priority on reading as a method of acquiring language. For instance, in writing about L1 users, Smith (1978) argues that 'children do more than learn to read through reading; they learn language' (p. 70). The writer's experience in the South Pacific has prompted him to hypothesize a similar case for L2 users. If there is truth in this hypothesis and if there is no reading done by children outside of their all-too-brief instructional periods, we can scarcely expect reading standards to be high. The dearth of children's books in Fiji is clear, and its significance should be obvious.

The English language instructional programme

The other factor which could well account for much of the Fijian children's difficulties with English is to be found in the instructional programme used in the elementary schools. The Tate Oral English Program prepared by Gloria Tate in the early 1960s is an audio-lingual approach, based on the principles of Fries and Bloomfield. It is a highly structured programme, founded on regular drills and patterned practice of a rigid sequence of structures. It starts with simple, frequently encountered structures and moves systematically through a succession of twice-daily oral lessons.

Regardless of the merits of this oral programme, it is more important in this context to examine the reading programme in the Tate scheme. In all handbooks of the Tate Program, reading is played down as a source of language learning. Tate (1971) says that 'children must not be exposed in print to language structures which they have not previously learned orally.' In fact, it is recommended that there be a gap of twelve months between the oral presentation of a structure and its presentation in print, this gap to narrow gradually to three months after Class 3 and disappear at the end of elementary school.

One consequence of such assumptions is that children rarely encounter unfamiliar words or structures in print. Therefore they seldom have the opportunity to practise the process of guessing the meaning of a word or structure, and confirming or revising their guess when they check the meaning of the sentence. This is the very process that is emphasized by such writers as Rubin, Clay, Goodman, Smith and other researchers who have thrown so much light on the nature of the reading process in recent years. If it is true that this guessing process is the key to rapid language growth, then it is little wonder that Fijian children are struggling with their reading.

This neglect of the printed word has little support in recent theory. Nor is it supported by the empirical research. Dodson

(1967), for instance, found that Welsh children learning second-language vocabulary learned more efficiently when the oral presentation was supplemented with the printed word. Nor did they show any tendency to repeat the erroneous guesses they made during learning. The current writer has found, more recently, that Fijian and Indian Grade 5 children are easily able to determine the meanings of large numbers of unfamiliar English structures when presented in the context of meaningful sentences (Elley 1979). In the Grade 6 test standardization study (see (3) above) it was found that typical Grade 6 pupils were able to infer the meanings of such rare words as 'edifice', 'grotesque', 'resentful', 'precarious' provided they were given the assistance of a meaningful context. Such findings suggest that the Tate Program underestimates the ability of FL learners to teach themselves through the printed word. In the writer's view, the restricted assumptions of this programme are unnecessary, and if they were dropped a more effective reading instruction programme might result.

The way ahead

Fijian children stand to gain considerably from an improvement in their English language. Entry to high school, to university, to teachers' colleges, to gainful employment and to many other avenues of personal fulfilment is won primarily by success in examinations conducted entirely in English. Without reasonable mastery of English, pupils cannot survive this series of competitive examinations; they are denied access to the worlds of English literature, of science, of government, and of keeping up with current events in their society and the world at large

The evidence reported above shows serious deficiencies in English reading skills, and points to some of the likely causes. Do the findings suggest a way ahead? In the writer's view, one profitable line to pursue is based on the assumption that L2 learners will acquire English more effectively and painlessly if greater emphasis is given to the role of reading in the school programme. This hypothesis has the support of several leading students of the reading process in the first language (e.g. Goodman 1976 and Smith 1978) and is consistent with the correlational studies which show that good readers in Fiji come from homes and schools with many books. Further studies of the effects of a book flood in Fiji should make possible a more controlled assessment of this hypothesis with L2 users.

In particular, it is suggested that a reading programme which emphasizes appealing stories as 'the basis' for classroom discussion and teaching would make a greater impact than the present highly structured reading programme which subordinates interest and meaning to a carefully controlled sequence of structures. The basis for this assertion is empirical and quite dramatic. In a recent investigation on the island of Niue (Elley 1979) Grade 3 children in six primary schools learned to read English much more quickly, and with more positive attitudes, when they were taught with the 'shared book experience' method, using locally produced stories with high interest levels and only limited controls over structure. A comparable sample of children working on the more structured but less interesting Tate Program showed very limited development.

In brief, the shared book experience method is designed to capture the interest of the children through an exciting story, and then to maximize the interaction between teacher and a group of pupils in exploiting the language potential of the story. The teacher chooses the story, 'blows up' the print and pictures so that it can be read by a group, and provokes discussion about its likely contents. She reads it to the children several times over a period of days, and the pupils join in wherever they can. Regular discussion takes place about the content and linguistic points in the story. The intrinsic interest of the story keeps motivation high, so that repeated readings are possible. Therefore there is little need for the contrived repetitions found in highly controlled instructional books.

The shared book method was developed and popularized in New Zealand primary schools (Holdaway 1979) with L1 users, but has recently shown much promise with the many L2 Pacific Islands migrant children in Auckland Schools. A comparative evaluation with Maori kindergarten children in Hamilton (Ritchie 1978) showed that the method was superior to two other well-known structured programmes, and the success of the programme in Niue has kindled interest in the method amongst educational authorities throughout the Pacific.

Conclusion

Improvement in the quality of reading in English in the South Pacific will no doubt be a slow process, with an occasional breakthrough and many disappointments. In coming to grips with the problem, the present writer would like to record a growing realization which has emerged from the kinds of empirical studies of reading described above. It is becoming increasingly clear that second-language learning has much more to learn from first-language learning than is commonly thought. We have found: first, a similarity in the reactions of L2 and L1 users to different reading tests; second, a similarity in the pattern of their errors; and third, a similarity in their attitudes and in their language development as a result of reading programmes derived from first-language settings. Clearly there are limits in the extent of these parallels, but the present writer has been more impressed with these similarities in the language growth of L1 and L2 users than with the differences. Perhaps there is more we can learn about these similarities that will enable us to improve the reading performance and general language proficiency of Fijian children and students.

Postscript on Elley

Most of the writers in this book treat reading as a means of acquiring information about academic subjects. Elley is unusual in viewing reading partly as a means of learning a second language. His position, however, is a very common one in EFL teaching. Many 'reading' textbooks contain language exercises, which often seem to take priority over comprehension questions. In fact, it is sometimes difficult to tell whether the texts are intended as reading passages or as convenient sources of language data.

There is common ground between Elley and Cooper, both in the situation they face, and at least in part in the remedies they suggest. One might argue that Cooper attributes his subjects' poor reading performance to their weakness in English, whereas Elley attributes his subjects' weakness in English to their lack of opportunity to read at an early stage. Both, however, recommend ample supplies of 'simple' FL reading material as a way of improving students' performance.

Cooper devotes a lot of attention to particular aspects of English likely to affect his students' reading performance. Elley does not examine this, but concentrates much more on the validity of his testing procedures. His reasons for examining the validity of cloze procedure as an L2 testing measure (p. 287) are readily comprehensible; apart from presumed differences between receptive and productive vocabulary, the standard cloze deletion procedure almost inevitably results in the deletion of a large number of structural items, the restoration of which would seem to require a good deal of productive syntactic knowledge. It is thus quite reasonable to correlate cloze scores with scores on multiple choice items, which would appear to test only receptive understanding. We must regard with some scepticism, however, the claim that it is possible to equate a level of cloze scores with a level of multiple choice scores (p. 289). In the cloze procedure, once a text has been selected, the tester's control extends only as far as choice of deletion rate (e.g. every fifth or every seventh word) and method of marking (e.g. original word or acceptable synonym). Once these have been selected, the difficulty of the test is out of the tester's hands. On the other hand, the difficulty of multiple choice items is to a large extent under the control of the item writer, and can be varied to some extent regardless of the text being used. Thus Bormuth and his associates are comparing tests of fixed difficulty with tests of variable difficulty, and it is surprising, to say the least, that a consistent statistical correspondence has been found. Presumably the answer lies in the type of multiple choice item used, and it would perhaps be interesting to examine this more closely.

On the whole, Elley's case for using cloze as a readability test in an L2 context makes good empirical sense. Of particular interest is his finding (p. 290) that there was a marked similarity between the L1 and L2 groups in the cloze items they found difficult. On the evidence, this would appear to be caused not so much by 'the inherent difficulties in the language' (p. 291) as by the difficulties of predicting utterances, that is, what is likely to be said about a particular situation. One might expect different cultural groups to vary in their predictions more than Elley found. The fact that they did not might be taken as evidence that the texts used contained little cultural bias with respect to the three groups being tested. It could, however, be due to the relative insensitivity of these cloze tests to cultural bias. Since these findings would seem to have very practical relevance to simplification of written tests, it would be valuable to have more evidence from this area.

As a remedy for his subjects' poor reading performance, Elley recommends early exposure to written material. As was stated above, there is a widespread belief that written material can be a valuable source of language data for the learner. In the 1950s and 1960s, however, reading was virtually banned in the early stages of FL learning by advocates of the audio-lingual method. They insisted not only that spoken language should take precedence over written language in the classroom, but that students should not be exposed at all to written language until some time after the introduction of spoken language. It is to this insistence that Elley attributes the poor reading ability of Fijian students.

It seems likely that the main motive for emphasizing the spoken language to such an extent was a wish to correct a previous over-emphasis on the written language. However, as theoretical justification for their beliefs, proponents of the method often appealed to linguistic views of the relationship between spoken and written language. So, although the audio-lingual method is no longer as dominant as it was a few years ago, it seems worthwhile at this point to examine these views.

There are two linguistic principles which appear to be relevant. The first is that in linguistics spoken language is considered to be primary (Lyons 1968; p. 38). Speech precedes writing in human history, and in the development of the individual. There are languages which still have no written form. Most writing systems are obviously based on speech. All this is uncontroversial, and makes the principle a valuable, in fact necessary, one for linguistics.

In some applied fields, however, the principle is less useful, particularly when stated as ' . . . writing is essentially a way of representing speech in another medium' (Lyons p. 38). This could be taken to mean that a reader must first decode the graphic message into sounds, before processing this 'speech'. This is the view put forward by Lefevre (1964), for whom writing is a 'mnemonic device' reminding the reader of word sounds, intonation, etc. (p. 4). It is not, however, a view likely to be accepted by many teachers of reading.

Even if one rejects this extreme position, however, the general principle of the primacy of speech, carried over uncritically from linguistics to FL teaching, could be taken as justifying the insistence that spoken language must precede the written form. If writing is essentially a way of representing speech, then it would seem that the teaching of speech must come first. To accept this uncritically, however, would be to ignore the fact that in modern English the written and spoken languages differ partly in form, but much more so in function.

The second relevant principle is the Saussurean dictum that language is form, not substance, and thus the 'same' language can be realized in sound, or visual symbols, or indeed any other suitable medium. According to Lyons (pp. 60–61) '. . . we can interpret this to mean that neither the sounds nor the letters are primary, but that they are both alternative realizations of the same formal units'. Writing can be seen, not so much as 'a way of representing speech', but as '. . . a medium for "encoding" language' (Lyons p. 63). It is perhaps worth noting that this is the view put forward strongly by Fries, a founder of the audio-lingual method (Fries 1963).

It is not necessary to consider these two principles as contradictory. For the linguist, speech is primary; in theory, at least, it provides him with his primary source of data. For the individual language user, at a particular moment in time, language can be medium-independent: he can receive and process a message in either medium without having to translate from one to the other. Linguistically, speech is primary; psycholinguistically, language may be medium-independent.

For the teacher of reading, this second principle is much more useful. The reader can be seen as processing information directly from written language, without an intervening vocalization stage, thus gaining considerably in speed, ability to skim, etc. The principle also allows the language teacher much greater flexibility. If the aim is to impart a reading knowledge of the FL, there is no theoretical objection to beginning with the written language. For young beginners, we may well concentrate on speech for the sake of the livelier classroom interaction it engenders. But if we want to introduce written language as a back-up, there is nothing in the theory to prevent us. Thus the decision when to introduce written language becomes an empirical one, to be decided according to particular situations.

Thus, as Elley recommends for the Fijian situation, written material can be introduced at an early stage, reducing the demands on the teacher to provide all the linguistic information, and providing students with a far richer source of language data. Whether such an exposure will result in greater proficiency in the FL is a matter of empirical measurement.

Bibliography

Adams-Smith, D. E. (1981) 'Levels of Questioning: Teaching Creative Thinking through ESP,' *English Teaching Forum*, January 1981, 15–17, 21.

Alderson, J. C. (1978) 'A Study of the Cloze Procedure with Native and Non-native Speakers of English.' Unpublished PhD. thesis, University of Edinburgh.

Alderson, J. C. (1979a) 'The Cloze Procedure as a Measure of Proficiency in English as a Foreign Language.' *TESOL Quarterly*, **13**, 219–227.

Alderson, J. C. (1979b) 'The Effect on the Cloze Test of Changes in Deletion Frequency.' *Journal of Research in Reading*, **2**, 108–119.

Alderson, J. C. (1980) 'Native and Non-native Speaker Performance on Cloze Tests.' *Language Learning*, **30**, 59–76.

Alderson, J. C., Bastien, S. and Madrazo, A-M (1977) 'A Comparison of Reading Comprehension in English and Spanish.' Research and Development Unit Report No. 9, mimeo, UNAM, Mexico City.

Alderson, J. C. and Richards, S. (1977) 'Difficulties which Students Encounter when Reading Texts in English.' Research and Development Unit Report No. 8, mimeo, UNAM, Mexico City.

Allen, D. I. (1970) 'Some Effects of Advance Organisers and Level of Questions on the Learning and Retention of Written Social Studies Material.' *Journal of Educational Psychology*, **61**, 333–339.

Allen, W. P. (1956) *Selecting Reading Materials for Foreign Students*. Rockville, Md.: English Language Service.

Allen, J. P. B. and Widdowson, H. (Series eds.) *English in Focus*. London: Oxford University Press.

Anderson, J. and Hunt, A. H. (1972) 'A Frame of Reference for Cloze Tests of Readability of English Learned as a Foreign Language.' *P.N.G. Journal of Education*, **8**, 184–188.

Anderson, J. R. and Reder, L. M. (1978) 'An Elaborative Process Explanation of Depth of Processing.' In L. S. Cermak and F. I. M. Craik (eds.), *Levels of Processing in Human Memory*. New York: Halstead Press.

Anderson, R. C. and Biddle, W B. (1975) 'On Asking People Questions about What they are Reading.' In G. Bower (ed.), *Psychology of Learning and Motivation, vol 9*. New York: Academic Press.

Anderson, R. C., Reynolds, R. E., Schallert, D. L. and Goetz, E. T. (1977) 'Frameworks for Comprehending Discourse.' *American Educational Research Journal*, **14**, 367–382.

Anderson, R. C., Spiro, R. J. and Anderson, H. C. (1978) 'Schemata as

Scaffolding for the Representation of Information in Connected Discourse.' *American Educational Research Journal*, **15**, 433–440.

André, T. (1979) 'Does Answering Higher-level Questions while Reading Facilitate Productive Learning?.' *Review of Educational Research*, **49**, 280–318.

Argyle, M. (1970) *The Psychology of Interpersonal Behaviour*. Harmondsworth: Penguin Books.

Aron, H. (1978) 'Comparing Reading Comprehension in Spanish and English by Adult Hispanics Entering a Two-year College.' Paper presented at the Third International Conference on Language Proficiency and Language Dominance Testing, Southern Illinois University, Carbondale, Illinois, September, 1978.

Atkin, J. M. (1969) 'Behavioral Objectives and Curriculum Design: a Cautionary Note.' In R. C. Anderson et al. (eds.), *Current Research on Instruction*. Englewood Cliffs, N.J.: Prentice-Hall, 65–69.

Augstein, E. S. (1971) 'Reading Strategies and Learning Outcomes.' Unpublished Ph.D thesis, Brunel University, London.

Ausubel, D. P. (1967) 'Learning Theory and Classroom Practice.' Bulletin No 1, Institute for Studies in Education, Toronto, Ontario.

Baldauf, R. B. and Propst, I. K. (1978) 'Preliminary Evidence Regarding the Validity of a Modified Cloze Procedure for Lower Elementary ESL Students.' *Education and Psychological Measurement*, **38**, 451–455.

Banton, M. (1965) *Roles: an Introduction to the Study of Social Relations*. London: Tavistock Publications.

Barik, H. and Swain, M. (1975) 'Three-year Evaluation of a Large-scale Early Grade French Immersion Program: the Ottawa Study.' *Language Learning*, **25**, 1–30.

Barrera-Vasquez, A. (1953) 'The Tarascan Project in Mexico.' In 'The Use of the Vernacular in Education,' *Monographs in Fundamental Education*, **8**, Paris: UNESCO. 77–86.

Barrett, T. C. (1968) 'What is Reading?' In T. Clymer (ed.), *Innovation and Change in Reading Instruction*. 67th Year Book of the National Society for Study of Education, University of Chicago Press.

Bates, J. A. (1979) 'The Relationships between Achievement Test Itemtypes and Measures of Cognitive Structure.' Paper presented at the meeting of the American Educational Research Association, San Francisco, April, 1979.

Beard, R. (1978) 'Reading and Learning in the Middle Years.' In D. Thackeray (ed.), *Growth in Reading: Proceedings of the 15th annual course and conference of the United Kingdom Reading Association*. London: Ward Lock.

Berman, R. A. (1978) 'Contrastive Analysis Revisited: Obligatory, Systematic and Incidental Differences between Languages, with Specific Reference to Modern Hebrew and English: *Interlanguage Studies Bulletin, Utrecht*: **3**, 212–233.

Berman, R. A. (1979) 'Postposing, Lexical Repetition and the like: a Study in Contrastive Stylistics'. *Journal of Applied Linguistics*, Israel **2**, 1.

Berne, E. (1968) *Games People Play*. Harmondsworth: Penguin Books. 2nd edn, 1970.

Bernstein, B. (1971) *Class, Codes and Control, vol 1*. London: Routledge and Kegan Paul.

Betts, E. A. (1946) *Foundations of Reading Instruction*. New York: American Book Co.

Bever, T. G. (1970) 'The Cognitive Basis for Linguistic Structures.' In J. R. Hayes (ed.), *Cognition and the Development of Language*. New York: Wiley.

Biggs, J. B. (1971) *Information and Human Learning*. Glenview, Illinois: Scott Foresman.

Bloom, B. (1980) 'The New Direction in Educational Research: Alterable Variables.' *Phi Delta Kappan*, **61**, 382–388.

Bloom, B. S., Engelhart, M. D., Furst, E. J., Hill, W. H. and Kratwohl, D. R. (1956) (eds.), *Taxonomy of Educational Objectives: Cognitive Domain*. David McKay, New York (See also Bloom, B. S. et al. (eds.), *Taxonomy of Educational Objectives. Handbook 1. Cognitive Domain*. London: Longman, 1977).

Bormuth, J. R (1966) 'Readability: a New Approach.' *Reading Research Quarterly*, **1**, 79–132. (See also Bormuth, J. R. (1964) 'Relationships between Selected Language Variables and Comprehension Ability and Difficulty.' US Dept. of Health, Education and Welfare).

Bormuth, J. R. (1968) 'Cloze Test Readability: Criterion Reference Scores.' *Journal of Educational Measurement*, **5**, 189–196.

Bormuth, J. R. (1971) 'Development of Standards of Readability.' Final Report, Project No. 9–0237, US Dept. of Health, Education and Welfare (See also Bormuth, J. R., and Klare, G. R. 'Research Critiques: Development of Readability Analyses.' *Elementary English*, **48**, 1971, 675–681).

Bransford, J. D. and Johnson, M. K. (1972) 'Contextual Prerequisites for Understanding: some Investigations of Comprehension and Recall.' *Journal of Verbal Learning and Verbal Behaviour*, **11**, 717–726.

Bransford, J. D. and Johnson, M. K. (1973) 'Considerations of some Problems of Comprehension.' In W. G. Chase (ed.), *Visual Information Processing: Proceedings of 8th Annual Carnegie Symposium on Cognition*. New York: Academic Press.

Bransford, J. D. and McCarrell, N. S. (1974) 'A Sketch of a Cognitive Approach to Comprehension: In W. Weimer, and D. S. Palermo (eds.), *Cognition and the Symbolic Processes*. New York: Halsted Press.

Bransford, J. D. (1979) *Human Cognition: Learning, Understanding and Remembering*. Belmont, California: Wadsworth Publishing Co.

Bransford, J. D., Stein, B. S., Shelton, T. S. and Owings, R. A. (to appear) 'Cognition and Adaptation: the Importance of Learning to Learn.' In J. Harvey (ed.), *Cognition; Social Behaviour and the Environment*. Hillsdale, N.J: Erlbaum.

Brown, R. and Gilman, A. (1960) 'The Pronouns of Power and Solidarity.' In T. A. Seboek (ed.), *Style in Language*. Cambridge, Mass.: MIT Press.

Brown, P. and Levinson, S. (1978) 'Universals in Language Usage: Politeness Phenomena.' In Goody 1978.

Bruner, J. S. (1974) *The Relevance of Education.* Harmondsworth: Penguin Education (Allen and Unwin, 1972).

Bull, S. G. (1973) 'The Role of Questions in Maintaining Attention to Textual Material.' *Review of Educational Research*, **43**, 83–87.

Burt, M. and Dulay, H. (1978) 'Some Guidelines for the Assessment of Oral Language Proficiency and Dominance.' *TESOL Quarterly*, **12**, 177–192.

Carey, S. T. and Cummins, J. (1979) 'English and French Achievement of Grade 5 Children from English and Mixed French–English Home Backgrounds Attending the Edmonton Separate School System English–French Immersion Program.' Report submitted to the Edmonton Separate School System, April, 1979.

Carpenter, P. A. and Just, M. A. (1977) 'Reading Comprehension as the Eyes See it.' In M. A. Just and P. A. Carpenter (eds.), *Cognitive Processes in Comprehension.* Hillsdale, N.J.: Erlbaum.

Carroll, J. B. (1972) 'Defining Language Comprehension: Some Speculations.' In R. O. Freedle and J. B. Carroll (eds.), *Language Comprehension and the Acquisition of Knowledge.* Washington: Winston. 1–29.

Charniak, E. (1972) 'Towards a Model of Children's Story Comprehension.' Doctoral dissertation, Massachusetts Institute of Technology, (Also MIT Artificial Intelligence Laboratory Tech. Rep. A1-TR, 266, 1972).

Chase, P. N., Johnson, K. R. and Keenan, J. B. (1977) 'A Survey of Cognitive Levels Programmed in Introductory and Educational Psychology Study Materials.' Unpublished survey, University of Massachusetts, Amherst.

Chen, A. (1982) 'Diagnosis of a Non-Native Reader of English Using Miscue Analysis and Introspection/Retrospection'. Mimeo, University of California.

Chihara, T., Oller, J., Weaver, K. and Chavez-Oller, M. A. (1977) 'Are Cloze Items Sensitive to Constraints across Sentences?'. *Language Learning*, **27**, 63–73.

Chitravelu, N. (1980) 'Strategies for Reading, University of Malaya English for Special Purposes Project.' *ELT Documents*, British Council.

Chitravelu, N. (1975) 'A Preliminary Report on the Reading Attainment Test, University of Malaya English for Special Purposes Project.' Mimeo, Language Centre, University of Malaya.

Chomsky, N. (1965) *Aspects of the Theory of Syntax.* Cambridge, Mass.: MIT Press.

Clapham, C. (1975) 'Test of English for Adult Learners (TEAL).' University of Edinburgh.

Clark, H. and Clark, E. (1977) *The Psychology of Language.* New York: Harcourt, Brace, Jovanovich.

Clark, R. (1975) 'Adult Theories, Child Strategies and their Implications for the Language Teacher,' in J. P. B. Allen and S. P. Corder (eds.),

Papers in Applied Linguistics, the Edinburgh Course in Applied Linguistics, vol 2, Oxford University Press.

Clarke, M. (1979) 'Reading in Spanish and English: Evidence from Adult ESL Students.' *Language Learning*, **29**, 121–150.

Clarke, M. (1980) 'The Short Circuit Hypothesis of ESL Reading — or when Language Competence Interferes with Reading Performance.' *Modern Language Journal*, **64**, 203–209.

Clay, M. M. (1973) *Reading: the Patterning of Complex Behaviour*. London: Heinemann.

Cleveland, L. (1970) 'The Admission of Overseas Students.' Unpublished mimeo, Victoria University of Wellington, New Zealand.

Coady, J. (1979) 'A Psycholinguistic Model of the ESL Reader.' In R. Mackay, B. Barkman and R. R. Jordan (eds.), *Reading in a Second Language*. Rowley, Mass.: Newbury House, 5–12.

Cohen, A. D. and Fine, J. (1978) 'Reading History in English: Discourse Analysis and the Experience of Native and non-Native Readers.' *Working Papers on Bilingualism*, **16**, 55–74.

Cohen, A. D., Glasman, H., Rosenbaum, P. R., Ferrara, J. and Fine, J. (1978) 'Reading English for Specialised Purposes: Discourse Analysis and the Use of Students.' Paper presented at the 12th Annual TESOL Convention, Mexico City, April 1978. Also *TESOL Quarterly*, **13**, 1979, 551–564.

Cohen, A. and Hosenfeld, C. (1981) 'Uses of Introspection/Retrospection in Learner-centered Research.' *Language Learning*, **31**, 285–313.

Cojocaru, G. (1977) 'Reading at the College Level.' Mimeo, Tel Aviv University term paper.

Cole, P. and Morgan, J. L. (eds.) (1975) *Syntax and Semantics, vol 3: Speech Acts*. New York: Academic Press.

Coleman, E. B. (1965) 'Learning of Prose Written in Four Grammatical Transformations.' *Journal of Applied Psychology*, **9**, 332–341.

Collins, A. M. and Quillian, M. R. (1972) 'How to Make a Language User.' In E. Tulving and W. Donaldson (eds.), *Organization of Memory*. New York: Academic Press.

Corder, S. P. (1981) 'Formal Simplicity and Functional Simplification in Second Language Acquisition.' In R. W. Anderson (ed.), *New Dimensions in Second Language Acquisition Research*. Rowley, Mass.: Newbury House.

Cowan, J. R. (1976) 'Reading, Perceptual Strategies and Contrastive Analysis.' *Language Learning*, **26**, 95–109.

Cowan, J. R. and Sarmad, Z. (1976) 'Reading Performance of Bilingual Children According to Type of School and Home Language.' *Language Learning*, **26**, 353–376.

Craik, F. I. M. and Tulving, E. (1975) 'Depth of Processing and the Retention of Words in Episodic Memory.' *Journal of Experimental Psychology, General*, **104**, 268–294.

Cripwell, K. (1976) 'What is a Cloze Test: How do I Use it?'. *Modern English Teacher*, **4**.

Crisswell, C. and Squire, S. (1976) *Living Hong Kong Social Studies 1C*. Hong Kong: Longman (Far East).

Crothers, E. J. (1972) 'Memory Structure and the Recall of Discourse.'

In R. O. Freedle and J. B. Carroll (eds.) *Language Comprehension and the Acquisition of Knowledge.* Washington: Winston, 247–283.

Cummins, J. (1976) 'The Influence of Bilingualism on Cognitive Growth: a Synthesis of Research Findings and Explanatory Hypotheses.' *Working Papers on Bilingualism,* **9,** 2–43.

Cummins, J. (1979) 'Cognitive/Academic Language Proficiency, Linguistic Interdependence, the Optimum Age Question and some Other Matters.' *Working Papers on Bilingualism,* **19,** 197–205.

Cziko, G. A. (1978) 'Differences in First and Second Language Reading: the Use of Syntactic, Semantic and Discourse Constraints.' *Canadian Modern Language Review,* **34,** 473–489.

Dahlgren, L. O. (1975) 'Qualitative Differences in Learning as a Function of Content-oriented Guidance.' *Acta Universitatis Gothoburgensis,* Göteborg.

Dalis, G. T. (1970) 'Effect of Precise Objectives upon Student Achievement in Health Education.' *Journal of Experimental Education,* **39,** 20–23. (Also *Dissertation Abstracts,* **30 (2-A),** 1969, 616–7.)

Darnell, D. K. (1968) 'The Development of an English Language Proficiency Test of Foreign Students Using a Clozentrophy Procedure.' Final Report, Colorado University, Boulder, DHEW Research Bureau No. BP-7-H-010.

Davies, A. (1964) English Proficiency Test Battery: Version A (unpublished). Birmingham University and British Council, London.

Davies, A. and Widdowson, H. (1974) 'The Teaching of Reading and Writing.' In J. P. B. Allen and S. P. Corder (eds.), *Techniques in Applied Linguistics, vol. 3.* Oxford University Press.

Davies, F. (1973) *Teaching Reading in Early England.* London: Pitman.

DeCharms, R. (1968) *Personal Causation.* New York: Academic Press.

Deci, E. (1975) *Intrinsic Motivation.* New York: Plenum Press.

De Leeuw, M. and E. (1965) *Read Better, Read Faster.* Harmondsworth: Penguin.

Dewey, D. (1913) *Interest and Effort in Education.* Boston: Houghton Mifflin.

Dodson, C. J. (1967) *Language Teaching and the Bilingual Method.* London: Pitman.

Dooling, D. J. and Lachman, R. (1971) 'Effects of Comprehension on Recall of Prose,' *Journal of Experimental Psychology,* **88,** 216–222.

Duchastel, P. C. (1972) 'Incidental and Relevant Learning with Instructional Objectives.' Technical Memo 66, CAI Centre, Florida State University, Tallahassee.

Duchastel, P. C. and Merrill, P. F. (1973) 'The Effects of Behavioral Objectives on Learning: a Review of Empirical Studies.' *Review of Educational Research,* **43,** 53–70.

Duchastel, P. C. and Brown, B. R. (1974) 'Incidental and Relevant Learning with Instructional Objectives.' *Journal of Educational Psychology,* **66,** 481–485.

Duchastel, P. C. (1977) 'Functions of Instructional Objectives: Organisation and Direction.' Paper presented at the meeting of the American

Educational Research Association, New York, April, 1977.

Duddington, C. L. (1966) *Seaweeds and Other Algae*. London: Faber and Faber.

Duell, O. K. (1974) 'Effect of Type of Objective, Level of Test Questions, and the Judged Importance of Tested Materials upon Post-test Performance,' *Journal of Educational Psychology*, **66**, 225–232.

Edfelt, A. E. (1976) 'Är det Meningsfullt med Studieteknisk Träning?' (Is there a Meaningful Study-skill Training?) *Forskning om Utbildning*, **3**, 15–24.

Elley, W. B. and Reid, N. A. (1969) 'Progressive Achievement Tests of Reading.' Wellington: New Zealand Council for Educational Research.

Elley, W. B., Watson, J. E. and Cowie, C. R. (1975) 'The Impact of a Book Flood.' Wellington: New Zealand Council for Educational Research.

Elley, W. B. and Thompson, J. (1978) 'The English Language Skills of USP Foundation Students.' Mimeo, University of the South Pacific, Suva.

Elley, W. B. (1979) 'Learning to Read in the South Pacific.' Paper presented at Annual Convention of International Reading Association, Atlanta, Georgia, April, 1979.

Elley, W. B. and Mangubhai, F. (1979) 'A Research Paper on Reading in Fiji.' *Fiji English Teachers' Journal*, **15**, 1–7.

Entwhistle, N., Hanley, M. and Hounsell, D. (1979) 'Identifying Distinctive Approaches to Studying.' *Higher Education*, **8**, 365–380.

Eskey, D. (1975) 'Advanced Reading: the Structural Problem.' *English Teaching Forum*, **XIII**, Nos. 3 and 4.

Faw, H. and Waller, T. G. (1976) 'Mathemagenic Behaviours and Efficiency in Learning from Prose.' *Review of Educational Research*, **46**, 691–720.

Ferguson, C. A. (1971) 'Absence of the Copula and the Notion of Simplicity.' In D. Hymes (ed.), *Pidginization and Creolization of Languages*. Cambridge University Press.

Ferster, C. B. (1968) 'Individualised Instruction in a Large Introductory Psychology Course.' *The Psychological Record*, **18**, 521–532.

Fransson, A. and Rovio-Johansson, A. (1973) 'University Studies in Teams, part 2.' Report from the Institute of Education, University of Göteborg, No. 101.

Fransson, A. (1978) 'Att Rädas Prov och att Vilja Veta. (To be Afraid of Tests and the Will to Learn).' *Acta Universitatis Gothoburgensis*, Göteborg.

Frase, L. T., Patrick, E. and Schumer, H. (1970) 'Effect of Question Position and Frequency upon Learning from Text under Different Levels of Incentive.' *Journal of Educational Psychology*, **61**, 52–56.

Fries, C. C. (1945) *Teaching and Learning English as a Foreign Language*. Ann Arbor: University of Michigan Press.

Fries, C. C. (1963) *Linguistics and Reading*. New York: Holt, Rinehart and Winston. (Reprinted 1981: New York: Irvington.)

Garfinkel, H. and Sacks, H. (1970) 'On Formal Structures of Practical Actions.' In McKinney and Tiryakian, 1970.

Gatbonton, E. C. and Tucker, G. R. (1971) 'Cultural Orientation and the Study of Foreign Literature,' *TESOL Quarterly*, **5**, 137–143.

Giles, H. and Smith, P. M. (1979) 'Accommodation Theory: Optimal Levels of Convergence.' In Giles and St. Clair, 1979.

Giles, H. and St. Clair, R. (eds.) (1979) *Language and Social Psychology*. Oxford: Basil Blackwell.

Gilliland, J. (1972) *Readability*. London: University of London Press.

Goodman, K. S. (1967) 'Reading: a Psycholinguistic Guessing Game.' *Journal of the Reading Specialist*, 126–135.

Goodman, K. S. (1973) 'Psycholinguistic Universals of the Reading Process.' In F. Smith (ed.), *Psycholinguistics and Reading*. New York: Holt, Rinehart and Winston, 21–29.

Goodman, K. S. (1974) 'Miscue Analysis: Theory and Reality in Reading.' Paper presented at 5th World IRA Congress, 1974. In Merritt, J. (ed.), *Proceedings, New Horizons in Reading*. International Reading Association, Vol. 19, 1976.

Goodman, K. S. (1976) 'Reading: a Psycholinguistic Guessing Game.' In H. Singer and R. B. Ruddell (eds.), *Theoretical Models and Processes of Reading*. International Reading Association, 2nd revised edn.

Goody, E. N. (ed.) (1978) *Questions and Politeness: Strategies of Interaction*. Cambridge University Press.

Granowsky, A. and Botel, M. (1974) 'Background for a new Syntactic Complexity Formula.' *The Reading Teacher*, **28**, 31–35.

Gregory, R. L. (1966) *Eye and Brain: the Psychology of Seeing*. London: Weidenfeld and Nicholson, 3rd revised edn, 1977.

Grice, H. P. (1975) 'Logic and Conversation.' In Cole and Morgan, 1975.

Halliday, M. A. K. and Hasan, R. (1976) *Cohesion in English*. London: Longman.

Harri-Augstein, E. S. (1978) 'Reflecting on Structure of Meaning. A Process of Learning-to-learn.' In F. Fransella (ed.), *Personal Construct Psychology*. London: Academic Press.

Harris, D. P. and Palmer, L. A. (1965) *A Vocabulary and Reading Test for Students of English as a Second Language*, revised edn. American Language Institute, Georgetown University, Washington, D.C.

Harrison, C. (1979) 'Assessing the Readability of School Texts.' In Lunzer and Gardner, 1979, 72–107.

Hatch, E. (1973) 'Research on Reading a Second Language.' UCLA Workspapers in *TESOL*, **VII**, 1–10. (Also *Journal of Reading Behaviour*, **6**, 1974, 53.)

Heritage, J. C. and Watson, D. R. (1979) 'Formulations as Conversational Objects.' In Psathas, 1979.

Hodges, J. C. and Whitten, M. E. (1962) *The Harbrace College Handbook*. New York: Harcourt Brace Jovanovich.

Holdaway, D. (1979) *The Foundations of Literacy*. Sydney: Ashton Scholastic.

Hosenfeld, C. (1977a) 'A Learning-Teaching View of Second-Language

Instruction: The Learning Strategies of Second-Language Learners with Reading Grammar Tasks.' Ph. D. thesis, Ohio State University.

Hosenfeld, C. (1977b) 'A Preliminary Investigation of the Reading Strategies of Successful and Non-successful Second Language Learners.' *System*, **5**, 110–123.

Hosenfeld, C. (1979) 'Cindy: a Learner in Today's Foreign Language Classroom.' In W. Born (ed.), *The Foreign Language Learner in Today's Classroom Environment*. Northeast Conference Reports, Northeast Conference on the Teaching of Foreign Languages, Middlebury, Vermont, 53–75.

Hosenfeld, C., Arnold, V., Kirchofer, J., Laciura, J. and Wilson, L. (1981) 'Second Language Reading: a Curricular Sequence for Teaching Reading Strategies.' *Foreign Language Annals*, **14**, 415–422.

Hosenfeld, C., Brinton, D. and Allwright, J. (1982) 'A Psycholinguistic Approach to Teaching a Beginning ESL Reading Class at UCLA Extension.' Videotape, University of California at Los Angeles.

Hosenfeld, C., Frankel, E. and Brinton, D. (1982) 'Reading Workshop for the 1982 UCLA Freshman Summer Program.' University of California at Los Angeles, May 11, 18, 25 and June 1, 1982.

Hudson, T. (to appear) 'The Effects of Induced Schemata on the "Short Circuit" in L2 Reading. Non-decoding Factors in L2 Reading Performance', *Language Learning*.

Huey, E. B. (1908) *The Psychology and Pedagogy of Reading*. New York: Macmillan. (Republished 1968, Cambridge, Mass: MIT Press.)

Hunkins, F. P. (1969) 'Effects of Analysis and Evaluation Questions on Various Levels of Achievement,' *Journal of Experimental Education*, **38**, 45–58.

Hunt, K. W. (1965) *Grammatical Structures Written at Three Grade Levels*. National Council of Teachers of English, Champaign, Illinois.

Hymes, D. (1968) 'The Ethnography of Speaking.' In J. A. Fishman, *Readings in the Sociology of Language*. The Hague: Mouton.

Jarvis, G. A. (1979) 'The Second Language Teacher: Reconciling the Vision with the Reality.' In W. Born (ed.), *The Foreign Language Learner in Today's Classroom Environment*. Northeast Conference Reports, Northeast Conference on the Teaching of Foreign Languages, Middlebury, Vermont, 77–104.

Johns, T. F. 'The Text and its Message: an Approach to the Teaching of Reading Strategies for Students of Development Administration'. In H. Faber and A. Maley (eds.), *Leseverstehen im Fremdsprachenunterricht*. Munich, Goethe Institut.

Jolly, D. (1978) 'The Establishment of a Self-access Scheme for Intensive Reading.' Paper presented at the Goethe Institute, British Council Colloquium on Reading, Paris, October, 1978.

Just, M. A. and Carpenter, P. A. (1980) 'A Theory of Reading — from Eye Fixations to Comprehension,' Psychological Review, **87**, 329–354.

Kaplan, R. and Rothkopf, E. Z. (1974) 'Instructional Objectives as Directions to Learners: Effect of Passage Length and Amount of

Objective-relevant Content.' *Journal of Educational Psychology*, **66**, 448–456.

Kaplan, R. and Simmons, F. G. (1974) 'Effects of Instructional Objectives used as Orienting Stimuli or as Summary/Review upon Prose Learning,' *Journal of Educational Psychology*, **66**, 614–622.

Kaplan, R. (1976) 'Effects of Grouping and Response Characteristics of Instructional Objectives on Learning from Prose,' *Journal of Educational Psychology*, **68**, 424–430.

Keller, F. S. (1968) 'Goodbye, Teacher . . .' *Journal of Applied Behavior Analysis*, **1**, 78–79.

Kelvin, P. (1971) *The Bases of Social Behaviour*. London: Holt, Rinehart and Winston.

Kintsch, W. and van Dijk, T. A. (1978) 'Towards a Model of Text Comprehension and Production.' *Psychological Review*, **85**, 363–394.

Klare, G. R. (1963) *The Measurement of Readability*. Ames, Iowa: Iowa State University Press.

Klare, G. R. (1974) 'Assessing Readability', *Reading Research Quarterly*, **X**, 62–102.

Klare, G. (1978) 'Assessing Readability.' In L. J. Chapman, and P. Czernewska (eds.), *Reading: from Process to Practice*. London: Routledge and Kegan Paul. Abridged version of Klare (1974).

Koch, S. (1956) 'Behavior as "Intrinsically" Regulated: Work Notes Towards a Pre-theory of Phenomena called "Motivational".' Paper presented at I. M. R. Jones Nebraska Symposium on Motivation, University of Nebraska, Lincoln.

Konold, C. E. and Bates, J. A. (1978) 'Applying the Episodic/Semantic Memory Distinction to the Study of Instructional Effects on Cognitive Structure.' Paper presented at the meeting of the American Educational Research Association, Toronto, March, 1978.

Kueneman, H. (1931) 'A Study of the Effect of Vocabulary Changes on Reading Comprehension in a Single Field.' Master's thesis, State University of Iowa.

Kueter, R. A. (1970) Instructional Strategies: the Effect of Personality Factors on Recognition Learning Using Statements of Behavioral Objectives as Opposed to no Statements of Behavioral Objectives prior to Instruction.' Doctoral dissertation, Indiana University.

Kulik, J. A., Jaska P. and Kulik, C.-L. C. (1978) 'Research on Component Features of Keller's Personalized System of Instruction.'*Journal of Personalized Instruction*, **3**, 2–14.

Labov, W. and Waletsky, J. (1967) 'Narrative Analysis: Oral Versions of Personal Experiences.' In J. Helm (ed.), *Essays on the Verbal and Visual Arts*. Proceedings of the 1966 Spring Meeting A. E. S., American Ethnological Society, N.Y.

Lackstrom, J. L., Selinker, L. and Trimble, L. (1972) 'Technical Rhetorical Principles and Grammatical Choice.' Paper presented at the 3rd International Congress of Applied Linguists, Copenhagen, August, 1972.

Ladas, H. (1973) 'The Mathemagenic Effects of Factual Review Questions on the Learning of Incidental Information: a Critical Review.' *Review of Educational Research*, **43**, 71–82.

Lambert, W. E. (1975) 'Culture and Language as Factors in Learning and Education.' In A. Wolfgang (ed.), *Education of Immigrant Students*, Ontario Institute for Studies in Education, Toronto.

Lapkin, S. and Swain, M. (1977) 'The Use of English and French Cloze Tests in a Bilingual Education Program Evaluation: Validity and Error Analysis.' *Language Learning*, **27**, 279–313.

Lautamatti, L. (1978) 'Observations on the Development of the Topic in Simplified Discourse.' In V. Kohonen and N. E. Enkvist (eds.), *Text Linguistics, Cognitive Learning and Language Teaching*. A Fin LA, Akateeminen Kirjakauppa Postilokero 128, 00101 Helsinki 10.

Lefevre, C. A. (1964) *Linguistics and the Teaching of Reading*. New York: McGraw-Hill.

Lloyd, K. E. (1971) 'Contingency Management in University Courses.' *Educational Technology*, **11**, 18–23.

Lunzer, E. and Gardner, K. (eds.) (1979) *The Effective Use of Reading*. London: Heinemann.

Lyons, J. (1968) *Introduction to Theoretical Linguistics*. Cambridge University Press.

McCarrell, N. S. and Brooks, P. H. (1975) 'Mental Retardation: Comprehension Gone Awry.' Paper presented at a Research Colloquium sponsored by the John F. Kennedy Center for Research on Education and Human Development, Nashville, Tennessee, September, 1975.

McConkie, G. W., Rayner, K. and Wilson, S. (1973) 'Experimental Manipulation of Reading Strategies.' *Journal of Educational Psychology*, **65**, 1–8.

McCrimmon, J. M. (1963) *Writing with a Purpose*. Boston: Houghton Mifflin.

McGaw, G. and Grotelueschen, A. (1972) 'Direction of the Effect of Questions in Prose Material.' *Journal of Educational Psychology*, **63**, 580–588.

McKenzie, G. R. (1972) 'Some Effects of Frequent Quizzes on Inferential Thinking.' *American Educational Research Journal*, **9**, 231–240.

Mackin, R. and Carver, D. (1968) *A Higher Course of English Study 1*. Oxford University Press.

McKinney, J. C. and Tiryakian, E. A. (eds.) (1970) *Theoretical Sociology*. New York: Appleton-Century Crofts.

MacNamara, J. (1970) 'Comparative Studies of Reading and Problem Solving in two Languages,' *TESOL Quarterly*. **4**, 107–116.

McNeill, W. H. (1963) *The Rise of the West*. University of Chicago Press and Mentor Books, New English Library.

Mager, R. F. (1962) *Preparing Instructional Objectives*. Palo Alto, California: Fearon. 2nd edn. 1975, London: Pitman.

Malott, R. W. and Suinicki, J. G. (1969) 'Contingency Management in an Introductory Psychology Course for a Thousand Students.' *The Psychological Record*, **19**, 545–556.

Mandelbaum, D. G. (1970) *Society in India*. 2 volumes. Berkeley: University of California Press.

Marenghi, E. and Frydenberg, G. (1980) 'A Reading Experiment with Native and Non-native Speakers of English: Chronological and Non-chronological Arrangements of Texts.' Term paper, University of Michigan.

Marquardt, W. F. (1967) 'Literature and Cross-cultural Communication in the Course in English for International Students.' *The Florida Foreign Language Reporter*, 5, 9–10.

Marquardt, W. F. (1969) 'Creating Empathy through Literature between Members of the Mainstream Culture and Disadvantaged Learners of the Minority Cultures.' *The Florida Foreign Language Reporter*, 7, 133–141, 157.

Marton, F. (1974) 'Some Effects of Content-neutral Instructions on Non-verbatim Learning in a Neutral Setting', *Scandinavian Journal of Educational Research*, 18, 199–208.

Marton, F. (1975) 'On Non-verbatim Learning: I — Level of Processing and Level of Outcome.' Report from the Institute of Education, University of Göteborg, No. 39, (Also *Scandinavian Journal of Psychology* 16, 1975, 273–279.)

Marton, F. and Säljö, R. (1976) 'On Qualitative Differences in Learning: I — Outcome and Process.' *British Journal of Educational Psychology*, 46, 4–11.

Marton, F. (1976) 'On Non-verbatim Learning: II — The Erosion Effect of a Task-Induced Learning Algorithm.' Report from the Institute of Education, University of Göteborg, 1976. (Also *Scandinavian Journal of Psychology*, 17, 1976, 41–48.)

Marton, F. and Säljö, R. (1979) 'Learning in the Learner's Perspective: III — Level of Difficulty Seen as a Relationship between the Reader and the Text.' Report from the Institute of Education, University of Göteborg, No. 78.

Mayer, R. E. (1975) 'Forward Transfer of Different Reading Strategies Evoked by Testlike Events in Mathematics Texts.' *Journal of Educational Psychology*, 67, 165–169.

Melton, R. F. (1978) 'Resolution of Conflicting Claims concerning the Effect of Behavioral Objectives on Student Learning.' *Review of Educational Research*, 48, 291–302.

Merritt, J. (1969) 'The Intermediate Skills: towards a Better Understanding of the Process of Fluent Reading,' in J. H. Morris (ed.), *The First R: Yesterday, Today, and Tomorrow*. London: Ward Lock.

Meyer, B. J. F. (1975) *The Organisation of Prose and its Effects on Memory*. New York: North Holland.

Miller, L. R. (1975) 'Predictive Powers of Multiple-choice and Cloze-derived Readability Formulas.' *Reading Improvement*, 12, 52–58.

Moag, R. F. and Moag, L. (1977) 'English in Fiji: some Perspectives and the Need for Language Planning.' *Fiji English Teachers' Journal*, 13, 2–26.

Modiano, N. (1966) 'Reading Comprehension in the National Language: a Comparative Study of Bilingual and all Spanish Approaches to

Reading Instruction in Selected Indian Schools in the Highlands of Chiapas, Mexico.' Doctoral dissertation, New York University.

Mountford, A. (1975) 'Discourse Analysis and the Simplification of Reading Material for ESP.' M. Litt. thesis, Edinburgh University.

Moyle, D. (1978) 'Readability: the Use of Cloze Procedure.' In L. J. Chapman and P. Czerniewska (eds.), *Reading: from Process to Practice*. London: Routledge and Kegan Paul.

National Council of Teachers of Mathematics (1980) *An Agenda for Action: Recommendations for School Mathematics of the 1980s*. The Council, Reston, Virginia.

Neisser, U. (1976) *Cognition and Reality: Principles and Implications of Cognitive Psychology*. San Francisco: W. H. Freeman.

Nemser, W. (1971) 'Approximative Systems in Foreign Language Learners.' *IRAL*, **9**, 115.

Nicholson, J. (1977) *Habits*. London: Macmillan, London: Pan Books, 1978.

Oller, J. W. (1973) 'Cloze Tests of Second Language Proficiency and What they Measure.' *Language Learning*, **23**, 105–118.

Olshtain, E. and Bejarano, Y. (1979) 'Learning Strategies and Reading for Comprehension.' Paper presented at the 10th Annual CATESOL State Conference, Los Angeles, April, 1979.

Orndorff, B. A. (1925) An Experiment to Show the Effect of Sentence Length upon Comprehension. Master's thesis, State University of Iowa.

O'Sullivan, P. (1978) 'English at USP: the Student's View.' Mimeo. University of the South Pacific, Suva.

Parker, D. H. (1959) *SRA Reading Laboratory, Student Record Book (IVa)*. Chicago: Science Research Associates.

Pask, G. (1969) 'Strategy, Competence and Conversation as Determinants of Learning.' *Programme Learning*, 250–267.

Paulston, C. B. and Bruder, M. N. (1976) *Teaching English as a Second Language: Techniques and Procedures*. Cambridge, Mass.: Winthrop.

Peterson, J., Paradis, E. and Peters, N. (1973) 'Revalidation of the Cloze Procedure as a Measure of Instructional Level for High School Students.' *National Reading Conference 22nd Yearbook*, 144–149.

Piaget, J. (1961) 'The Genetic Approach to the Psychology of Thought.' *Journal of Educational Psychology*, **52**, 275–281.

Popham, W. J. (1969) 'Probing the Validity of Arguments against Behavioral Goals.' In R. C. Anderson et al. (eds.), *Current Research on Instruction*. Englewood Cliffs, N.J: Prentice-Hall.

Psathas, G. (ed.) (1979) *Everyday Language: Studies in Ethnomethodology*. New York: Irvington.

Ragni, J. (1979) 'Primary and Secondary Schools Library Questionnaire: Results and Recommendations.' *Fiji English Teachers' Journal*, **15**, 23–27.

Rankin, E. F. and Culhane, J. W. (1969) 'Comparable Cloze and Multiple-choice Comprehension Scores.' *Journal of Reading*, **13**, 193–198.

Richards, J. (ed.). (1974) *Error Analysis: Perspectives in Second Language Acquisition*. London: Longman.

Rickards, J. P. (1979) 'Adjunct Postquestions in Text: a Critical Review of Methods and Processes.' *Review of Educational Research*, **49**, 181–196.

Rigg, P. (1977) 'The Miscue ESL Project.' In H. D. Brown, C. A. Yorio and R. H. Crymes (eds.), *Teaching and Learning ESL: Trends in Research and Practice*. (On TESOL '77), Washington, D.C., TESOL, 106–118.

Ritchie, J. (1977) *Tamariki Maori*. Centre for Maori Studies, University of Waikato.

Ritchie, J. (1978) *Chance to be Equal*. Cape Catley, Queen Charlotte Sound, N. Z.

Rivers, W. M. (1968) *Teaching Foreign Language Skills*. Chicago: University of Chicago Press.

Rivers, W. M. and Temperly, M. S. (1978) *A Practical Guide to the Teaching of English as a Second or Foreign Language*. New York: Oxford University Press

Robin, A. L. (1976) 'Behavioral Instruction in the College Classroom.' *Review of Educational Research*, **46**, 313–354.

Robinett, B. W. (1979) *Teaching English to Speakers of Other Languages*. New York: McGraw-Hill.

Robinson, F. P. (1961) *Effective Study*. New York: Harper and Row, 4th revised edn, 1970.

Rohwer, W. D., Jr. (1966) 'Constraints, Syntax and Meaning in Paired Associate Learning.' *Journal of Verbal Learning and Verbal Behaviour*, **5**, 541–547.

Romer, A. S. (1954) *Man and the Vertebrates, vol. 1*. Harmondsworth: Penguin Books.

Rosenthal, R. (1969) 'Interpersonal Expectations: Effects of the Experimenter's Hypothesis.' In R. Rosenthal and R. W. Rosnow (eds.), *Artefacts in Behavioral Research*. New York: Academic Press.

Rothkopf, E. Z. (1966) 'Learning from Written Instructive Material: an Exploration of the Control of Inspection Behavior by Test-like Events.' *American Educational Research Journal*, **3**, 241–249.

Rothkopf, E. Z. and Billington, M. J. (1974) 'Indirect Review and Priming through Questions.' *Journal of Educational Psychology*, **66**, 669–679.

Rothkopf, E. Z. and Bisbicos, E. (1967) 'Selective Facilitative Effects of Interspersed Questions on Learning from Written Material.' *Journal of Educational Psychology*, **58**, 56–61.

Rothkopf, E. Z. and Kaplan, R. (1972) 'Exploration of the Effect of Density and Specificity of Instructional Objectives on Learning from

Text,' *Journal of Educational Psychology*, **63**, 295–302.

Rubin, J. (1975) 'What the Good Language Learner can Teach us.' *TESOL Quarterly*, **9**, 41–52.

Rumelhart, D. E. (1975) 'Notes on a Schema for Stories.' In D. B. Bobrow and A. M. Collins (eds.), *Representation and Understanding: Studies in Cognitive Science*. New York: Academic Press.

Rumelhart, D. E. (1977) *Introduction to Human Information Processing*. New York: Wiley.

Rumelhart, D. E. and Ortony, A. (1977) 'The Representation of Knowledge in Memory.' In R. C. Anderson, R. J. Spiro and W. E. Montague (eds.), *Schooling and the Acquisition of Knowledge*. New York: Halsted Press.

Säljö, R. (1975) 'Qualitative Differences in Learning as a Function of the Learner's Conception of the Task.' *Acta Universitatis Gothoburgensis*, Göteborg.

Saltz, E. (1971) *The Cognitive Bases of Human Learning: From Association to Concepts*. Homewood, Illinois: Dorsey Press.

Sanford, A. J. and Garrod, S. C. (1981) *Understanding Written Language: Explorations of Comprehension beyond the Sentence*. New York: Wiley.

Saville-Troike, A. M. (1979) 'Reading and the Audio-lingual Method.' In R. Mackay, B. Barkman and R. R. Jordan (eds.), *Reading in a Second Language*. Rowley, Mass.: Newbury House.

Schank, R. C (1975) *Conceptual Information Processing*. Amsterdam: North Holland.

Schank, R. C. (1972) 'Conceptual Dependency-theory of Natural Language Understanding.' *Cognitive Psychology*, **3**, 552.

Schank, R. C. and Abelson, R. P. (1977) *Scripts, Plans, Goals and Understanding*. New York: Halsted Press.

Schlesinger, I. M. (1968) *Sentence Structure and the Reading Process*. The Hague: Mouton (Janua Linguarum 69).

Schumann, J. (1976) 'Social Distance as a Factor in Second Language Acquisition,' *Language Learning*, **26**, 138–143.

Selinker, L. (1972) 'Interlanguage.' *IRAL*, **10**, 209.

Shavelson, R. J., Berliner, D. C., Ravitch, M. M. and Loeding, D. (1974) 'Effects of Position and Type of Question on Learning from Prose Material: Interaction of Treatments with Individual Differences.' *Journal of Educational Psychology*, **66**, 40–48.

Smith, F. (1971) *Understanding Reading*. New York: Holt Rinehart and Winston, 2nd edn, 1978.

Smith, F. (1978) *Reading*. Cambridge University Press.

Smith, P. E. and Kulhavy, R. W. (1974) 'The Influence of Adjunct Rules and Objectives on Learning from Text Material.' Paper presented at the meeting of the American Educational Research Association, Chicago, April, 1974.

Stamp, D. (1979) 'A Readability Survey of UNDP Material using the Cloze Procedure.' *Directions (Fiji)*, **2**, 23–28.

Steffensen, M. S., Joag-Dev, C. and Anderson, R. C. (1979) 'A Cross-cultural Perspective on Reading Comprehension.' *Reading Research Quarterly*, **15**, 10–29.

Stein, B. S., Morris, C. D. and Bransford, J. D. (1978) 'Constraints on Effective Elaboration.' *Journal of Verbal Learning and Verbal Behavior*, **17**, 707–714.

Stein, B. S. and Albridge, U. (1978) 'The Role of Conceptual Frameworks in Prose Comprehension and Recall.' Mimeo, Vanderbilt University.

Stein, B. S. and Bransford, J. D. (1979) 'Constraints on Effective Elaboration: Effects of Precision and Subject Generation.' *Journal of Verbal Learning and Verbal Behavior*, **18**, 769–777.

Stein, B. S., Bransford, J. D., Owings, R. and McGraw, W. (to appear) 'Individual Differences in the Spontaneous Utilization of Knowledge and Skills'.

Stern, H. H., and Cummins, J. (1981) 'Language Teaching/Learning Research: a Canadian Perspective on Status and Directions.' In J. K. Phillips (ed.), *Action for the '80s: A Political, Professional and Public Program for Foreign Language Education*. Skokie, Illinois: National Textbook Company.

Sticht, T. G. (1972) 'Learning by Listening.' In R. O. Freedle, and J. B. Carroll (eds.), *Language Comprehension and the Acquisition of Knowledge*. Washington: Winston, 285–312.

Stock, R., Kol, S. and Berman, R. A. (1979) *English for Speakers of Hebrew — Advanced Language, Book Two*. Tel Aviv: Techerikover Publishers.

Stockwell, R. P. (1977) *Foundations of Syntactic Theory*. Englewood Cliffs, N.J: Prentice-Hall.

Strang, R. (1972) 'The Nature of Reading.' In A. Melnik and J. Merritt, (eds.), *Reading Today and Tomorrow*. Open University, Milton Keynes, 67–117.

Svensson, L. (1976) 'Study Skill and Learning.' *Acta Universitatis Gothoburgensis*, Göteborg.

Svensson, L. (1977) 'On Qualitative Differences in Learning: III — Study Skill and Learning.' *British Journal of Educational Psychology*, **47**, 233–243.

Swain, M., Lapkin, S. and Barik, H. C. (1976) 'The Cloze Test as a Measure of Second Language Proficiency for Young Children.' *Working Papers on Bilingualism*, **11**, 32–42.

Tate, G. M. (1971) *Oral English Handbook*. Wellington: Reed Education.

Taylor, W. L. (1953) 'Cloze Procedure: a New Tool for Measuring Readability.' *Journalism Quarterly*, 415–433.

Thaman, K. (1977) 'Community Survey of Students' Unmet Educational Needs — Tonga.' Paper presented to General Meeting of Suva Institute for Educational Research, September 1977.

Thomas, L. F. (1968) 'A Flow Diagram Technique for Describing the "Meaning Structure" of a Text.' Mimeo, Centre for the Study of Human Learning, Brunel University.

Thomas, L. F. (1969) 'McQuitty: a Computer Program for Hierarchical Cluster Analysis.' Mimeo, Centre for the Study of Human Learning, Brunel University.

Thomas, L. F. and Augstein, E. S. (1972) 'An Experimental Approach to the Study of Reading as a Learning Skill.' *Research in Education*, **8**, 28–46.

Thomas, L. F. and Augstein, E. S. (1973) *Developing Your Own Reading*. Milton Keynes: Open University Press.

Thomas, L. F. and Harri-Augstein, E. S. (1974) 'Reading to Learn.' In J. Merritt (ed.), *New Horizons in Reading, Proceedings of 5th World IRA Congress, Delaware, 1974*. International Reading Association, **19**, 1976.

Thomas, L. F. and Harri-Augstein, E. S. (1975) 'Structure of Meaning: a Kit.' Centre for the Study of Human Learning, Brunel University.

Thomas, L. F. and Harri-Augstein, E. S. (1976) 'The Self-Organised Learner and the Printed Word.' Mimeo, Centre for the Study of Human Learning, Brunel University, and Final Report to SSRC on Techniques for the Further Development of Reading as a Learning Skill.

Thomas, L. F. and Harri-Augstein, E. S. (1977) 'Learning-to-learn. The Personal Construction and Exchange of Meaning.' In M. J. A. Howe (ed.), *Adult Learning: Psychological Research and Applications*. London: Wiley.

Thomas, L. F. and Harri-Augstein, E. S. (1978a) 'Comprehending Reading. The Dynamics of Learning Conversations.' In D. Thackeray (ed.), *Growth in Reading: Proceedings of the United Kingdom Reading Association 15th Annual Course and Conference*. London: Ward Lock.

Thomas, L. F. and Harri-Augstein, E. S. (1978b) 'The Kelly Repertory Grid as a Vehicle for Eliciting a Personal Taxonomy of Reading Purposes.' *Journal of Research in Reading*, **1**, 53–66.

Thomas, L. F. and Harri-Augstein, E. S. (1978c) 'Is Comprehension the Purpose of Reading?.' In E. Hunter-Grundin, and H. U. Grundin (eds.), *Reading: Implementing the Bullock Report*. London: Ward Lock.

Thomas, L. F. and Harri-Augstein, E. S. (1978d) 'The Art and Science of Getting a Degree.' Mimeo, Centre for the Study of Human Learning, Brunel University.

Thomas, L. F. and Harri-Augstein, E. S. (1979a) 'Self-organised Learning and the Relativity of Knowing.' In P. Striner, and D. Bannister (eds.), *Constructs of Sociality and Individuality*. London: Academic Press.

Thomas, L. F. and Harri-Augstein, E. S. (1979b) 'Learning Conversations: a Person-centred Approach to Self-organised Learning.' *British Journal of Guidance and Counselling*, **7**, 80–91.

Thomas, R. M. and Titiali'i, T. F. (1973) *A Study of Unmet Educational Needs in American Samoa*. Dept of Education, Pago Pago, American Samoa.

Thorndike, E. L. (1917) 'Reading as Reasoning: a Study of Mistakes in Paragraph Reading.' *Journal of Educational Psychology*, **8**, 323–332.

Thorndyke, P. W. (1977) 'Cognitive Structures in Comprehension and

Memory of Narrative Discourse.' *Cognitive Psychology*, **9**, 77–110.

Tommola, J. (1979) Some Parameters of Simplification. Communication Studies Paper, MSc in Applied Linguistics, Dept. of Linguistics, University of Edinburgh, mimeo, 1979.

Trabasso, T. (to appear) 'On the Making and the Assessment of Inferences during Reading.' In J. T. Guthrie (ed.), *Reading Comprehension and Education*. International Reading Association, Newark, Delaware.

Ulijn, J. M. and Kempen, G. A. M. (1976) 'The Role of the First Language in Second Language Reading Comprehension. Some Experimental Evidence.' In G. Nickel (ed.), *Proceedings of the 4th International Congress of Applied Linguistics, vol 1*. Hochschulverlag, Stuttgart, 495–507.

Ulijn, J. M. (1978) 'Conceptualisation in Second Language Reading.' Paper presented at the 5th International Congress of Applied Linguistics, Montreal, August, 1978.

University of Malaya (1980) *English for Special Purposes Project, Skills for Learning*. International edn, Nelson and the University of Malaya Press, 1980 and to appear.

Urquhart, A. H. (1981) 'Operating on Learning Texts.' In L. Selinker, E. Tarone, and V. Hanzeli, (eds.), *English for Academic and Technical Purposes*. Rowley, Mass.: Newbury House, 211–222.

van Dijk, T. A. (1977) *Text and Context: Explorations in the Semantics and Pragmatics of Discourse*. London: Longman.

Watts, G. H. and Anderson, R. C. (1971) 'Effect of Three Types of Inserted Questions on Learning from Prose.' *Journal of Educational Psychology*, **62**, 387–394.

Weaver, C. (1980) *Psycholinguistics and Reading: From Process to Practice*. Cambridge, Mass: Winthrop.

Widdowson, H. G. and Urquhart, A. H. (1976) 'K.A.A.U. English for Academic Purposes Project, 1st Yearly Report,' Mimeo, University of Edinburgh, K.A.A.U. Reading Research Project.

Widdowson, H. G. (1978) *Teaching Language as Communication*, Oxford University Press.

Widdowson, H. G. (1979) *Explorations in Applied Linguistics*. Oxford University Press (includes 'The Process and Purpose of Reading').

Williams, A. I. (1977) 'Community Survey of Students' Unmet Educational Needs.' Paper presented to General Meeting of Suva Institute of Educational Research, September, 1977.

Williams, R. C. (1980) 'Longman Readability Pilot Study: Report of the Project Director.' Mimeo.

Williams, R. C. (1981) 'Lexical Familiarisation in Content Area Textbooks.' In L. J. Chapman (ed.), *The Reader and the Text, Proceedings of the 1980 UKRA Conference*. London: Heinemann.

Winne, P. H. (1979) 'Experiments Relating Teachers' Use of Higher Cognitive Questions to Student Achievement.' *Review of Educational Research*, **49**, 13–50.

Winter, E. O. (1977) 'A Clause-relational Approach to English Texts — Study of some Predictive Lexical Items in Written Discourse.' *Instructional Science*, **6**, Special Issue, 1–92.

Wodarski, J. S. and Buckholdt, D. (1975) 'Behavioral Instruction in the College Classroom; a Review of Methodological Procedures.' In J. Johnston (ed.), *Behavior Research and Technology in Higher Education*. Springfield, Illinois: Charles C. Thomas.

Wood, C. T. (1974) 'Processing Units in Reading.' Doctoral dissertation, Stanford University.

Wright, C. W. (1965) *An English Word Count*. National Bureau of Educational and Social Research, Pretoria.

Yorio, C. A. (1971) 'Some Sources of Reading Problems for Foreign Language Learners.' *Language Learning*, **21**, 107–115.

Yousef, F. S. (1968) 'Cross-cultural Testing: an Aspect of the Resistance Reaction.' *Language Learning*, **18**, 227–234.

INDEX